Chains of Finance

Chains of Finance

How Investment Management
is Shaped

Diane-Laure Arjaliès, Philip Grant, Iain Hardie,
Donald MacKenzie, and Ekaterina Svetlova

OXFORD
UNIVERSITY PRESS

OXFORD
UNIVERSITY PRESS

Great Clarendon Street, Oxford, OX2 6DP,
United Kingdom

Oxford University Press is a department of the University of Oxford.
It furthers the University's objective of excellence in research, scholarship,
and education by publishing worldwide. Oxford is a registered trade mark of
Oxford University Press in the UK and in certain other countries

First Edition published in 2017
Impression: 1

Published in the United States of America by Oxford University Press
198 Madison Avenue, New York, NY 10016, United States of America

British Library Cataloguing in Publication Data
Data available

Library of Congress Control Number: 2016962488

ISBN 978–0–19–880294–5

Printed and bound by
CPI Group (UK) Ltd, Croydon, CR0 4YY

Acknowledgements

This book reports the results of a research project, 'Evaluation Practices in Financial Markets', supported by the European Research Council under the European Union's Seventh Framework Programme (fp7/2007–2013)/ERC grant agreement no. 291733). Additional funding was received from the DFG project 'Economic Calculations. Creation of Calculative Realities in the Financial Markets' (Svetlova).

We would also like to thank Frances Burgess and Caroline Laffey at the University of Edinburgh; Arjen van der Heide for his work on the references; Clare Kennedy and David Musson at Oxford University Press; our copy editor, Joanna North; our indexer, Moyra Forrest; Elakkia Bharathi and Jayasri Janarthanan from SPi Global; and our proofreader, Denise Bannerman; colleagues who participated in our mini-conferences in Edinburgh where we discussed the writing of the book; and the anonymous reviewers of our book proposal.

Two notes of special thanks go, first of all, to all of those we interviewed or worked alongside and without whose willingness to share their time, views, expertise, and experience, this book would not have come into existence; and second, to Éric Loiselet, the 'politician' of Chapter 7, who was highly supportive of the research on which the chapter is based and who sadly passed away just before the completion of our manuscript.

Contents

List of Figures	ix
List of Tables	xi
1. Investment Management and the Investment Chain	1
2. Chains of Freedom: The Investment Chain inside the Investment Management Firm	25
3. Fund Managers and Their Investors	47
4. Quantitative Asset Managers and Their Chains	76
5. Entangled Trading: Fund Managers and Dark Pools	98
6. Bringing Society Back into the Investment Chain: Responsible Investing during the Financial Crisis	120
7. Trapped in Resistance: Collective Struggles through the Investment Chain	138
8. Conclusion	156
Appendix: A Brief Roster of Intermediaries	169
References	175
Index	189

List of Figures

1.1 The investment chain   5

1.2 The unit cost of financial intermediation in the United States,
    1884–2012   12

4.1 The investment chain within the investment management firm   77

4.2 The development of the quantitative investment product and the
    relevant chain partners   88

List of Tables

2.1 Enabling and constraining in the investment chain   44

5.1 The additional set of interviews drawn on in Chapter 5   102

5.2 Approximate average daily transaction volumes on leading
US dark pools (September 2009)   114

7.1 The investment chain and the attempted transformation of
Corporate X's attitude towards unionization   150

1

Investment Management and the Investment Chain

We may be entering 'the age of asset management', suggested the Bank of England's Director of Financial Stability and now Chief Economist, Andrew Haldane, in an April 2014 speech. The amounts of assets (shares, bonds, and other investments) controlled by investment management firms change from day to day, as money flows into and out of those firms and asset prices fluctuate; exact definitions of the sector also vary. However, in 2013–14, researchers for the finance industry body TheCityUK provided rough but plausible estimates of the total sums managed by the world's pension funds, insurance companies, and mutual funds: $87 trillion at the end of 2012, rising to $97 trillion by December 2013 (TheCityUK 2013, 2014).

As Haldane said, $87 trillion—about the equivalent of a year of global GDP—was around 40 per cent of all the world's financial assets in 2012, as estimated by the McKinsey Global Institute (2013). Many of the world's top banks have shrunk in the wake of the financial crisis and tighter regulation, while the assets controlled by investment management firms have been growing. Investment managers' $87 trillion in 2012 was roughly equal, Haldane pointed out, to three-quarters of the total assets on the balance sheets of the world's banks.[1] BlackRock, the world's largest investment management firm, illustrates the sector's rise. By 2014, BlackRock's total investments were larger than the assets of any bank in the world; indeed, its portfolio, now approaching $5 trillion, comfortably exceeds the GDP of Germany (a comparison first made by Kolhatkar and Bhaktavatsalam in 2010, when BlackRock was less than three-quarters of the size it now is).

---

[1] Haldane (2014). Note, however, that there is no absolute boundary between investment management and banking. Some investment management firms are owned by banks, and banks are quite often involved directly in investment management (as in the case of the continental European mutual funds whose management is discussed in Chapter 4).

The decisions made by investment managers therefore determine how a vast sum of money is used. Some activities, some firms, and some governments are financially supported, and others are not. As an indicator of how consequential this is, consider the level of additional global investment in renewable energy needed annually to head off dangerous levels of climate change, which has been estimated at between one and two trillion US dollars (Fulton and Capalino 2014; Randall 2014). That is a very large amount of money—a trillion is a million millions—but, if the incentives were right, is potentially affordable in the context of an investment sector that manages nearly $100 trillion.

Some of those who control investment management's huge accumulations of capital now earn as much as those at the pinnacle of global banking. In 2014, with the aid of insiders, the Bloomberg journalist Barry Ritholtz estimated the remuneration of the two highest-paid staff of PIMCO, the Pacific Investment Management Company. Bill Gross, PIMCO's co-founder and manager of its Total Return Fund, earned a bonus in 2013 of $290 million. PIMCO's then chief executive, Mohamed El-Erian, took home $230 million. Admittedly, a quirk of PIMCO's history—a profit-sharing arrangement with Allianz, the German insurance company that bought a majority stake in PIMCO in 2000—made those figures atypically large: for instance, Black-Rock's chief executive and co-founder, Larry Fink, earned a mere $22.9 million in 2013 (Ritholtz 2014). Nevertheless, average pay at investment management firms is high. Research by the think tank New Financial (Wright 2015) estimates the average for 2014 as $263,000, which was within touching distance of the $288,000 average for global investment banking.

Haldane's aim in diagnosing an 'age of asset management' was to start a discussion of the latter's potential risks. Because losses on shares, bonds, and other investments are passed on by investment management firms to those whose money is being managed, most such firms are much less likely than banks to become insolvent (although firms such as hedge funds that invest borrowed money are vulnerable to insolvency). However, the decisions made even by investment managers who do not invest borrowed money may be dangerously pro-cyclical: they may amplify both bubbles and crashes in the financial system. For example, research at the Bank of England showed that between 1996 and 2012, both US and French life insurance companies added, in relative terms, to their portfolios of shares as the prices of the latter rose, and reduced them as share prices fell (Haldane 2014: chart 6). There also seem to be frequent 'mini' booms and crashes in respect to particular investment funds and styles of investing. As a fund manager we interviewed put it to us, 'quite often a fund will do well: let's say it's up 25 per cent one year . . . then it'll do well the second year, and then suddenly the fund selectors . . . will start to recommend the fund . . . Now the fund will grow. It's now ten times the size it was before. Then the fund struggles to invest to the same scale or it isn't as lucky ... '. This can mean that the returns to the average investor in a fund can be lower than the average performance of the fund might suggest, because there are more investors and more money in the fund at the point at which its performance starts to deteriorate.[2]

Sudden withdrawal of capital by investors in response to deteriorating performance can also have the effect of making that performance even worse. If a fund or an entire investment sector is in trouble, and prices are falling, the investment management firm or firms involved may face large-scale withdrawal of capital by those whose money they manage, and may therefore have to sell assets at fire-sale prices, so worsening the price fall. Following the 2016 vote to leave the European Union, for example, funds investing in UK commercial property faced exactly this danger. Fortunately, however, those funds' rules allowed their managers to slow the pace of withdrawals, and at the time of writing a fire sale seems to have been averted.

The Financial Stability Board, based in Basel, guides the global regulation of financial markets. It has considered adding the world's biggest investment managers, such as BlackRock and PIMCO, to the list of the thirty banks and nine insurance companies that it considers 'Sifis' (systemically important financial institutions) and subjects to enhanced scrutiny and an additional layer of capital requirements. Eventually, though, the Board decided not to, but—reportedly—not for an entirely reassuring reason. There are established ways of regulating banks and insurance companies, but the Board 'did not know how it would regulate' investment management firms, beyond some simple measures to reduce the risk of fire sales (Jopson et al. 2015).

The Financial Stability Board is not alone in its puzzlement when confronting investment management. As Haldane put it, '[a]nalysing and managing the behaviour of asset managers is ... a greenfield site' (2014: 14). While that is an exaggeration (we outline the findings of the existing research on investment management later in this chapter), research is much sparser than might be expected given the size and importance of the investment management sector. This matters. Failure to understand the detailed dynamics of investment management can lead to serious policy errors. For example, the coalition government that ran the UK from 2010 to 2015 seems to have underestimated the institutional dynamics—for example, the effects of the accounting rules governing the valuation of pension funds' and insurance companies' liabilities—that have created continuing healthy demand for gilts (UK

---

[2] Thus low-cost fund provider Vanguard calculates (using data from the fund raters Morningstar) that 'large-capitalization funds as a whole produced an average return of 6.93% over the ten years ended December 31, 2013. The average annual investor return in those funds, however, was 5.54%—a lag of nearly 1.4 percentage points' (Zilbering 2014). Note that this effect is separate from the effect of fees on investors' returns, for which see the section 'Why the Chain Matters'.

government bonds), despite the hugely increased issuance of the latter. This underestimation may well have been a contributor to harsher austerity measures than many macroeconomists would have regarded as optimal (see, e.g., Wolf 2011).

The Investment Chain

In January 2016, we were interviewing a manager of what is called a 'retail' fund: in other words, one in which members of the general public invest. 'One of the things, I think, that's most remarkable about the job', he said, is that the expression 'retail fund' means 'that Mr and Mrs Smith on Acacia Avenue invest in the fund. Yet, in the job, you almost never see them, meet them, hear from them, have any contact whatsoever with them.' This manager is not an introvert. He spends quite a lot of his time talking to people, but they are nearly always other financial professionals, not the individuals who invest in his fund.

What he was pointing out was the salience in his working life of what we call the 'investment chain', which is the organizing theme of this book. Investment is no longer primarily a matter of individual savers directly choosing which shares or bonds to buy. Rather, most of their money flows through a chain: a sequence of intermediaries (see Figure 1.1). What we mean by the 'investment chain' is the sets of intermediaries that 'sit between' savers and companies or governments, along with the links between those intermediaries.[3] The investment chain is thus a subset—a particularly crucial subset, we would argue—of the multiple, dense network links that connect actors in financial markets. The central argument of this book is that investment management is shaped profoundly by the opportunities and constraints that this chain creates. To understand the behaviour of any one set of intermediaries (such as the 'fund managers' who normally play the most direct role in selecting firms or government debts to invest in, and who are our main focus empirically), we must therefore examine those intermediaries' links to those who occupy other intermediary roles in the investment process.

---

[3] Readers who know the work of Bruno Latour will notice that (because we want to follow normal usage among those who write about finance) we use the word 'intermediary' when he would say 'mediator'. Financial intermediaries do not 'transport...meaning or force without transformation' (which is Latour's notion of 'intermediary'); rather, like Latour's mediators, they 'transform, translate, distort, and modify the meaning or the elements they are supposed to carry' (Latour 2005: 39).

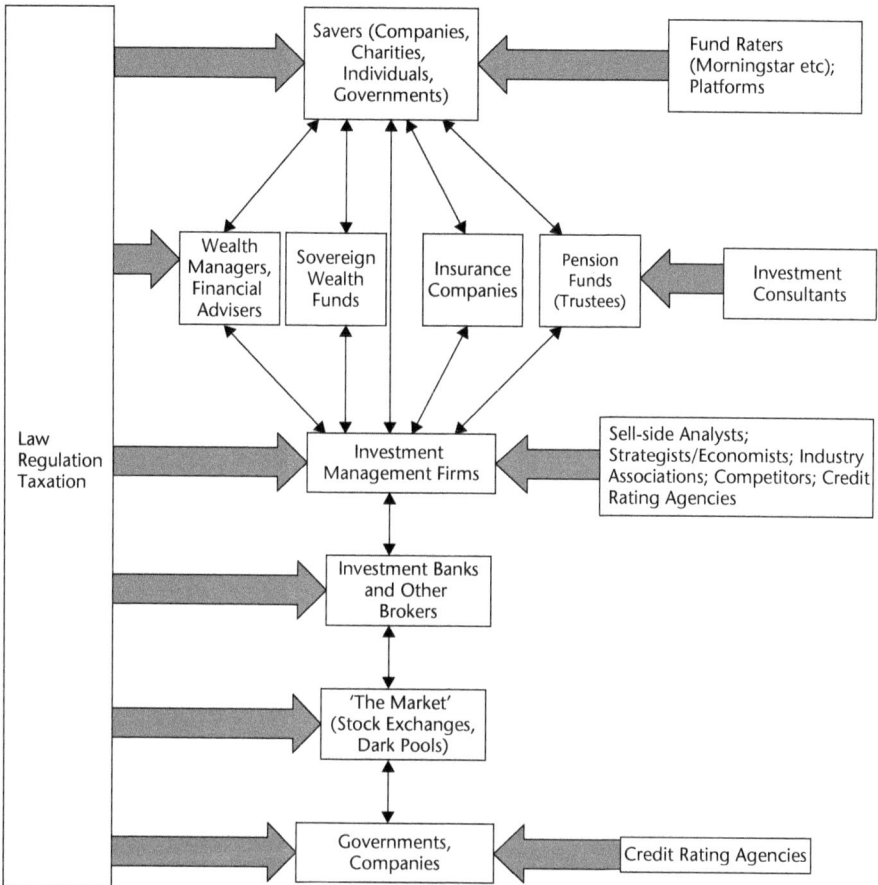

Figure 1.1 The investment chain

From Savers to Investment Management Firms

Let us begin at one end of the investment chain, with savers. They can include governments (investing, for example, via sovereign wealth funds such as Norway's 'Oil Fund'), companies, charities, and other bodies, but to start to flesh out what the 'investment chain' encompasses, consider an individual saver. She can, of course, simply build up a stash of banknotes, or put her money into a bank account. But let's assume she becomes an investor. It's now very unusual to invest without some use of an intermediary: even if, for example, she were to decide 'directly' to buy a company's shares, she would in practice nearly always need to use a firm of brokers to make the purchase. Furthermore, as depicted in Figure 1.1, it is now typical for her money to flow through the hands of (or decisions about it to be taken by) at least one further layer of intermediaries.

She could, for example, decide to put her money into a mutual fund, run by an investment management company, which pools the money of multiple investors and uses it to buy a portfolio of shares, bonds, or other assets.[4] She could herself directly choose a fund. In many countries, however, there is a bewildering variety of funds from which to choose, so she may well seek guidance from—or in practice de facto delegate the choice of fund or funds to—a financial adviser. If she is well enough off, she can delegate further, paying a 'wealth management' firm continuously to manage her investment portfolio (or, if she is among the super-rich, create what's called a 'family office' dedicated exclusively to the management of her investments). Even if she herself chooses a mutual fund in which to invest, nowadays she will often use (and pay fees to) an online investment platform that pre-selects a set of preferred funds for her to choose among.

For many savers, furthermore, by far the most important form of saving is putting money into a pension. Sometimes, they do this individually (in the form of a 'private pension' as it is called in the UK), in an arrangement that enjoys tax advantages and involves limitations on the timing of any withdrawals, but otherwise can be similar to putting money into a mutual fund. Many such private pension arrangements are managed by insurance companies, and when the saver retires she will also often turn to an insurance company to buy an annuity, thus turning her accumulated pension pot into an income stream. The role of insurance companies in pension provision makes them important financial intermediaries, and the scale of their presence in financial markets is also increased by them themselves investing the insurance premiums they earn from other aspects of their businesses such as life insurance, property insurance, and so on.

Much pension provision, however, is not via individual investment arrangements but via occupational pension schemes. Their collective aspects make these pension funds more complex than individual arrangements, especially when (in 'defined benefit' schemes) the levels of pension they will provide are determined by pre-set rules. Pension funds' liabilities—in other words, what they must pay their pensioners—stretch many decades into the future, and require the accumulation of very large investment portfolios (nowadays often designed carefully to match their liabilities), making those funds also crucial financial intermediaries.

---

[4] The most popular type of mutual fund is called an 'open-ended investment company' in the European Union; the older UK term was 'unit trust'. The expression 'mutual fund' is used in North America, but we use it throughout the book for the sake of convenience to refer to similar funds in all jurisdictions.

Some intermediaries such as pension funds and insurance companies thus directly form part of the investment chain: savers' money passes through their hands, and they take decisions as to what happens to that money. Other financial firms influence what goes on the chain, without playing such a direct role in it, and we give some examples on the right-hand side of Figure 1.1. For instance, individual savers may be influenced in their choices of mutual funds by specialist firms such as Morningstar and Standard & Poor's that give such funds ratings ('gold', 'silver', etc.), based not just on their performance but on the perceived rigour of their internal processes. In the United States, for example, 'any rating [of a mutual fund] other than five stars [from Morningstar] will lead, other things being equal, to outflows. Having one star—the lowest category—will tend to drive outflows equivalent to 2.3 per cent of a fund's assets every month', an outcome that, if it continues month after month, means the fund will close (Authers 2015).

Another very important influence on the investment chain is investment consultancy firms. Pension funds usually delegate the detailed selection of stocks, bonds, and other assets to fund managers employed by investment management companies (although very large pension funds often have their own in-house fund management function as well). Pension funds typically pay investment consultants to help them decide which managers to use, as well as to advise them on other aspects of their work. (Being a pension fund trustee is a responsible position, with serious penalties—in the extreme, a jail sentence—if one is deemed negligent. It is unsurprising, therefore, that trustees often seek external professional advice, and regulators sometimes also pressure them to do so. One trustee to whom we spoke, who was a fund manager in his day job, had been responsible for a learned society's surplus funds of around £1 million. Given the modesty of that sum by financial sector standards, he felt that he and his fellow trustees—who included, for example, an actuary—were well able to manage it. However, they received a letter from the UK Financial Services Authority pointing out that they employed no financial adviser, and then felt compelled to appoint one.) Investment consultants indeed often move from being influences on the investment chain to becoming a direct part of it: pension trustees quite frequently delegate the administration of a pension fund to an investment consultancy firm, which then decides how to allocate the fund's money among different classes of financial asset and which fund managers to use.

Within Investment Management Firms

As the previous section has suggested, and as we depict in Figure 1.1, investment management firms sit right in the centre of the investment chain. They channel money from institutional investors such as pension funds towards the market, choosing shares, bonds, and other forms of investment. Private investors' stock market and bond market investments are also, as noted earlier, nowadays more usually made via investment management firms than more directly.

As well as thus being central to the overall investment chain, large investment management firms also contain an internal chain. At its heart are fund managers (who, as noted, are the people who take the most immediate decisions about which shares, bonds, or other assets to have in the investment portfolios they manage). But a big investment management firm will also employ marketing staff and client service personnel (who interact more directly with clients than fund managers ordinarily do), traders (who implement managers' decisions to buy or sell), and sometimes asset allocators who channel money from the firm's clients to the firm's particular internal funds. Also shaping a firm's investment processes will be risk managers, compliance officers, and sometimes economists (see the roster in the Appendix at the end of this book). The work of many of those staff members is shaped by and/or oriented towards other intermediaries. Thus the marketing staff in investment management firms seem often to devote the bulk of their efforts to influencing fellow intermediaries in the investment chain, not our interviewee's 'Mr and Mrs Smith on Acacia Avenue'.

Investment management firms also often delegate some of their responsibilities to further specialist intermediaries in separate firms. For example, encouraged by regulators, most investment management firms employ custodians, which are separate companies (often large, well-established banks), which hold the shares or bonds bought by investment management firms. Nowadays, investment management firms often also hire specialist 'proxy voting' companies to advise them how they should vote on contested shareholder issues, or even simply to cast their votes for them.

Between the Investment Management Firm and the Market

The investment chain stretches beyond what market participants call the 'buy side' (investment management firms and associated intermediaries). When, for example, a fund manager decides to buy or sell shares or bonds, her firm's traders usually do so not directly but via 'sell-side' intermediaries: brokers or dealers, in particular those who work for big investment banks. Although the names sound similar, what an investment bank does is quite different from an investment management firm.[5] Among many services provided, an

---

[5] Again, though, we should note that some investment banks have investment management divisions, and many also act as wealth managers.

investment bank arranges new issues of shares or bonds on behalf of corporations and sometimes governments, often selling those shares or bonds to investment management firms. It sells services to investment management firms, such as the execution of their orders for shares or bonds, as well as providing research reports on matters such as likely price movements. (That investment management firms are usually the purchaser in arrangements such as these is why those firms are described as 'buy side'.) An investment bank will also advise on corporate mergers and take-overs, and often act as a 'market-maker', continually quoting prices at which it will buy and sell financial instruments. These crucial roles make investment banks among the most important and best informed financial intermediaries.[6]

What one of our interviewees, a trader working for a buy-side firm, called 'relationship value' (the extent to which trading reinforces relations of reciprocity between investment management firms and investment banks) often trumps cost as a determinant of how those firms choose to trade. Reciprocity can involve the investment bank being prepared to use its own capital and act as a dealer (selling the stocks or bonds in question directly to the investment management firm, or buying them directly from it), rather than simply acting as a broker, merely channelling the firm's order to the market. It almost always involves the investment bank or other broker providing 'free' research or other services to the investment management firm in return for trading via it, an issue that we examine in Chapter 5.

Why the Chain Matters

The investment chain is already lengthy and complex, and seems to be becoming more so. Sometimes, regulators demand the use of intermediaries, and some markets can be accessed only via intermediaries, but a basic reason for employing an intermediary is specialized knowledge and expertise. For example, private or individual investors (as already noted, the standard industry term for them is 'retail') put their money into a pooled investment vehicle such as a mutual fund not just because that is an easy way of diversifying their investments across multiple corporations—which is certainly sensible—but also because they often believe that the fund's manager or managers have their finger on the pulse of the markets. (The latter belief may be less well

---

[6] It is worth noting that in most jurisdictions the different functions of investment banks are separated by internal controls (sometimes known as 'Chinese walls') regulating the flow of information and the ability to collaborate between employees of different departments. For example, employees advising a company on a merger are not allowed to communicate this to colleagues working as brokers or investment managers, in order to prevent so-called 'insider trading'.

founded. The efficient market hypothesis of financial economics suggests that—trading on the basis of insider information aside—genuinely superior knowledge and therefore a manager having the capacity systematically to beat the market are probably unlikely.) Those fund managers—even if very knowledgeable about investment opportunities—cannot, however, be expected to follow the minute-by-minute flow of the buying and selling of shares or bonds, and thus to know the least costly way to execute a big trade. That is the reason why all but the smallest investment management firms typically employ traders (and/or computerized trading algorithms) as well as fund managers. As just noted, these 'buy-side' traders, in their turn, often trade not directly but via investment bank dealers or brokers. One reason for doing so is that a dealer or broker experiences the flow of buying and selling more directly than a buy-side trader does, and will also often have some insight into what other big players in the market are trying to do.

The proliferation of intermediaries, however, has effects that go far beyond making specialized expertise available and thus—hopefully—improving investment decisions. First, it fragments ownership (which is, in a sense, the central institution of a capitalist, 'free enterprise' society). Who owns a public company, asks the economist John Kay (2015b):

> The answer is that no one does . . . It makes little sense even to ask who owns shares in a company. One name is recorded on a share register; someone else makes a decision to buy or sell; someone else decides how the shares are to be voted; and someone else benefits from the returns from the company's activities. It is not only possible today, but usual, for all these rights to be exercised by different people.

Second, intermediaries' situations in the investment chain can create incentives for them to act in ways that are detrimental to the interests of those whose money they manage, as John Kay also emphasized in his influential 2012 review of the market for UK shares. (The review was commissioned by the then Secretary of State for Business, Innovation and Skills, Vince Cable.) The most systematic tension between the interests of investment management firms and their clients was spelled out twenty years ago by the economists Judith Chevalier and Glenn Ellison. 'Investors would like [an investment management] company to maximize risk-adjusted fund returns', they wrote. However, those returns to investors typically benefit investment management companies and their senior staff only indirectly: their income is usually determined much more directly by the total amounts of capital they manage and the fees they charge for doing so. So they have 'an incentive to take actions that increase the inflow of investments' (Chevalier and Ellison 1997: 1167), even if those actions reduce the returns to those who invest in their funds, for example by expanding the size of a fund beyond the scale of genuine investment opportunities available to the strategy it is pursuing.

Third, intermediation is expensive, an issue that requires more attention from our academic field, the 'social studies of finance': the application to finance not just of economics but of wider social science disciplines such as anthropology, human geography, politics, science and technology studies, and sociology. The field has made exciting progress, as documented for example in the handbook edited by Knorr Cetina and Preda (2012). It has often done so by focusing on issues that had received insufficient attention in earlier research on finance, issues that range from how traders cultivate 'selves' appropriate to their immersive, stressful, risky work (Zaloom 2006) to the effects that mathematical models and other 'market devices' have on the markets in which they are deployed (Callon et al. 2007; MacKenzie 2006). However, attention to issues such as those now needs to be complemented, we believe, by a greater focus on the basic issue of how money is made within the financial system, and with what consequences. The fees charged and expenses incurred by the various layers of intermediaries in the investment chain are a very important aspect of this.

Since the middle of the nineteenth century, financial intermediation as a whole (i.e. financial services of all kinds, including banking and money transfer, not just investment management) has expanded substantially, both in absolute terms and as a proportion of GDP. By 2005, financial intermediation made up over 6 per cent of GDP in several countries, including the US, UK, Japan, Canada, Australia, and the Netherlands (Philippon and Reshef 2013). Although a complex modern economy clearly needs a large amount of financial intermediation, it is far from clear that the size to which the financial sectors of some countries have grown since around 1980 is either necessary or beneficial, or that the proliferation of specialized intermediaries actually saves money or improves investment decisions.

There is, for example, evidence that—perturbingly—the overall efficiency of financial intermediation, as measured by its unit cost, has not grown through time, despite the huge advances in the underlying technology of information processing: see Philippon (2015) and our Figure 1.2 for the US; and Bazot (2014) for Europe.[7] Remarkably, for example, Philippon finds that the unit

---

[7] Estimation of the 'unit cost' of intermediation can be explained thus: imagine you have savings of £100. You want them to be safe and to have ready access to them. You therefore need what an economist would call 'liquidity services', and a bank can provide them. Let's say that when your savings are deposited in the bank they earn 1 per cent a year. Let's assume there is also someone who needs 'credit services'. She wants to borrow £100. The bank lends her that amount, charging her 5 per cent per year, or £5. So it earns £4 per year acting as an intermediary, standing in between you and her. Altogether, the bank has provided £200 of intermediation services (£100 of liquidity services to you; £100 of credit services to her) at a cost to the consumers of those services of £4. So the unit cost of financial intermediation is £4 divided by £200, i.e. 0.02 or 2 per cent per year. Working out the unit cost of intermediation for an entire financial system involves doing the same three things as in this example: first, calculating the total amount of intermediation services provided in each year; second, working out the total annual cost of those services; and finally

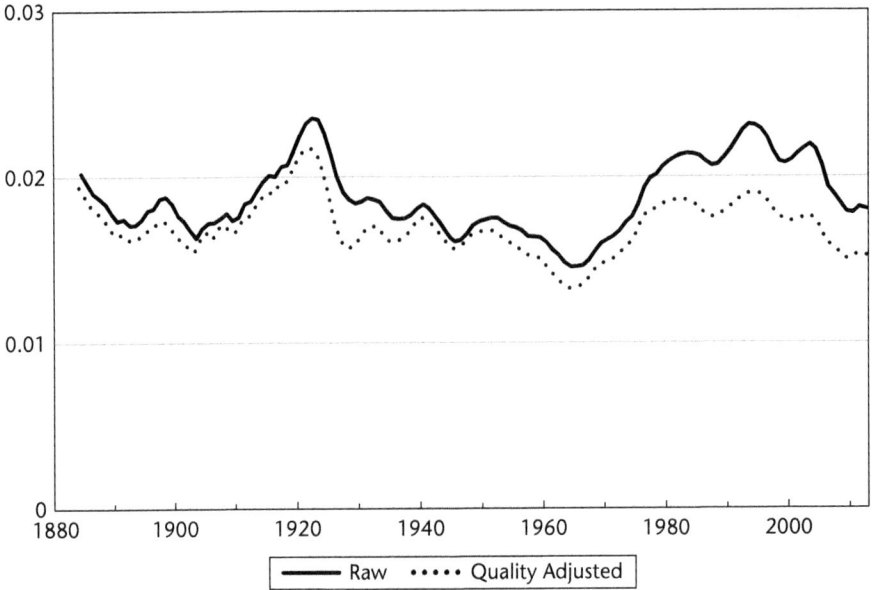

Figure 1.2 The unit cost of financial intermediation in the United States, 1884–2012
Data courtesy Thomas Philippon. For details, see note 7 and Philippon (2015).

cost of financial intermediation in the US has scarcely declined since the 1880s, the time of pens and paper ledgers, when a 'computer' was a human being, equipped at best with a mechanical calculator. Instead, much of the economic benefit of technological improvements seems to have been captured by senior staff in financial firms in the form of higher pay, both in absolute terms and relative to their counterparts in other sectors (see Philippon and Reshef 2012 for the case of the US), a process that has most likely contributed to increasing inequality. Much of the growth in earnings at

dividing the result of the second calculation by that of the first. Philippon (2015) does the first calculation by adding together the sums of money involved in four broad financial activities: the total amounts held in bank accounts and similar 'safe' deposits; the money lent to firms and the value the market gives their shares; the money lent to households; and the total value of corporate mergers and acquisitions. He does the second calculation (working out the total annual cost of intermediation) by adding up the profits and staff salaries of the entire gamut of financial intermediaries: banks, investment management companies, insurance companies, private equity firms, and so on. (Not all the business of insurance companies is financial intermediation, so Philippon subtracts from his total income estimate an estimate of expenditure on health, household, motor, and 'other transportation' insurance. See Philippon 2015: 1432–3.) The lower line in Figure 1.2 is Philippon's estimate of the unit cost corrected for the changing aggregate level of the difficulty of the task of intermediation. For example, investing wisely in start-ups involves more screening and monitoring—and is thus intrinsically more expensive—than buying the shares of established corporations with lengthy track records, while making a single big loan to a wealthy household is cheaper per dollar lent than making multiple smaller loans to less well-to-do households. Adjusting the unit cost of intermediation to take this into account produces a picture of change through time that is somewhat better, but not dramatically so.

the top of the income scale that has fuelled increased levels of inequality in the US and Europe in recent years is in the earnings of intermediaries (not just senior bankers, investment managers, and the like, but also related professionals such as top accountants and corporate lawyers): see, for example, Tomaskovic-Devey and Lin (2011) for the case of the US, Godechot (2013) for France, and Bell and Van Reenen (2010) for the UK.

The rise of investment management contributes to the overall growth of financial intermediation. The high level of aggregation in existing data on intermediation means that it can be difficult unequivocally to identify how much of that growth results from the rise of investment management, but there is clear evidence from the US, where Greenwood and Scharfstein (2013) find the rise of investment management to be one of the top two drivers of the growth of the financial sector (the other driver is increased lending to households, especially in the form of mortgages).

In the US, the unit cost of investment management of the mainstream kind discussed in this book seems to have declined—in particular, the rates of fees charged by mutual funds have fallen considerably (French 2008)—although perhaps not to the extent one might have expected given the greatly increased scale on which investment management now operates. (Part, but not all, of the decline in fees is the result of investors shifting from high-fee 'active' managers—who pick the shares or bonds to include in investment portfolios, which is the form of fund management that we focus on in this book—to lower-fee 'passive' management, which involves seeking simply to track an overall market index such as the S&P 500.) Unfortunately, however, from the viewpoint of the overall cost of intermediation, the US has also seen a sharp rise in the use of alternative investment vehicles such as hedge funds, a process that French (2008) finds has cancelled out most of the reduction in the cost of mainstream investment management. While the amount of capital managed by hedge funds is still much lower than the amount controlled by the mainstream investment management firms we focus on in this book, hedge funds charge very much higher fees.[8]

Costly financial intermediation matters to the non-financial economy because it acts in effect as a tax on it, slowing its growth. It also impacts directly on the returns received by savers: apparently small levels of fees and of other expenses can have a large cumulative impact. Consider, for example, an example given by the *Financial Times* (Rovnick 2015): an employee who over a forty-year working life saves £2,000 per year towards her pension, and is fortunate enough to invest that into a fund that makes a steady return of

---

[8] Thus French (2008: 1556) notes that, in the US, '[t]he fees hedge fund and fund of fund clients pay to invest 458.6 billion dollars in 2006, for example, are 36% higher than all the costs institutions pay to invest [$] 6.18 trillion'.

6 per cent each year, not adjusting for inflation. If fees and other expenses were no more than 0.5 per cent per year, her pension pot would total £273,211 when she retires, which the *Financial Times* calculates—very optimistically—could translate into an annual pension of nearly £23,000. If, however, the total annual expenses of her fund were 2 per cent, her pot would be almost a third lower—£190,051—meaning a pension estimated by the *FT* as no more than around £14,000 (Rovnick 2015). Differences of that size are, obviously, deeply consequential for the kind of life that can be enjoyed in retirement.

What flows through the investment chain is, therefore, above all money, with 'leakage' throughout the chain in the form of explicit fees and other expenses (in particular, trading costs) whose size is harder to determine. (One estimate of the total annual fees and expenses in the UK is £67 billion: see Boffey 2011. Even if that figure is inflated, it gives a sense of the possible scale of the issue. As a point of comparison, the 2015–16 budget for the National Health Service in England was £116.4 billion.)[9]

The performance that at least some intermediaries (especially fund managers) deliver in return for the fees they charge and the expenses they incur is measurable, and achieving good performance 'numbers' is a constant concern of investment managers, as we discuss in Chapter 2. Performance, though, is not simply a matter of numbers: the investment chain is also a sequence of impression management performances in the sense of Goffman (1959). Above all, what is performed is the financially competent self, and the best performance is that which is seamless: that does not appear to be a performance. Fund managers, for example, have to convey personal expertise and insight both in meetings internal to their firms and in external encounters with fellow intermediaries. They also have to portray themselves to investment consultants and ratings firms as rigorous followers of a formalized, auditable decision-making process. Sometimes, too, intermediaries indulge in what market participants call 'fronting': giving the appearance of having more influence than actually is the case.

What circulates through the investment chain, then, is not only money. It also includes performance numbers (measures of intermediaries' performance); self-presentations as competent, insightful, rigorous, influential professionals; quantitative models and other ideas for investing and trading; other forms of research; information such as 'market colour' (who is buying or selling what and why); emotions (the chain can involve friendships and trust, but also distrust, discrimination, even sometimes hatred); and much else beside. Their circulation through the links in the investment chain is interwoven intimately with that of money. Of equal importance is what does

---

[9] See <http://www.kingsfund.org.uk/projects/nhs-in-a-nutshell/nhs-budget>, accessed 24 January 2016.

not circulate through the chain. Sometimes, for example, the wishes and interests of end-investors seem to become diluted, almost to vanishing point, as their money passes from hand to hand.

A word is needed on the metaphor of 'chain' that we have chosen. One ordinary connotation of the word is constraint, and our book will highlight ways in which intermediaries in the investment chain are not free to act as they wish. For example, as we have already emphasized, the most important audiences who judge intermediaries' performances are often not the ultimate beneficiaries of their research and of the investment decisions based on it, but fellow intermediaries. Their implicit demands can be hard to ignore. For instance, as Svetlova discovered in ethnographic observation, effective impression management typically requires financial analysts and fund managers to give numerically precise predictions with a specific time-horizon— 'the target price for the share in 2017 is $85'—even though such predictions are hugely unreliable (see, e.g., Hägglund 2000) and those making them may privately have little confidence in them.

A chain, however, is a resource as well as a constraint: its links can be a source of strength; it can make possible action that otherwise would be infeasible. That second meaning of 'chain' is, for example, clear in the relationship between fund managers and client-service personnel explored in Chapter 2: they need each other as well as constrain each other. The chain's role as enabler as well as constraint was also evident, for instance, in an episode directly witnessed by one of us (Arjaliès) in which representatives of end-investors—that is to say, of the ultimate beneficiaries of pension funds— were mobilized in an attempt to influence corporations in whose shares the funds invested. As we show in Chapter 7, in that case the chain both made political action possible but also limited the forms that action could take.

Whether a chain constrains or enables, however, it always joins and entangles, tying intermediaries to each other. Indeed, that is the overall message of our book: investment management is shaped profoundly by these relations of entanglement in the investment chain.

What We Already Know about Investment Management

Although our field, the social studies of finance, has been growing rapidly, investment management has often received less attention from researchers in it than topics such as trading, financial derivatives, investment banks, and the causes of the 2007–8 and Eurozone financial crises. Nevertheless, especially if one takes a sufficiently broad view of the social studies of finance (to include, for example, the work of economists addressing sociological issues such as the tendency of investment managers to 'herd', that is to say, to take similar investment decisions), there is a reasonable body of existing research findings to draw upon.

Five broad clusters of findings stand out. First, how investment is organized has substantial effects on the structure and behaviour of companies. One of the pioneering books that showed this was Michael Useem's *Investor Capitalism* (1996), which argued that as institutional investors' holdings of the shares of US corporations had grown—they first surpassed the holdings of individuals in 1990—the relationship between investors and firms had changed. An individual investor dissatisfied with the performance of a corporation could simply sell her or his shares. An institutional investor trying to sell a big holding, however, would face losses caused by the very act of selling (as discussed in our Chapter 5), so rather than doing so institutional investors were increasingly—and successfully—pressuring corporate management to act in ways that they wished. Useem's book (along with Neil Fligstein's 1990 *The Transformation of Corporate Control*) helped spark one of the two main strands of existing broadly social studies of finance research on investment management: the examination of how the rise of investment management and of ideas of 'shareholder value' has changed American corporations. That change has involved the wholesale break-up of the multi-industry conglomerates of the 1960s and 1970s, and their replacement by 'lean', 'focused' firms (often formed by consolidation within an industry, with associated 'downsizing' and large-scale worker lay-offs). These firms took on more debt than their predecessors, and raised the cash to service it—and to generate the near-term profit increases that institutional investors were looking for—by aggressive cost-cutting, other measures such as lowering pension contributions, and sometimes cutting back on capital spending that would not have a short-term pay-off (Jung and Dobbin 2012: 62 and *passim*). Broadly analogous research has now emerged on Europe: see, for example, Goyer's analysis (2011) of the way in which short-termist Anglo-American investment managers prefer France's centralized corporations to Germany's more consensual corporate governance, with the voice it provides to employees.

Second, how firms are classified for the purposes of financial analysis is consequential. (The work of financial analysts is the second of the two main foci of such social studies of finance research on investment management as has been conducted—see the chapter on research on analysts [Wansleben 2012] in the *Oxford Handbook of the Sociology of Finance*—and accordingly this book focuses more on other intermediaries.) Typically, for example, sell-side financial analysts specialize in coverage of one or more specific economic sectors. Firms whose business does not fit neatly into those sectors sometimes attract less coverage by these analysts, and then pay a stock price penalty: their shares trade at lower prices than those of firms with similar levels of earnings and sales and similarly valued assets that are covered by more analysts

(Zuckerman 1999). This, in its turn, creates a pressure on firms to change their businesses so that they 'present a coherent product identity in the stock market' (Zuckerman 2000: 591). Furthermore, which sector a firm is classed as falling primarily within can strongly influence its valuation. For example, as Beunza and Garud (2007) noted, analysts' valuations of Amazon during that firm's rise were affected hugely by whether they saw it as an Internet company or a bookseller. Even the valuation of the shares of the best-known corporations can be influenced by how they are classified. In 2016, for example, Apple engaged in a major effort to persuade fund managers, many of whom saw the firm mainly as a hardware vendor, to view it primarily as a software and Internet business, and thus value its shares more highly.

Research in these first two areas—the effects of investment management on corporate behaviour and the importance of how firms are classified for financial analysis—is now relatively well established. The other clusters of findings are more tentative, but interesting nonetheless. The third is that career considerations strongly shape fund managers' decisions. Thus Chevalier and Ellison (1999) show that—most likely because of their more precarious career situations—younger fund managers tend to make more conventional decisions than their older counterparts: their portfolios of shares resemble those of others more than is the case for their older counterparts. (Hong et al. [2000] similarly demonstrate that the forecasts made by early-career analysts are closer to the average of others' forecasts.) Fund managers' educational formation also seems to matter. Thus Dincer et al. (2010) show that fund managers with business-school MBAs construct riskier portfolios than their counterparts with the main professional qualification, Chartered Financial Analyst (CFA), which is normally achieved primarily by independent study, often by those already employed in investment management.

Fourth, because fund managers' perceived performance matters to their career prospects and income, there are persistent temptations to manipulate how others in the investment chain perceive that performance, using techniques that go beyond effective Goffmanesque self-presentation. The most common technique seems to be 'window dressing': changing a portfolio of shares or bonds just before the date at which the portfolio's composition has to be reported to clients. Window dressing a portfolio of shares usually involves selling what clients will see as 'duds'—shares that have fallen in price—and buying shares that have risen in price and that clients will view as 'winners' (for econometric evidence of price movements consistent with window dressing, see Lakonishok et al. 1991). The window dressing of fixed income portfolios (portfolios of bonds or bond-like investments) typically involves temporarily replacing risky bonds whose high yields have boosted portfolio performance with less risky government bonds, so as to make the portfolio look safer (Morey and O'Neal 2006). Another technique is 'leaning for the tape': buying shares already held, just before portfolio performance is reported to investors, so that the 'market impact' of those purchases boosts the price of existing holdings and thus temporarily improves measured performance (Carhart et al. 2002).

Fifth, the gender of investment managers seems to matter, not to performance in the sense of the returns on the funds they manage, but to their capacity to attract investment. It might be expected that women and men would be equally good at the professional management of investment funds, and the detailed analysis of single-manager US mutual funds between 1992 and 2009 by Niessen-Ruenzi and Ruenzi (2015) suggests that is indeed the case. (Male *lay* investors tend actually to perform worse than women, apparently because over-confidence in their capacity to predict price movements leads them to trade too often, incurring costs that eat into their investment returns: Barber and Odean 2001.) However, despite their similar performance, mutual funds managed by women attracted inflows of capital a third lower than those managed by men (Niessen-Ruenzi and Ruenzi 2015).

Because capital inflows—not investor returns per se—are the key determinants of the profitability of investment management firms, these lower inflows (perhaps along with other forms of discrimination within the firms for which they work) may help explain how few women fund managers there are: for example, only 2 per cent of the fund management assets in the US are managed by women, a percentage that has been falling in recent years (Newlands 2015). In experimental settings, even the choice among index funds (which, as noted earlier, simply track the S&P 500 or a similar stock market index, and so if tracking the same index differ in performance in only very minor ways) is affected by the manager's gender, with male experimental subjects investing less in index funds run by women (Niessen-Ruenzi and Ruenzi 2015; their experiment is a variant of that first conducted by Choi et al. 2010).[10] This evidence is consistent with strong gender effects found outside financial markets, for example Kricheli-Katz and Regev's (2016) discovery that women sellers received around 20 per cent less on average than men did when selling identical new items on eBay.

There has been only limited direct focus on the investment chain in the research that underpins these five clusters of findings. However, we are not the first authors to examine the chain. For example, Gordon Clark's *Pension Fund Capitalism* (2000) identified determinants of the growing importance of pension funds in Anglo-American economies and examined decision-making, competitive processes, and organizational structure within the sector

---

[10] It might be thought that this indicates lack of understanding of the nature of an index fund, but Niessen-Ruenzi and Ruenzi (2015: 19) find the effect to be marginally stronger among subjects with higher levels of knowledge of finance.

(including its use of investment consultants and investment management firms). Clark's pioneering study has spawned further work by him (e.g. Clark 2003) and others (e.g. Dixon 2008). Indeed, although Clark did not explicitly employ the notion of 'investment chain' (the most influential use of the concept has been in Kay 2012, but see also, e.g., Wong 2010; Svetlova 2013; Kay 2015a; and Garratt and Hamilton forthcoming), Clark certainly discusses intermediaries and their role in the investment process: e.g. Clark (2000: 79).

Another noteworthy contribution to our understanding of the investment chain is Paul Langley's *The Everyday Life of Global Finance* (2008), which included (as well as an extensive discussion of borrowing) an analysis—broadly inspired by Michel Foucault—of the shift in Anglo-American economies from 'thrift' and 'insurance' to 'investment', especially via mutual funds and defined-contribution pension funds. In our terms, Langley traced the investment chain back into everyday life; in contrast, we focus more strongly on the layers of intermediaries through which investors' money passes. We share, however, an interest in the contradictions that afflict 'investment', including those evident in 'responsible investment' (see our Chapters 6 and 7).

A further major social stud of finance contribution to our understanding of the investment chain is Horacio Ortiz's *Valeur financière et vérité* (2014), which involved extensive ethnographic work, for example in a New York brokerage that supplies investment management firms with research (paid for, although Ortiz does not elaborate the point, by 'soft dollars' of the kind discussed in our Chapter 5). Ortiz focuses in particular on the tensions involved in participants' efforts to ascribe a fair or true value ('vraie valeur') to shares. That shares do have such a value—the present value of the future income stream to which they are an entitlement—is widely believed, but the uncertainty of future income makes any calculation of that value a precarious process of prediction. Participants typically think that worthwhile estimates of value must be personalized: they must be the 'sincere' product of personal 'convictions' (Ortiz 2014: 57). For a valuation to 'tell the truth' (Ortiz 2014: 54), however, those personal convictions must stand the test of how prices will move in efficient, competitive markets, and those markets—notoriously—render it difficult or impossible consistently to make profitable predictions. We too have witnessed this and related tensions in our fieldwork; they are discussed especially in Chapter 2.

Our Underlying Research

Although each of our chapters has a partially distinct empirical base (sketched in each chapter), the overall empirical evidence we draw upon in our examination of investment chains is of two main types. The first is semi-structured interviews with fund managers and other intermediaries in 'buy-side' investment chains. Altogether, we have conducted 234 such interviews, mainly in the UK, France, Germany, Switzerland, and the US. Furthermore, when in Chapter 5 we follow the chain into the 'sell-side' world of trading, we draw upon a further 181 interviews with traders (especially 'high-frequency' traders, who specialize in large volumes of ultra-fast, automated buying and selling), brokers, the staff of exchanges and other trading venues such as 'dark pools' (see the next section), the suppliers of technology to trading firms, etc.

The second form of research we have employed is participant observation. Arjaliès spent two and a half years working as a participant observer in an investment management firm with a responsible investment mandate; her observations especially inform our discussion in Chapters 6 and 7 of that form of investment. Svetlova similarly spent three months as a participant observer in the investment management and quantitative departments of a Swiss private bank and in a big German investment house. In addition to this formal participant observation, we also draw occasionally (especially in Chapter 2) on the personal experiences of Grant and Svetlova in their previous working lives—of five years and six years, respectively—in investment management.

The Chapters that Follow

Chapter 2 begins our more detailed examination of the investment chain. It draws on our interviews, but also (as just noted) on Grant's time working as an investment manager, to introduce some of the main sets of intermediaries and what their jobs are. The chapter sketches how those intermediaries enable and constrain each other and form audiences for each other's presentations of self.

Behind the pervasive 'front stage' presentations of an orderly, rigorous investment process, suggests Chapter 2, there lies a normally hidden, more messy, Goffmanesque 'back stage' of failures, uncertainties, and sometimes dissent. The chapter also highlights the way in which the numbers that measure investment performance obscure the ethical-political, labour, and legal conditions that make them possible—'responsible investment' still remains on the margins of investment management (see Chapters 6 and 7)—and are the focus of a pervasive, albeit again normally hidden, anxiety. As financial economics predicts, it is at best very hard for high-fee 'active' fund management (which, as noted before, is the form of management discussed in this book, and involves the selection of shares or bonds, rather than simply the less costly tracking of an index) consistently to outperform the relevant index. Implicitly, fund managers have to live their working lives in the shadow of that stubborn reality.

Chapter 3 examines the mechanisms through which clients impact fund managers' practices and vice versa. Our discussion in that chapter encompasses fixed income investment as well as investment in shares (the latter is the almost exclusive focus of the existing literature). In both fixed income and shares, clients can include both institutional investors (such as pension funds) and retail investors (private individuals, though often guided by financial advisers). Because fund managers' incomes and careers are heavily dependent on the amount of money they manage, their priority is to retain their existing clients and to attract new clients. However, fund managers cannot achieve this by concentrating exclusively on maximizing the performance of the funds they manage. Those who invest in funds are heterogeneous. Their reasons for investment vary, leading to different time-horizons on their decisions, different ways of measuring performance, and different forms of interaction with the rest of the investment chain. An important segment of institutional clients wants fund managers to focus not on maximizing returns but on meeting the client's liabilities, especially pension funds' contractual obligations to pensioners. The sophistication of clients varies, including their information-gathering capacity and their understanding of the complexities of financial markets, as does their reliance on various forms of advisers: investment consultants, independent financial advisers, and fund-rating companies.

Variations of these kinds among their clients influence fund managers' investment decisions, whether intentionally or not. Those decisions cannot properly be understood by focusing simply on a fund manager's beliefs about particular securities or markets: it is necessary to take into account also the broader investment chain context within which decisions are made. One thread in the existing literature on investment management is the incentives for 'agents' (investment managers) to act against the interests of their 'principals' (those whose money the agents manage): see the earlier discussion of 'window dressing' and 'leaning for the tape'. To focus too much on abuses of this kind is, however, unfair to the many fund managers who act honestly, as well as analytically simplistic. The client–fund manager relationship is not a simple principal–agent problem, but a multi-faceted, contextually dependent, malleable matter. Institutional investor clients such as pension funds have the power to set the terms of investment to constrain fund managers. Simultaneously, fund managers can also reshape what their clients take their interests to consist of, influencing their clients to align their goals with those of the managers.

Chapter 4 discusses a particular set of fund managers and analysts, those who run funds whose investment strategies are based on quantitative research or who advise on how the results of this research can improve investment performance. They might be expected to be more solitary in their practices and less enmeshed in relations to clients and to other intermediaries than their colleagues who rely on more qualitative reasoning. We find, however, that this is not so. Although quantitative managers certainly test ideas themselves, those ideas often (perhaps usually) come from others in the investment chain. Brokers and sell-side analysts are one major source, and the traditional way in which they are rewarded is by investment management firms choosing to buy and sell via them even when doing so is relatively expensive (see Chapter 5). Another source of ideas is those occupying similar roles in other firms. Despite efforts at secrecy, there is circulation of ideas among different firms—one of our interviewees talked openly about 'stealing' ideas from others—and some of this circulation is caused by managers' need to 'market' ideas to existing or potential clients. Indeed, basing a quantitative investment strategy around an idea that is already in circulation eases the task of marketing, because clients will typically already have heard of it from others. However, successful self-presentation to external audiences can cause internal frictions, and internal processes are again often much messier and less stringently rule-bound than they are portrayed as being to external audiences.

Chapter 5 is where we follow the investment chain from the 'buy side' of investment management into the 'sell side' of brokers and traders. Again, we do not attempt to do so in any comprehensive way. Rather, we organize our discussion in Chapter 5 by following historically a single thread in the trading of US shares (changes in how they are traded have had a huge influence on share trading in Europe and elsewhere), although we also discuss the trading of bonds more briefly. The thread we follow is the development of 'dark pools', which are private share-trading venues in which subscribers can bid to buy shares or offer to sell them without those bids or offers being visible to the market at large.

Originally, access to dark pools was restricted to investment management firms, and the pools were intended to permit those firms to buy or sell large blocks of shares among themselves at low cost and without the 'market impact' (adverse effect on market prices) of trading in the public markets. The history of dark pools, however, shows how hard it has been to cling to that vision in the face of investment chain entanglements. The entanglement on which we focus most is what are known colloquially in the US as 'soft dollars'. The term refers to the dominant way in which buy-side investment management firms pay for research by sell-side analysts, who typically work for brokers such as big investment banks. Buy-side firms channel their buy and sell orders via those brokers, even though the latter's fees mean that this is usually a more expensive way to trade than direct dealing via the original dark pools. The point of soft-dollar arrangements (which, although the term is

American, have been common in Europe too, although they are increasingly constrained by European Union regulations) is that the costs of trading are charged to the funds being managed, while if research had to be paid for directly it would most likely have to be the investment management firm itself that paid. Entanglements of this kind, Chapter 5 shows, have shaped the history of dark pools profoundly.

In Chapters 6 and 7—which are based primarily on Arjaliès's participant-observation research—we show how responses to the demand for responsible investment, a demand that has greatly increased since the financial crisis, are shaped both by the dynamics of the investment chain and by systematic differences in investment managers' entrenched practices and their ways of conceiving their accountability to their clients and to society at large.

Chapter 6 focuses on one of the paradoxes of responsible investment, which has not been prominent in previous discussions of the area, because they have focused too exclusively on shares. Responsible investment is much less influential in fixed income (bonds and bond-like investments) than in shares, so a company's bonds are often in practice treated as 'ethically' quite different from its shares. In Chapter 6, we find fixed income fund managers who were close to contemptuous of responsible investment, clinging to established tools, practices, and priorities, and (for example) continuing to invest heavily in Greek government bonds, because of the high yields these offered, despite warnings from their responsible investment colleagues that Greece's finances were not sustainable. The sophisticated mathematical tools available to help fixed income managers profit from pricing discrepancies seemed to divert their gaze from the more basic relationship between fixed income markets and the broader economies and societies of which they are part.

Chapter 7 extends the discussion of responsible investment by describing an episode in which parts of the investment chain were mobilized to seek a change in corporate policy, in this case overseas car companies' habit of banning trade unions in their plants in Mississippi (a major location of new car plants in the US). The episode reveals that such efforts at mobilization can attract attention and influence, but it also suggests that legal constraints and conflicts of interest are pervasive. Nearly all the members of the investment chain involved in the mobilization were constrained in some way. Fund managers, for example, wanted to be seen as responsive to clients' concerns, but had to bear in mind that they also managed investments in the same corporations for other clients whose priorities were different; in some cases, they might also be involved in managing the pension funds of the corporations that might be criticized. Trade union representatives on the boards of end-investors (in this case, public pension funds) were sympathetic to the demand for trade union rights, but also aware of the sensibilities of their colleagues who worked for the corporations that might be 'named and shamed'. The investment chain, in other words, can indeed be used to exert a force to change policies and practices, but the effects of its links are complex and contradictory.

Chapter 8, the conclusion, emphasizes how much more needs to be discovered about how the entanglements of intermediaries in investment chains shape investment management. We consider what are perhaps the three most common responses to the problems caused by investment chain entanglements: demands for increased information disclosure; calls to shorten the investment chain; and the continuing shift from the 'active' investment management discussed in this book to 'passive' index-tracking. Individually, none of these offers, we argue, a silver bullet. Perhaps, however, an appropriate combination of elements of all three—along with much greater emphasis on responsible investment—might offer a promising way forward.

2

Chains of Freedom

The Investment Chain inside the Investment Management Firm

Investment management isn't really about investment managers, whether understood as freestanding individuals or as part of teams of investors analysing and buying and selling and making money for their clients. It is about investment chains. As this book argues, investment managers are part of an investment chain. Chains bind: they constrain, restrict, compel, subject. Yet they are also (but not always) strong: through their binding they link, connect, enable, reinforce.

This chapter explores a particular set of links in the investment chain, drawing on both auto-ethnographic and interview materials. In focusing on the chain as a set of relationships, it continues work by other scholars of the social studies of finance. In particular, Horacio Ortiz has demonstrated in his ethnographic study of a New York broker and a Paris fund manager that the work of investment managers is usually reduced to that of putatively autonomous and individual 'investors' (2014). His ethnography shows that we ought instead to regard decision-making as 'disseminated' among fund managers, sell-side analysts, traders, and the financial press (2014: 137).

The metaphor of the chain allows us to complement the idea of disseminated decision-making, or of the 'distributed framing' we have found elsewhere in the financial industry (Hardie and MacKenzie 2007). Within the investment management industry, chains enable the staging of professional competence, whilst also requiring it to give an account of itself, and at times of crisis actively calling it into question. They also enable the activity of investment itself, through the way in which the labour of investing, far from being concentrated in individual investors, is distributed across multiple, linked roles. At the same time, these relationships impose limits on what can be done and how.

In the ethnographic account we give in this chapter, the investment managers are anything but individualized 'investors' processing information and taking decisions autonomously. Whilst investment management is a hierarchical space, and the place in the chain occupied by portfolio managers highly prestigious, these managers are nonetheless subject to a multitude of pressures from those in adjacent roles: internal client service personnel, investment consultants advising clients, and the clients themselves. Fund managers participate in a regime of visibility that means they have to justify themselves constantly to these parties, whose scrutiny, when it leads to a positive evaluation, means that fund managers and their firms retain existing or attract new funds—the condition of their continuing to exercise their prestigious and well-remunerated profession.

Moreover, ever present in investment management, integral to the architecture of constraint and enablement, are numbers. They make possible investment managers' daily routine of buying, selling, and measuring and reporting performance and risk, even as they constrain managers to think about, carry out, and present their work in certain ways and not others. Because of their claim to objectivity, they serve both to demonstrate the truth of the value of investment managers' activities, when those activities can be demonstrated to others in the chain to have led to 'good numbers', and to demonstrate the truth of managers' failings when other links in the chain can use numbers to challenge managers' performance of competence and experience.

Numbers are also a link to wider considerations of truth and value of the sort raised by Horacio Ortiz in his ethnographic study of financial markets (2014). He argues that we live in a world saturated with the assumptions and conclusions of financial economics, in particular concerning rational, autonomous investors, the efficient market hypothesis, and intrinsic value as potentially calculable. These assumptions shape the forms of investment that count as correct and legitimate (and therefore 'true'). In so doing, they conceal the processes by which value came to be understood in this fashion, the social relations necessary for this conception of value to be performatively effective, and the political consequences that ensue in terms of the allocation of credit and distribution of income and wealth. All of this is hidden from sight, because from the financiers' perspective these stand outside the regime of truth in which they are expert.

What this chapter seeks to achieve, then, is to trace some of these processes quasi-ethnographically. For five years (prior to Grant's training as an anthropologist) he worked in the financial industry in the City of London, first as a graduate trainee in various departments of a well-regarded but fairly small investment bank and institutional stockbroker (with around 1,000 employees, most in London), and then, from 1999 to 2003, as an assistant fund manager in its investment management arm, which had at the time around £10 billion of assets under management.[1] Had he known he would later become a researcher in the social studies of finance, he would have kept an ethnographic diary of these years. As it is, he draws here on his memory, faulty like all memory though it is, but having aided this memory by two visits to his former firm during the course of later research, and by a number of conversations and interviews with former colleagues, some still working there, others having moved on to other firms. He also conducted twenty-five interviews with equity investment management professionals at other firms in London, Edinburgh, New York, and Los Angeles, as well as participant observation at a conference for investment managers in New York. In what follows, then, he draws extensively on his own experiences, having found that these conversations and interviews tend to confirm both the value of his memories mobilized as auto-ethnographic material, and the relevance of these insights for the subsequent period and for other firms. To avoid artificiality in the remainder of this chapter, he uses the first person when discussing events and processes he directly participated in or observed.[2]

Chains of Freedom: Links in the Chain, c.2000

When I first began to work in fund management in 1999, I started as a trainee on the client service team for our charity clients. While a medium-sized fund manager, with just over £10 billion in assets under management at the time, we had a leading position in the UK charities market, although institutional pension funds nonetheless constituted the largest proportion of our assets. A transfer (or rather escapee) from the world of corporate finance, I was told that this was the only place available for me. I would be assisting two senior client service managers. One of them, Robert, also had a part-time role as a fund manager and investment team analyst, and would regularly come and go between our sixth-floor desk, where everyone sat in quiet or had hushed conversations about presentations to clients and how best to put our case, and the fifth floor, the 'investment floor', where teams of portfolio managers and sector analysts sat grouped according to geographical focus, the phones rang more often, the dealing team sat in the corner, and decisions to buy and sell, often involving millions of pounds per transaction, were taken.

---

[1] Assets under management of course fluctuate both in accordance with market fluctuations and portfolio performance (generally closely tied to broader market performance, which is the problem!) and with inflows and outflows of client funds. The years 1999–2003 being volatile times for equity markets in particular, this figure ranged between £9 and £14 billion across this period, but was more often than not in the region of £10 billion, making the firm a medium-sized investment management house by the standards of London at the time.

[2] We adopt this convention in subsequent chapters (4, 6, and 7) where we similarly draw on ethnographic data.

Determined to make a good impression, I nonetheless felt at sea in the world of client service. Robert quickly sensed that I would have preferred to be in the world of investment analysis and decision-making. Indeed, he said as much: a young, ambitious, apparently intelligent man like me should be working downstairs. I sensed that he would also like to work full-time on the investment team. A relatively recent recruit from a larger investment house, he was one of the rare employees of our firm to have an MBA. Together with the Chief Investment Officer, with whom I would frequently see him in intense conversation, he was working on an overhaul of the firm's investment process, seeking to ground it in 'scientific' data drawn from academic financial economics. A new process would both make it more likely that our funds outperformed the equity markets[3] they were invested in around the world, and demonstrate to investment consultants and potential clients that we were among the most professional and credible in this competitive business. He began to involve me in this process, sending me huge spreadsheets to analyse (they did not fit on the three-inch 'floppy' discs we still used at the time), even as he dropped hints to his senior colleagues on the floor below that they might transfer me to the UK Equity team once an opening appeared.

Staff turnover at our firm, as elsewhere in the industry, being reasonably high, this opportunity duly transpired and I bade farewell to the world of client service to become a utility sector analyst and assistant UK institutional equity fund manager. I had arrived.

Robert also became more and more active on the fifth floor, provoking grumbling and humorous but sarcastic asides from his sixth-floor colleagues. The new investment process was duly rolled out within the firm at a series of internal meetings, with attendance compulsory and the firm's top brass present. As well as being a serious 'demonstration' of the efficacy of the new process, with series of graphs and tables, it was also a marketing call to arms: go out and sell this with confidence to clients. The Chief Investment Officer even declared that we could now afford to be 'arrogant', that investment consultants did not want to hear fund managers in presentations cautiously averring 'I think that...'. Then we hit the Internet bubble, and performance, hitherto promising, became dreadful: not only in absolute terms, but relative to falling markets too.

One of the investment team's roles was to explain the rationale of our investment decisions to client service teams so that they could themselves deal with any awkward questions from clients whose first point of contact they were. Part of our underperformance stemmed from our over-investment in various 'tech' stocks, principally telecommunication service providers and

---

[3] 'Equity markets' is the standard industry term for the markets in the shares (or in the US, 'stock') of companies listed on an authorized stock exchange.

software makers. Our investment process was designed to stop what one fund manager we later spoke to called 'thrashing around', volte-faces in fund positioning in an attempt to catch up with a market sentiment that we had hitherto misjudged. Our investment decisions were supposed to be rigorous and consistent. There was an internal 'audit trail', one-page notes describing the investment case for each stock we invested in and available on the firm's internal computer network or intranet. Buy and sell decisions would also be communicated to client service teams at meetings each day after the end of trading. Once made, we were not supposed to reverse our decisions unless something 'material' had changed to affect our investment case, for instance a company's strategy or management had changed, or had revised down its profit forecasts (a 'profit warning').

Yet we increasingly found we reverted to 'thrashing around' (although we were loath to admit it), selling 'tech' stocks we had not long previously bought at higher prices, much to the chagrin of client service managers who had to deal with baffled, bewildered, even angry clients questioning our judgement and competence. I sometimes accompanied Robert as he reported back to the charity team, and saw increasingly irate staff gesturing to presentation packs outlining our investment process and asking, as Robert explained we had reduced positions in yet another falling 'tech' stock, 'What has changed? What has changed?'

By 2002 Robert, the Chief Investment Officer, and several other senior investment personnel had been made redundant, in an involuntary reduction of staff that was unprecedented in the history of our firm and which affected all business areas, not just fund management. Personally, however, this meant more responsibility for me, with new industry sectors to analyse, and new bosses to impress as I sought to make my mark in the 'engine room' of the investment floor.

Think of investment management, and chances are the portfolio managers themselves will come to mind, as both emblematic of and embodying investment itself, seated at their desks analysing, taking decisions, buying, selling, making money for their clients. Certainly the most prestigious part of investment management is the portfolio management role. In my firm, as in other smaller and medium-sized firms, this was combined with the role of sector analyst, and for me and my colleagues on the investment floor, the job offered the right combination of intellectual stimulation and the excitement of actually making successful buy or sell decisions.

No moment was happier in my career than when I advised the manager of our 'concentrated' UK institutional equity fund, one with a lower number of stocks and a higher risk profile, to buy more Viridian. Viridian was the privatized Northern Irish electric utility. Few analysts, whether on the sell or the buy side, bothered to follow this company, since it was small and operated in different regulatory and political conditions to other UK utilities. I had spent some time researching it, reading brokers' reports, talking to the limited number of sell-side analysts who covered it, and meeting the company management. I had played around with profit forecasts in a simple spreadsheet and concluded that it was undervalued, recommending that our concentrated fund take a small position. One day, however, the company issued a profit warning and its shares fell. The fund manager who had bought the shares on my recommendation sent off some expletives in my direction on seeing the news, but then, manager of a higher risk fund that he was, asked me whether I should buy some more. I hummed and hawed. He goaded me to come to a decision. I went off and played around with the numbers again. The profit warning related to ancillary consulting businesses, not to the utility business itself. Even assuming continuing losses on the consulting side, the whole company was worth considerably more than the market price implied. The dividend was secure. 'Buy some more', I said, reasonably confidently, and my colleague duly did. Over the next three months the stock outperformed the market considerably, helping his fund outperform and enhancing my reputation within the team. 'Good call on Viridian', he shouted at me across the desk; my immediate supervisor and the team head occupied two of the desks between us.

Enabling and Constraining

Analysing the division of labour at investment consulting firms, Pierre de Larminat noted a clear hierarchy between 'quantitative' and 'qualitative' analysts (2013). The former analysed the performance records of investment managers with the aid of computer software; the latter, while still in fact making use of quantification, saw their role as bringing to bear on the quality of investment managers the shrewd judgement that was the fruit of years of industry experience. Demonstrating one's ability to analyse the 'numbers' was only a prelude to becoming the more prestigious 'qualitative' type of analyst who could evaluate the future and therefore uncertain performance of investment managers, a future not amenable to the kind of statistical analysis the 'quantitative' analysts applied to past performance data.

He observes, following Bruno Latour (1987), that different forms of authority adhere to the products of the two forms of analysis: quantification enables circulation of reified things between agents sharing the same conventions of calculation; qualification acquires the authority of its being the result of the judgement of experienced persons. Extending this analysis to the world of investment management itself, Larminat notes that while portfolio managers invoke the technical effectiveness of their management (as evinced by risk-adjusted portfolio outperformance), the fact that managers often fail or that statistical analysis shows that luck plays an important part threaten this claim, whence a tendency to downplay quantitative in favour of qualitative reasons for success. They can show that their selections conform to professional norms, therefore obeying a procedural rationality, even if they turn out to be failures. In this way, distinctions such as that between the qualitative and quantitative help professional investors (the managers) retain control over investors (their clients), who often don't know what is entailed by such distinctions.

This ethnographic excursion enables us to confirm and extend Larminat's analysis, but also to complicate it. The division of labour inside a fund management house is both spatial and hierarchical. The firm's business is, after all, investment management, and those who manage the investments sit together and provide the rationale for the labour of all the other employees in the building. To me, as to my senior colleague Robert, the investment floor seemed the most prestigious part of the firm; to invest—to analyse, persuade, take decisions, and subsequently to be shown to be justified—was why we came into the business. The Chief Investment Officer's background was in portfolio management. There was a concentration of personnel with senior job titles in the various investment teams.

Unlike in Larminat's example of the progression from quantitative to qualitative analyst, however, there was not a clear progression from other parts of the business to the investment teams. Client service teams—there were three sets, dealing with pension funds, charities, and wealthy private clients—were also prestigious 'front office' groups, including a number of senior personnel. Nonetheless, there was an assumption, if only discreetly voiced (for instance by junior investment staff over drinks on a Friday night after work), that the well-liked senior portfolio manager who was transferred to pension fund client service would not have undergone this fate had he and his team's performance been better. Those older client service staff who had had previous experience of investment decision-making in the days when the division of labour had not been so clear and investment processes not so clearly demarcated often showed signs of frustration that they could no longer make investment decisions, all such decisions being made by the investment teams; this frustration (all of whose subjects were well-remunerated, middle-aged men with relatively senior positions but not at, or likely to reach, the top of the hierarchy) made their critiques of investment team performance all the more piquant.

This hierarchical relationship between client service personnel and investment managers was premised on the prestige that accrued to the investment teams by virtue of their execution of the 'core function' of an investment management firm: investment. Nonetheless, client service staff, by virtue of their client-facing role, remained prestigious 'front office' staff; so too the marketing personnel, who in various ways dealt with investment consultants and were therefore integral to bringing in more funds—essential in a business where revenues are for the most part based on a percentage of funds under management, and where senior management regularly issue ambitious targets for growth in funds.

More clearly hierarchically subordinate were the staff working in the valuations department (occupying a lower floor in the building), whose job was to produce the printouts of portfolio valuations sent out to clients each quarter, and to answer any queries pertaining thereto in the interim.[4] The image of hierarchy should not lead us astray, however: links in the chain stand in (often subtle) hierarchical relation to one another, but subordinate links constrain superordinate ones as much as they enable them. Client service managers, marketing staff, even valuations departments, both strengthen and limit investment managers. The first two in particular act as voices of the clients within the firm itself, even as in their outward-facing roles they act as voices of the investment teams, explaining and justifying their decisions.

One fund manager I interviewed in 2012, a senior portfolio manager with eighteen years in the industry at the time, put the influence client expectations have over his investment decisions in the following terms:

> The funds that are the lower risk ones…the institutional market, the trustee-based marketplace, I think it's dangerous to think about them too much, but I think you'll find most people think about them. Segregated funds, people think about the clients a lot more. It's really—sorry that I'm doing your job for you—that's really behavioural. At the end of the quarter, I've bought some atrocity, and 'it's been awful, you, you idiot'—it could ruin the relationship if you do something that looked quirky and odd but turned out to be, 'where's your judgement?' That could damage you even though your fund's done well. With retail money and hedge fund money, obviously I have the retail experience, and hedge fund I'm only a contributor, it's a bit more—there are many ways to skin a cat. 'If the numbers are good, I don't care how you got them.'…I've made it…deliberately…exaggerated, but there is a spectrum across how clients feel about you. When you're not doing as well, clients get a bit more granular and microscopic on you, and that of course creates its own pressure, because you're, because in that case it goes wrong. When you're doing well, you often take the view that you can, that you've got a bit of a cushion, so I'll have a go at this slightly odd thing, because if it blows up I'm still alive.

[4] Smaller firms like the one described here cannot afford the split between portfolio managers and research analysts that is common at larger firms. Our impression from interviewing investment professionals from the latter is that both these functions are prestigious and regarded as central to the firm's business; at many of these firms, demonstrating one's capability to use one's research to make good recommendations is a necessary step to becoming a portfolio manager (see Chapter 6); but for at least one analyst we interviewed, the labour of research was itself sufficiently prestigious and rewarding that he had no desire to become a portfolio manager.

Clients here are a sort of amalgam of two celebrated figures in social thought, Adam Smith's imaginary spectator (Smith 1976) and Clifford Geertz's ethnographer looking over the 'native's' shoulder (Geertz 1973). For Smith, our own judgements concerning our moral conduct necessarily take shape with reference to how we imagine others' sentiments towards them. For Geertz, commenting on Malinowski's canonical claim that ethnographers should seek to adopt the 'native's point of view', ethnographers can at best look over the shoulders of their informants and describe their world in terms which both elicit the richness and distinctiveness of the culture being described and yet remain foreign to it.

For the portfolio manager just quoted, an imaginary client is ever-present, especially when it comes to his largest, institutional, that is to say pension fund clients: he may find it dangerous to think too much about them, but his opinion is that most managers do so anyway. When performance is poor, or even if just one particular investment decision appears to contradict what clients and their consultants have been told about rigorous investment processes, clients are imagined exerting pressure and questioning their managers' judgement—a question which strikes at the root of investment managers' professional identity. At the same time, there is a subtext which suggests that clients can never fully grasp the fund manager's world. Perform well, and client pressure is reduced: they are unlikely to conduct fine-grained analyses of the reasons for this outperformance, or phone their investment manager and ask for a justification of the deals that led to this outperformance.

In my experience, inherent in many of the discussions between fund managers, or between fund managers and marketing staff or client service managers, is a concern to present the previous quarter's or year's activities in the best possible light, to explain and thereby to justify the positions taken or the macroeconomic outlook which will prove the fund's positioning right in the months to come. It is as if clients are both able to understand, and indeed, deserve an explanation, and yet by virtue of not having themselves participated in the discussions leading to investment decisions, can never fully understand. Further explanation is always possible, and never comprehensive.

Within the firm itself, client service managers are a less imaginary form of spectator. At my firm, these managers visited our floor occasionally, or called on the internal phone network, but the main point of contact was formal daily meetings at 5 p.m., half an hour after the closure of European stock markets, during which designated investment team managers would pass on information about the investment teams' dealings and discussions during the day, and respond to any questions. In times of poor performance—for us the aftermath of the Internet bubble in 2001–2 was one such period—this could be a harrowing experience, with the investment manager's competence coming under fire.

Murmurs of discontent—themselves reflections of the difficult job client service managers have when having to defend poor performance to concerned clients—crystallized into barely suppressed protest on one occasion when a mid-level fund manager was asked to explain what the company Cable & Wireless Communications did now that it had been demerged from its parent Cable & Wireless. 'Not Cable & Wireless' came back the blustering reply, to rolls of eyes and angry mutterings from the audience. With this in mind, later on, when I had the task of reporting to our private client managers, I always made sure that I had a couple of sentences prepared to explain what any company we had invested or might invest in did and how it made money, and once or twice client service managers approached me to explain they appreciated my taking them seriously—a sort of successful 'internal marketing' discussed further in Chapter 4.

My more senior colleague (who later moved to another firm, but not as a fund manager) was not, however, incompetent. It would be wiser to interpret his lapse as a momentary failure of performance. Fund management is like much Western bourgeois social interaction as long ago diagnosed by Erving Goffman, fundamentally reliant on a careful presentation of the self (1959). Working in an organization whose output, as crystallized quantitatively in its performance numbers, belied its claims to professional competence, my colleague was no doubt under considerable stress and had responded to a reasonable question with the kind of answer that ought to have been reserved for the 'back stage' in Goffman's terminology. Even a fund manager specializing in a single market such as London has a universe of 350 companies, and it is impossible to have an up-to-date detailed working knowledge of all of them. Around the investment team desk (back stage) he could have asked a colleague, for instance the telecoms sector analyst, or called up a broker or read a broker's report, and there would have been no issue in his admitting his ignorance. In front of his audience, however, this was out of the question.

When all functions well, this performance comes across as confidence, as reassuring, as not being a performance at all. Indeed, it has performative effects, inducing continuing trust in the fund manager on the part of clients. A client service manager at an Edinburgh firm with £50 billion under management told us that it was often necessary for him to 'educate' clients on their approach, which focused on long-term growth opportunities. He would explain to clients that quarterly or even annual underperformance was to be expected given the long-term orientation of the firm's funds, and that they should judge the firm on its five-year track record. Those clients who wanted what his firm offered, he told us, accepted this, while those who were seeking a racier short-term performance took their money elsewhere.

Whilst allowances must be made for investment professionals' presentation of self to visiting social scientists, the picture he painted of his role in the firm, mediating carefully between investment managers and clients, understanding the worlds and concerns of both and keeping both sides adequately informed of each other, implied a serenity that might be possible in a firm with a stable or growing client base and solid performance numbers, but difficult to manage when performance is poor and clients are heading for the door. Here it is important to recall the simultaneously enabling and constraining agency of the investment chain: clients impose limits, but also, when all is going well, enable the performance by portfolio managers of their job, abetted by client service managers.

The Edinburgh client service manager quoted here described his job as 'letting [portfolio managers] get on with it' by keeping their interactions with clients to a minimum. Conversely, one senior fund manager at a medium-sized London firm told us that he liked meeting clients, that once he had a presentation prepared this would serve for twenty-five meetings, and that a good meeting with a client gave him 'positive energy' and confidence that the rationale for his management of his funds was a sound one.

This performance is a performance of expertise. Presentations of fund management teams to the outside world—whether on websites accessible only to consultants and institutional clients, or in presentations designed for these groups, or in 'retail' material, that is to say marketing material designed for independent financial advisers and small investors (discussed further in Chapter 3)—invariably emphasize individuals' 'investment experience', in the first instance measured in years. After about four years in the industry, having done my regulatory and professional exams, with plenty of experience of analysing stocks and making and executing recommendations, confident in leading our meetings with company executives over twice my age, apparently respected by my investment team colleagues, having good relationships with a number of sell-side analysts, I nonetheless counted for little when it came to presentation to the parts of the chain on the client side of the office walls. 'Four years of investment experience' was a meagre sum to put on a presentation to consultants; at best I and my junior colleagues were there in order to demonstrate to potential clients that we had 'strength in depth', that our firm's professionalism included its ability to train the experienced fund managers of the future. The marketing employee (and former consultant) who dealt with the investment consultants would happily consult me or my fellow assistant fund manager if she wanted to know what the rationale for a particular transaction or position was, but she preferred to consult the fund manager when available, and it was only he who was whisked away for urgent consultations on forthcoming presentations. At the time I thought I had more or less learnt everything useful to know about investment. Some years later, then, I was astonished to hear from one of my interviewees, head of European equities at a large London fund manager owned by an even larger US firm, that 'fund management is a craft, and can only be learnt on the job. No one really knows what they're doing until they've been doing it for at least fifteen years'. For equity investing at least, professional exams like the CFA, he acknowledged, were useful; a formalized system for monitoring risk was essential; but neither of these could replace the 'judgement' developed after thousands of days at the desk and in meetings.

As noted earlier, this self-presentation as experienced professionals able to make sound judgements in a way others cannot in part stems from the industry's structural flaw, namely the impossibility that most of its participants might outperform benchmark markets on a consistent basis. The numbers do not lie, but as Mary Poovey (1993) noted with regard to statistics, they always require a narrative to explain them, and this narrative usually includes an attempt to demonstrate ongoing professional competence through providing a rationale for fund performance that in the case of underperformance involves a plausible projection of the reasons for one's outperformance into the near future, thus allaying client and consultant concerns.[5]

Together with my fellow assistant, one of my tasks was to write a one-page quarterly report sent out to smaller clients to update them on the progress of our funds. In incredibly lapidary style, during a prolonged period of underperformance our task was to explain the positions we had taken, why they had not provided us with outperformance during the quarter, express due contrition, but at the same time inspire confidence that we would be proved right very soon thanks to our intelligent reading of macroeconomic trends, our careful analysis of valuations, and our perspicacious interpretation of stock market cycles.

Behind this presentation to the outside world lay what I referred to earlier as the 'audit trail', designed in the first instance for internal consumption. Following the implementation of our new investment process, for every stock we bought or sold a one-page summary of the rationale had to be posted on the firm's intranet. The author was the investment team member responsible for the analysis of the company's industry sector. The summary included various valuations, a target price, a summary of the company's business and strategic positions, and a brief explanation of why we were buying or selling, increasing or decreasing our holding. This audit trail might be of value to other

---

[5] Although as we discuss in Chapter 4, fund managers using quantitative models in order (so they claim) to screen out fallible human judgement are offering an alternative narrative, one in which numbers and their putative objectivity are the narrative—a fiction which cannot ultimately be sustained.

investment team members wanting to refresh their memories of our discussions, but it was especially valuable to client service teams seeking to understand why we were managing our portfolios in the way we did. As I indicated previously, especially in times of underperformance, suspicion crept into relations between investment and client service personnel, and this virtual paper trail could be used as evidence: if our view on x date about y stock was positive, with z target price, why were we now selling at price $z-50$? The audit trail constrained us, since it offered a reduced and objectified rationale for decisions which had generally been made in more fluid and lengthy circumstances, the fruit of numerous conversations across the desk and in meetings, meetings with company management, discussions with sell-side analysts and sales staff, with our in-house economist and strategist. These circumstances could not be recapitulated in a five-minute conversation with a perplexed client service manager.

At the same time, the audit trail, and the investment process of which it was part, enabled us as fund managers by allowing us collectively, aided by client service managers and marketing staff, to present ourselves as professional and rigorous to the outside world. If internally this trail could at times be messy and lead to sceptical scrutiny of our actions, externally we could offer its existence as proof of our rigour and then cherry-pick examples to demonstrate how good we were as fund managers. Similarly, when during interviews we have asked fund managers and buy-side analysts to talk us through a particular share purchase, we have invariably been presented with a systematic and rigorous series of steps: industry sector reviews, review of sell-side reports, analysis of absolute and comparative valuations, testing of valuations under various macroeconomic or industry-specific scenarios, analysis of the company's strategic position, meetings with company management, establishment of share price targets, recommendations or actual decisions to buy or sell or ignore for the time being, and how much relative to the portfolio. The actual steps and their order do vary somewhat, but the impression usually given is of a clear-headed, ordered, rational process in harmony with well-established firm procedures. Indeed, when we asked one senior Edinburgh fund manager we had interviewed, and who had offered to help us further, whether one of us could come and observe an investment meeting, we were told that the firm's policy was never to have outsiders in these meetings on the grounds that they didn't want the consultants making the same request, as they felt that the presence of observers would hinder their performance. Reading between the lines, having participated in many such meetings as an employee, what is being protected here is the image of the clear and rational flow of the 'process', in reality a good deal messier and more improvised.

Euro-American values, wrote Marilyn Strathern, unlike Melanesian ones, privilege knowledge as the circulation of information and the demonstration to one's peers that one has this knowledge (2000: 312). She had in mind anthropologists and other academics rather than fund managers, but the phrase 'audit trail' easily crosses domains, from finance to academia to government and beyond, as part of a more general 'audit culture', the presumption that making visible, 'transparency', ensures greater organizational efficiency and effectiveness. This presumption is likewise constitutive of the investment chain: clients, consultants, client service and marketing personnel, and to some extent investment managers seek to demonstrate the rigour of their process through making it visible, or seek visibility of that process in order to confirm or call into question its rigour. Playing the role of a fund manager, an experienced investment professional capable of exercising a finely tuned and difficult to acquire judgement also requires an audience that sees the manager performing.

We say 'to some extent investment managers', because, as we have seen, investment managers are aware of the actual messiness of process and are, up to a point, keen to defend it from the outside gaze. Strathern suggests we ask what visibility conceals (2000: 310). Here the technology of visibility, the audit trail, or associated presentations to consultants, makes one version of the investment process available, of the kind that will retain and attract clients, but it conceals beneath its transparent façade the moments of dissent and uncertainty, of improvisation and contradiction that are as much part of the investment business as rigorous and logical analysis. Moreover, transparency renders invisible both its own transparent material (the audit trail is not shown for its own sake, but in order to reveal how the process works—see also Chapter 4) and the ideological agendas that subtend it (Pelkmans 2009: 426–7) in favour of an impression that there is no ideology at work at all except for faith in the powers of the market and public accountability as an end in itself (Levine 2005).

Chains of Numbers: Performance and other Figures as Agents

For all the importance of narratives and their 'framing' (Hardie and MacKenzie 2007) in financial market participants' evaluation practices, and despite investment managers' carefully professional presentation of self, 'the numbers', as performance figures are often referred to colloquially, are what fund managers and their firms are judged by first and foremost. Moreover, they are judged frequently. Most fund managers we interviewed have access to their portfolios in real time, meaning that they can call up a spreadsheet with live price links that tells them not only the valuation of each holding and of the portfolio as a whole, but also profit and loss, and, most importantly, performance relative to their benchmark index over a variety of time-scales. These spreadsheets will also give them various conventional measures of risk such as tracking error or the information ratio. The former is a calculation of the standard deviation of the difference between the portfolio's returns and those of the benchmark over a given time period, while the latter measures how much of a portfolio's excess return is generated from the manager's excess risk taking against the benchmark. These tools enable managers to see when large active positions get 'too large', possibly requiring action to reduce the risk, or even triggering a visit from the chief investment or risk officers in search of an explanation. Portfolio managers check these frequently; as one manager told us 'not too often, but several times a day'.

Portfolio managers therefore have a keen sense of how they are performing on a daily and even intra-daily basis. The writing of quarterly reports, presentations to clients and consultants, and the publication of performance data then compiled and ranked by various fund analysis services (particularly important in the retail market, as indicated in Chapter 1), as well as internal controls and lines of reporting (monitoring by heads of teams and chief investment officers) all involve the fixing of this performance in the form of a limited quantity of numbers which convey the truth of how well or poorly the fund, the team, the firm in question is doing its job. All the complexity of analysis and the messiness of decision-making are reduced to this simple form. It is true that performance numbers are immediately subjected to interpretation: 'this quarter's not looking good, but year-on-year performance is still first quartile [of the universe of comparable fund managers]', or 'a few more quarters like this and the three-year numbers won't look so awful any more'. Even so, it is the numbers which demand such a response, or rather the knowledge that they will be taken seriously by other parts of the chain— internally (client service managers, marketers, supervisors, including when deciding on employees' remuneration packages) and externally (clients, consultants, future employers if the manager is thinking one day of moving to another firm). Numbers are chains of subjection for those whose actions help to generate them, who indeed can only flourish if these numbers are 'good', i.e. indicate outperformance.

As already noted, for the majority of fund managers what matters is relative performance, that is to say, relative to a benchmark index. There is no immediate contradiction here between the standard justification of equity market investing—to earn a higher return than would be possible from less risky assets—and the spectacle of fund managers in periods of falling equity markets vaunting the fact that their fund has fallen only 13.75 per cent when the relevant index has fallen 14.75 per cent, since this fall in markets is assumed to be part of the risk (volatility of returns) taken on board by equity investors; in all likelihood the upside will be greater still. Nonetheless, a focus on relative numbers and on short reporting time-scales (with the basic unit being the quarter) means that this situation can frequently feel absurd, including to many fund managers themselves (Ortiz 2014: 142–3). The fact that clients pay substantial fees to have well-remunerated specialists manage their money; the fact that once these fees are subtracted, even clients of many outperforming managers do not see any outperformance; the fact that it is close to statistically impossible for all fund managers to outperform; the fact that it is probably impossible to predict which fund managers will outperform, or for any fund manager, however good their 'track record', to guarantee consistent future outperformance; the fact that a variety of index-tracking or replicating funds are available at a much lower cost to anyone who thinks that over time equity markets will appreciate more than other asset classes (and why pay someone more on the off-chance they might be able to eke out an extra couple of per cent?)—all these combine to make the absurdity of the situation weigh heavily on the industry.

Professionals along the investment chain are aware of this. Chatting informally around the desk one maxim that would crop up from time to time was 'you can't eat relative performance'. Active fund managers are keenly aware of the threat to their business from index funds. The persistent bear market of the early 2000s, the first since the 1970s, prompted many otherwise cautious, long-only fund managers, like the one Grant worked for, to set up hedge fund offerings for disgruntled clients looking for positive absolute returns (although these returns were no more guaranteed than the standard promise of steady relative outperformance).

Still, long-only active fund management not only persists, but controls trillions of dollars' worth of assets. Critics from within the industry often argue that investors ought to split their funds, with the majority placed in index trackers and the rest in absolute return funds—on the basis that the former capture long-term rises in equity markets at a low cost, the latter offer the possibility of gains well above market gains (albeit at a much higher risk)— and have even gone so far as to argue that to invest in so-called 'active' funds (in reality often 'passive' since many try to replicate and then slightly exceed their benchmark indices, so-called 'closet benchmarking') is a betrayal of fiduciary duty (Bernstein and Hawley 2014). Fund managers we spoke to were aware of this criticism: one described it as a 'pincer movement' that threatened his fund, at least in theory, but he nonetheless insisted there was a place for long-only, active management.

We conducted the interview in question in 2012, and so far he continues to be right, however difficult the persistence of the fund management industry in its current guise despite the implausibility of consistent outperformance can be to explain. The aura of professionalism, the suasive power of well-rehearsed narratives and the mathematically sophisticated academic financial theory which underpins them (Ortiz 2014), the way in which institutions across the chain but outside the firms themselves, from regulators to consultants to pension fund trustees to governments are deeply invested (affectively as well as financially) in it, the sheer difficulty of unwinding such a vast and unwieldy assemblage surely all play their part.

The shaky foundations of investment management have something of the quality of the 'public secret', Michael Taussig's term (1999) for that which everyone knows but no one articulates, or that which, even if articulated, is nonetheless not destroyed. Wherever numbers show up along the investment chain—and they are numerous—a public secret lurks in full view. Valuations of client portfolios, stock market indices, league tables of investment management houses' performance, the share prices of individual companies and their movements, macroeconomic data and forecasts: all proclaim at least a partial truth about some phenomenon: X's portfolio, the level of 'the market', the skills of fund managers, the fair value of such-and-such an enterprise, the size and direction of 'the economy', but all are subject to challenge. A portfolio valuation is an artificial fixing of that value at a given moment, already outdated by the time the client will have read it, and not corresponding to what they would receive were they to liquidate the portfolio and convert it into cash (because of the likely impact of sales on market prices: see Chapter 5). Indices are at best a proxy for all listed stocks rather than an infallible summary of their value, and still less do they stand for all economic value, despite often being conjured up as such in public discourse (Goede 2005). Thus the share price movements which underpin portfolio valuations and therefore performance statistics are on some level driven by supply and demand ('more buyers than sellers', one of our dealers liked to joke when asked if he had any information about a particular price rise), but they are also driven by company news, rumour, economic data, and a host of other pieces of often affectively charged information in ways which both confirm and exceed the theory of efficient markets (Ortiz 2014). Economic data are liable to revision; forecasts turn out wrong as often as not. All this investment professionals know, yet the torrent of reporting of these numbers, followed by careful analysis and their insertion into more or less performative stories of what they mean and how they affect, justify, or call into question a fund's positioning carries on regardless.

Numbers and their relation to investment managers are thus as much a link in the chain as client or consultant relationships. Despite the different ethical status of these agents—numbers are in no sense responsible or accountable, although they often empower or incite responsibility and accountability—when seen from the perspective of constraint and enablement they are ontologically similar to the other actors treated here;[6] they are 'actants', actors whose actions modify those other actors, to use the terminology of so-called actor-network theory (Latour 2004: 75).

What is more, numbers are highly effective agents. Talking of the marketization of post-communist Romanian healthcare, Sabina Stan noted 'a mystique of numerical and quantitative rationality' advanced by healthcare 'reformers' in the country (2007: 259). Being able to command this rationality made them highly influential and difficult to challenge, even as it hid other important dynamics—reformers' assumptions that individuals were motivated by self-interest and greed and could only be regulated by markets, aided by transparency, to which some opponents at least responded with 'occult cosmologies' purporting to explain what was really going on (Stan 2007: 264–70). In a similar way, the investment chain links groups of people all analysing and mobilizing sets of numbers, developing their own narratives and challenging others'. Given their training, many of these people are quite capable of challenging the mystique of any particular set of numbers, but the overall rationality of quantification is not called into question, nor its apparent lack of substantive justification; as Theodore Porter pointed out, numbers persuade both because they accumulate and link users who become invested in them, and because they have a long association with rationality and objectivity (1995: 417). In this sense, the apparatus of numerical presentation and evaluation in investment management also resembles double-entry bookkeeping, in that it is an *ex post* technique for justifying decisions which, through the way in which quantification appears to embody rationality itself, endows those decisions with the semblance of total rationality—even where the numbers reduce the complexity of all the interpretations and judgements that make them possible (Carruthers and Espeland 1991: 57–61).

This situation also has a lot in common with what Jane Guyer describes under the heading of 'composite price' (2009). Price, she writes as an anthropologist, is always composite. Following Marx (the fetishism of commodities concealing social relations) and Polanyi (land, labour, and capital as 'fictitious commodities'), she remarks that 'the concealment of composition would then be one of the main functions of price ideologies, since it dampens reasonable doubt about worth, and circumvents the moral and political commentary that might ensue from close analysis' (Guyer 2009: 204). Since the 1980s, however, we have witnessed in various parts of the world the rise of a composite price from the consumer's point of view, for instance in the breakdown of airline

---

[6] Nevertheless, as Martin Messner has (2009), following Judith Butler, pointed out, even (human) accountable agents are not accountable ad infinitum: our selves are opaque and mediated, and therefore limited in their capacity to give accounts of themselves.

price components to indicate how much is due to tax, fuel surcharges, security surcharges etc. She describes this as 'a moral economy of transparent prices, which nonetheless retain the mystery of their components' (Guyer 2009: 205). People are aware of prices as narrative fictions, in ways that go beyond Marx or Polanyi, and yet their decomposition of these prices only goes so far. So too, in investment management, with the quantification that takes place through the nexus of price, valuation, and performance. Everyone knows it is a narrative, and offers competing analyses of it, but ultimately it is what matters, what is presented as evidence of success or failure.

The reduction of the factors—by no means merely economic—that determine the values represented by particular numbers (whether stock prices, portfolio valuations, or performance figures) into those numbers is a process the examination of which lies outwith the scope of this chapter. One prominent attempt within the industry to make some of these factors more transparent is the movement for responsible investment dealt with elsewhere in this book (see Chapters 6 and 7). For present purposes it is sufficient to notice that numbers, despite the way in which they are invoked and manipulated in order to present an objective, measurable truth supposed to correspond unproblematically to empirical reality—what historian of statistics Alain Desrosières (2008) called 'metrological realism'—nonetheless construct certain truths while simultaneously concealing others. In making and concealing truth, they, like other actors in the chain, both empower investment managers to act in the way they do, and restrain them from acting in other ways.

In summary, it is possible to present the links in the chain considered here in schematic fashion (Table 2.1). Here we consider only the relations between investment managers (portfolio management and investment analyst functions conflated) and a small number of influential actors, thereby giving the impression that investment managers are central to the entire process.

In one sense they are, since many of the links considered here are to personnel whose task is either to assist them or to assist their clients. From this perspective indeed it makes sense to describe the key relationship as that between clients providing funds and investment managers managing them, even while mediated, influenced, reinforced, held in place, and sometimes weakened or threatened by the other relationships described in this chapter.

In another sense, however, neither they nor even their relationship with their clients are central. The chain extends beyond the scheme presented here, and some of these other links are dealt with elsewhere in this book. Given the scale of the chain and the complexity of the interdependence of its constituents, it would be absurd to claim that all of this apparatus—from individual pensioners to state-backed regulators, from market-makers to index providers, exists for the sake of investment managers, to make their job possible. It is this

Table 2.1 Enabling and constraining in the investment chain

Link	Enabling actions	Constraining actions
Client Service Personnel (CS) to Investment Managers (IM)	CS let IM focus on analysis/portfolio construction.	CS demand accountability from IM, act as voice of clients: justification of decisions, explanation of failures.
Marketing Staff (MK) to IM	MK assists IM in bringing in money, dealing with clients, fund raters, and consultants	IM must explain actions in terms of schematized process as presented to clients, advisers by MK.
Fund Raters and Investment Consultants (FRIC) to IM	When FRIC evaluate IM positively, they raise their individual/firm profiles, contribute to raising funds, boosting their professional standing.	FRIC expect a certain presentation of self of IM, and demand good numbers.
Clients (CL) to IM	CL provide money to IM, validation of their professional credentials and authority through the very act of entrusting investment of funds to IM rather than attempting it themselves.	CL are imaginary spectators, looking over IM shoulders. When IM take decisions they ask 'what would clients think?', especially in times of underperformance.
Numbers (N) to IM	N demonstrate truth about IM's performance and therefore professional competence; when N are good they offer IM opportunity to present narrative of self as outperforming because of experience, other personal and firm qualities (e.g. of investment process or philosophy).	Truth demonstrated by N may be poor performance of IM which no amount of narrative can rescue, leading to pressures on IM to take decisions in a certain way (e.g. 'short-termism'), or fund outflows, reduction of professional standing.

complex interdependence, the heteronomous quality of this assemblage of diverse actors, that should give us pause before assertions, however well reasoned (Kay 2012), that the main problem facing the investment industry is the excessive length of chains of 'intermediation' such as the investment chain (see Chapter 8).

Numbers, Truth, and Value: Concealing and Revealing

Numbers tell the truth about value, whether of companies listed on a stock exchange or of the performance of a particular fund. At the same time these truths require narrative elucidation, which can in turn be challenged by other interpretations. The constitution of the investment chain is such that such challenges are intrinsic to it: enabling and constraint once again. Numbers, and their configuration through the chain, also reveal and conceal, however: they can be manipulated to demonstrate the superiority of one asset class or one fund manager over another, or mobilized to project a hoped-for superiority in the future. They stand as signs of value, or as value itself, but in doing so they cover over the social relations, the inequalities, the conflicts, the exploitation or the environmental damage that are so often their condition of possibility. In so doing they also occlude the question of until when the present relationship of truth and value is sustainable, or whether indeed it is desirable at all.

Horacio Ortiz, commenting on Foucault's theorization of the 'birth of biopolitics', remarks that the political objective of neoliberalism is to constitute social organization so that justice depends on techniques of economic calculation, themselves defined as lacking all political or moral content (2014: 149). As we have seen, these calculative techniques obscure the ethico-political problems that make them, and the reality they produce through their calculations, possible. Openness and secrecy are the mutually constituting surface and depth of contemporary politics (Schumann 2007: 858). Ortiz observes that in this context, the price of shares exchanged, and the monetary gains made, indicate a social as well as individual wealth, which it is just to distribute. Price is truth, both as product of the application of investment and evaluation procedures, and as the legitimacy of the social hierarchy that is its consequence.

Writing in French, it is easier for Ortiz to make the connection between truth and value, since what is known in English as 'fair value' is in French 'vraie valeur', true value, but these are really two sides of the same coin. The English has clear moral connotations, even if these are obscured in contemporary investment practice. Truth is what is right, both in the technical sense of the correct answer to a question, and in a moral sense, where it rejoins the Anglophone notion of fairness.

Heidegger, whose work underpins the Foucauldian accounts of truth and its conditions of possibility drawn on here by Ortiz, famously challenged traditional philosophical ideas of truth as either correspondence (of a statement to an object, a reality described) or coherence (logically speaking, internally of a set of ideas). He formulated an alternative account of truth as variously a movement of concealing and revealing, and (by way of an etymology of the ancient Greek term usually translated as truth, *aletheia*, 'un-forgetting') the event of emergence from forgetting. The originary character of Heidegger's truth or its often tortuous German formulation need not detain us here. What is important is the heuristic value of the concept of truth as something beyond correspondence or coherence and as including a double movement of concealing and revealing. The numbers (valuation, performance) deployed in investment management are not simply the truth of what is 'out there', an objective reality to be observed, evaluated, interpreted, summed up by an analysing subject. Moreover their coherence is ensured not through some logical self-sufficiency, but by concealing other sections of reality, whether through the narrative arts (e.g. the interpretation of performance figures) or through an insistence that in the end, the number (price, performance) is what matters, not the labour or legal structures that make it possible. Challenges to particular narratives conceal as much as they reveal; more fundamental challenges to the justificatory narrative of mainstream active fund management still leave the political implications of the relationship of truth and value unexamined. Focusing on enabling and constraining in the investment chain opens the way to such an examination.

3

Fund Managers and Their Investors

The analytical frame of the investment chain draws attention to the relationships that make financial decisions possible. This chapter discusses the relationship between fund managers and the investors who provide the funds that fund managers manage. We aim to demonstrate the value of moving away from a focus solely on fund managers making investment decisions about particular securities or markets, divorced from the broader context within which those investment decisions must be made. In particular we highlight the extent to which investors influence fund managers' investment decisions, whether deliberately or not.

This chapter therefore examines a particular part of the investment chain, the link between 'savers/investors' and 'investment management firms' (Figure 1.1). A common framework within which these issues are analysed is principal–agent theory. Investors are conceptualized as principals who hire fund managers (agents) to manage their money. This results in various conflicts of interest: fund managers might not work hard enough to achieve the principals' goals; they might buy stocks for reasons other than future expected returns; they could, despite its illegality in many jurisdictions, 'front-run' against the fund (buy stocks on private account before they conduct the same transaction in the fund); and they might not minimize costs (Shah and Fernandes 2000; Woolley and Vayanos 2012). Furthermore, asset managers charge fees to asset owners, based mainly on the volume of assets under management. More active and apparently sophisticated investment processes are likely to have higher fees, with passive 'index-following' investment having the lowest. Fund managers sometimes claim to manage money actively, justifying higher fees, while actually hardly deviating from the index (so-called 'closet benchmarking'; Authers 2014).

As a result, principal–agent theory expects investors to focus on identifying the skills of fund managers and measuring their performance. It is tricky, however, to identify a genuinely good agent and monitor their performance. It is nearly impossible to know if returns reflect the fund manager's ability or are simply the result of good or bad luck. Shah and Fernandes (2000: 7) discuss the low 'signal to noise ratio' in fund management that makes performance measurement problematic: 'genuine ability in fund management tends to get drowned in the noise of market fluctuations'. Thus, it does not make much sense to judge fund managers based solely on current performance. Still, principal–agent theory claims that if fund managers fail to deliver performance, investors will exit. The story told is one of control and punishment, the latter nearly always in the form of withdrawal of funds.

This chapter shows that the relationship between asset managers and asset owners is more nuanced than a straightforward principal–agent approach suggests. We argue in particular that there is no 'uniform' principal. To illustrate this, we focus first on the contrast between individual ('retail') and 'institutional' investors. We consider the contrast between, on the one hand, the perception of individual investors as 'flighty' and prone to be influenced by short-term performance, and on the other hand their loyalty to those, such as wealth managers and independent financial advisers (IFAs), who decide on investments on their behalf. We argue that it is the additional links in the chain—the various types of intermediaries between retail investors and fund managers—that are the main reason for this perception of individual flightiness.

We then focus on the heterogeneity of institutional investors in funds. Here, our main contrast is between investors whose main priority is to match their liabilities as closely as possible, and those seeking to maximize returns. We also consider in this section the role of investment consultants, who represent both a significant influence on the investment chain, and increasingly another link in the chain. We see this additional link as increasing short-termism, even when the initial investors are likely to have a long-term investment perspective. Individual and institutional investors are heterogeneous, a diversity which includes their reasons for investing, their investment time-horizons, their 'sophistication', for instance their understanding of the complexities of financial markets, and, closely related, their information-gathering and information-processing capacities. Investors also differ in how they interact with the rest of the investment chain.

Individual investors may invest directly into equities or bonds, but increasingly entrust these decisions to others, thereby creating new links in the investment chain. This delegation does not, however, remove all decision-making: individual investors still have to decide to whom they will delegate. Similarly, institutional investors may either invest directly into equities or bonds, or delegate. Institutional investors are companies and organizations that either seek to invest their own money (e.g. churches, charities, endowments, etc.) or money they hold on behalf of others (so-called asset gatherers: pension funds, insurance companies, banks, etc.). This results in investment chains of varying length and complexity, with a crucial link usually a fund manager making specific investments on behalf of others. These others are investors into his or her fund, who either buy shares (or 'units') in the fund, or, for all but the smallest institutional investors, through a dedicated arrangement (see discussion under the heading 'Maximizing Returns'). We concentrate here on the implications of the heterogeneity of these investors into funds for the decisions fund managers make.

Investors' heterogeneity, we argue, has a material influence on the decision-making of those who manage their investments. In particular, the varied likelihood of investors selling their holdings in a fund—the likelihood of exit—has an impact on fund managers' freedom to make investments (Shleifer and Vishny 1997). In considering the variations in the likelihood of exit, our analysis supports Hirschman's analysis of the principal–agent problem, and in particular considers the issue of loyalty. Hirschman (1970: 98) sees *conscious* loyalty as 'the reluctance to exit in spite of disagreement with the organization', and *unconscious* loyalty as resulting from 'the general difficulties of recognizing change' (1970: 91), which can apply to ill-informed investors. The latter, as we show, can also apply to individual investors investing directly into funds and not exiting despite poor performance. Conscious loyalty potentially applies to wealth managers as well as to institutional investors, 'understood in terms of a generalized concept of penalty for exit' (Hirschman 1970: 91). Indeed, many institutional investors will demonstrate greater loyalty, both as a result of these penalties for exit, but also because of their greater knowledge regarding, and control of, what the fund managers are doing. These information disadvantages can result in unconscious loyalty from individuals, but in contrast overcoming them is likely to increase loyalty amongst institutional investors. The discussion in this chapter is based on empirical data from the study of three different kinds of investors: retail clients, mainly in the UK but also elsewhere in Europe as well as North America, who use the service of intermediaries such as wealth managers; UK pension funds using external managers; and mutual fund managers themselves. We draw on the relevant subset of our overall interviewing described in Chapter 1, which includes thirty-nine interviews with forty-nine financial market professionals, conducted in Europe and North America from July 2012 to October 2015. Interviewees included pension fund managers, managers of both primarily retail and institutionally targeted mutual funds, hedge funds, investment consultants, fund management client service managers, wealth managers, regulators, and market analysts.

Investment Intermediaries

Individuals will generally utilize two main types of intermediaries: wealth managers and IFAs (the UK term for a profession which has counterparts in many countries). 'Wealth manager' here describes organizations that manage individuals' investments, taking decisions on asset allocation (the percentage of investments in equities and bonds, or in the US or Japan, for example) and selecting the individual funds in which to invest within those asset classes. IFAs, in contrast, provide advice rather than managing investments directly. Interviewees made it clear, however, that this is an idealized distinction. If the individual client always follows the IFA's recommendations, including asset allocation, there is little practical difference from a wealth manager. Control of asset allocation can therefore potentially lie at different stages of the investment chain. This is important, as two different decisions will influence the moneys fund managers receive: first, asset allocation weightings dependent on the market views of these intermediaries; second, the latter's choices of which funds to buy and sell within asset classes. Both can result in substantial investment flows.

A third group of intermediaries for individuals is also important in a number of countries: fund 'platforms' allow individuals to deal, usually online, in the funds of their choice from vast lists on the platform's website (examples of UK platforms include Fidelity and Hargreaves Lansdown). These are 'execution only' services, but nevertheless influence investor decisions regarding the funds they buy, because some funds (including the platform's own) receive higher profiles on the websites, or for example, new fund launches by those companies are advertised.[1] Platforms are increasingly important, and are used by both individuals and IFAs.

Institutional investors vary in the extent to which they manage funds by themselves, and the advisers who influence that management. Many pension funds, especially in the US and UK, employ investment consultants to advise on investment strategy and choosing fund managers. Consultants are meant to guard the principal's interests, but, like all agents, also have their own interests. Investment consultants are large organizations with considerable influence on investment practices, but this influence varies depending on the pension fund they advise. We discuss investment consultants further in the following.

Investment is directed to fund managers not only by consultants, external advisers, or rating agencies but also—within fund management companies— by internal 'asset allocation funds' that allocate investments to the fund management company's specialist funds. This is part of the investment chain within the fund management company discussed in Chapter 2 (and

---

[1] At time of writing, for example, <http://www.fidelity.co.uk> highlights three Fidelity funds on the company's 'Select List' and <http://www.hl.co.uk> advertises the launch of a new Hargreaves Lansdown fund. In the US, Charles Schwab offers funds managed by its own investment arm as one of five options for potential purchasers of mutual funds: <http://www.schwab.com/public/schwab/investing/accounts_products/investment/mutual_funds>.

also illustrated by Figure 1.1). Within companies, we would expect asset allocation decisions to involve close cooperative relationships between the decision-makers, but Chapters 2 and 4 highlight potential areas of conflict in the internal investment chain.

However, the relationship between fund managers and investors is also often far from hostile, or even arm's-length, when two different organizations are involved. We show that the relationships investment management companies have with their investors can allow the former to influence the latter. As a result, the principal–agent relationship between fund managers (or/and client service managers or salespeople)[2] and their clients, as documented elsewhere in this book, is not simply an arm's-length interaction between principal and agent where the principal seeks the information necessary to judge, and the means to control, the agent. Rather, the influence on behaviour goes in both directions and can constitute a cooperative relationship. A stable, long-term relationship often builds up. Asset owners and asset managers may even cooperate in an attempt to trigger change among issuers and potentially society more broadly (see Chapter 7).

Individual Investors

Retail investors' importance has grown constantly during the last decades, led by the US and UK, as their range of savings has increased. The percentage of American households owing shares or funds increased from 19 per cent in 1983 (Nadler 1999) to 52 per cent in 2001 (Preda 2009). However, this increasing ownership of shares has coincided with the institutionalization of that ownership. Direct individual ownership of shares has fallen in both the US and UK, the two countries with the strongest tradition of retail equity investment. Individuals in the UK directly owned only 10.7 per cent of UK quoted shares at the end of 2012, down from 54 per cent in 1963.[3] Part of this decrease is because of increased foreign ownership of UK shares (now over half), but is mainly the result of individuals' use of investment intermediaries. In the US individuals still own 34 per cent of equity (many of them being founders and managers of companies), but the trend is also towards greater institutionalization of savings. Institutionalization has also occurred in bond markets. At the end of 2014, individuals owned only 5.4 per cent of US Treasury

---

[2] There is a trend to less personal contact between a fund manager and an institutional client. The division of labour has become clearer: the fund manager generates performance, the account manager or salesperson who acquired the mandate communicates with the client.

[3] Source: Office of National Statistics: <http://www.dmo.gov.uk/index.aspx?page=Gilts/Data>.

securities.[4] Household ownership of UK gilts is even lower.[5] The British image of a rentier class individually collecting interest on 'Dividend Day at the Bank of England'[6] and thereby influencing government policy in their interests (Stasavange 2003) has been replaced by fund managers (Hager 2014). Individuals and their decision-making as direct investors remain important, but focus should be on their investments into funds.

Individual investors face significant challenges acquiring and processing the information needed for investment decisions. For analytical purposes, we divide such investors by one of the ways in which they deal with information costs, even if in practice the two groups overlap. Some individual investors decide to invest and to trade themselves in shares, and—particularly in parts of continental Europe—bonds, and even in derivatives on those (Preda 2009; Roscoe 2013). Such individuals may do all they can to overcome information problems and investment biases, for example by devoting all their time to 'day trading', or effectively ignore the problem. This chapter is focused on individuals who seek a different solution, and delegate all or part of the investment decision to others. This does not entail, as noted, the avoidance of all decision-making, even if it involves inaction;[7] it is nevertheless this delegation which creates principal–agent issues.

Delegation takes many forms. Investors may rely in part on companies that evaluate the quality of particular funds, such as Morningstar, that are outside influences on this link in the investment chain. Interviewees recognized that marketing by large fund managers creates brand loyalty, and the reputation of high-profile 'star managers' and 'media made' investment gurus has an effect in encouraging investment into these funds. These are heuristics investors use as they aim to achieve future investment performance.

The most important delegation is to those who make investment decisions. Retail investors either invest in funds directly or more usually access the market via intermediaries, as described earlier. In other words, individuals may add further links to the investment chain, most commonly more than one. In the UK in 2014, for example, direct net sales by mutual fund companies to retail investors (one extra link) fell to just 7.5 per cent of their total sales, with 55 per cent taking place through fund platforms, and a further 38 per cent through wealth managers, stockbrokers, or IFAs (Investment Association 2015: 68). Although literature on finance has recently focused on disintermediation of banks, this disguises a dramatic process of reintermediation of

---

[4] Source: Securities Industry and Financial Markets Association (SIFMA).
[5] Source: Office of National Statistics: <http://www.dmo.gov.uk/index.aspx?page=Gilts/Data>.
[6] A painting by George Elgar Hicks: <http://www.bbc.co.uk/arts/yourpaintings/paintings/dividend-day-at-the-bank-of-england-50212>, accessed 17 August 2015.
[7] An example is where individuals can opt out of the employer-recommended investment strategy for defined contribution pensions. Most don't.

savings by often very large institutional investors (e.g. Useem 1996) and other investment intermediaries. The relationships between individual investors and the other links in the investment chain are therefore an important question in our analysis. This section starts by presenting some stylized views of retail investors as investors in funds and as clients of wealth managers and IFAs.

Two consistent views emerge regarding individual or retail investors amongst most fund managers interviewed: first, investments from individuals are 'flighty', quick to exit funds or sectors with a recent history of poor relative performance; second, individuals investing into funds through intermediaries such as wealth managers or IFAs demonstrate high levels of loyalty to those intermediaries. These observations are apparently inconsistent in that they suggest that individuals are both quick to exit as direct investors in funds, but unlikely to exit from the intermediaries ultimately responsible for their investments. We first set out these views in more detail, before suggesting that the explanation for the inconsistency lies in the workings of the investment chain. It is, we suggest, an additional link in the chain—wealth managers or IFAs—that explains the increased likelihood of exit by 'retail' investors.

Flighty Retail, and 'Winner Takes All'

Nearly all fund managers interviewed seemed clear about retail investors' reaction to adverse performance or events. 'They just take the money out', as one senior figure in an investment management company put it to us. Institutional investors into funds, discussed in the following, share this view of flighty retail, and, according to someone responsible for attracting institutional investors to his company's funds, are uncomfortable investing in funds with too high a proportion of retail clients:

> [I]f 80 per cent of the money is retail in the fund and they own like 20 per cent, they know that money is not sticky. So, institutional clients, if they invest in a fund they often will ask how much of the money is institutional, we can't give client names, we can say 40 per cent institutional 60 per cent retail, that will give them the comfort they need.

Fund management companies emphasize attracting new investment. Fund managers' confidence in good performance leading to inflows is certainly justified. Retail investment is concentrated in a very small number of leading funds, particularly in the UK, but also elsewhere, as a number of interviewees observed and the empirical evidence confirms. A senior manager responsible for marketing to retail investors suggested:

A very clear 'winner takes all' phenomenon where people are increasingly allocating flow to very few funds. So last year in the UK I think the eventual number for net sales in the UK retail market was £30 billion, I think six funds took two thirds of that. It's amazing... two and a half thousand funds [are] currently available in the UK. Comparatively few are bought in any size.

What is more, this perception that retail investors are flighty and that the 'winner takes all' influences how fund managers actually manage their funds.

First, if a fund is set up to invest into a particular market or sector, managers understand that the performance of this market or sector influences the performance, and therefore the flow of money into or out of the fund. Fund managers can do little about the performance of the particular sector their funds are invested in. If, for example, a given sector of the corporate bond market falls by 10 per cent, a manager of a fund investing in this market, however well the fund performs relative to its benchmark, has to expect poor (absolute) performance and consequently outflows from their fund. As one fund manager explained, 'this summer we had in the industry sixteen consecutive weeks of money flowing out of emerging market bond funds... the whole industry has to adapt to that... global asset allocation decision'. The possibility of such outflows means fund managers have to maintain sufficient levels of liquid assets—securities that can be sold immediately with minimal losses—to meet any outflows (see Shleifer and Vishny 1997). This constrains investment in less liquid—often longer maturity—assets. If retail fund managers cannot rely on their investors to make long-term investments, then they have to limit their own long-term investment.

Second, fund managers are inevitably influenced by how their performance is judged. Interviewees were consistent in their view that retail investors 'buy past performance'; the result that matters and can be influenced is performance against the relevant peer group: 'you've got to try and be in [the] top quartile on a one to three year working basis. That's the holy grail of what we do'. The vast majority of managers obviously cannot be top quartile.

This comparison of performance to peers is also institutionalized. In the UK, the industry body the Investment Association[8] categorizes fund managers into various sectors across equity, bond, and other markets. These sectors divide investment funds into groupings of funds that follow similar investment strategies, and it is performance against peers in the same sector that matters. Requirements for inclusion in a particular sector constrain what the fund manager can do, the aim being that the fund does what it claims to, and investors do not find that a fund they thought bought safe UK government

---

[8] Until recently the Investment Management Association (IMA).

bonds (gilts) had instead invested in risky technology equities. To be included in the Gilt Fund sector, for example, a fund must be at least 80 per cent invested in UK government bonds. We see the Investment Association, and similar industry bodies elsewhere, as an additional external influence on the fund manager part of the chain. Along with the greater economic efficiency of a standardized approach, the result is that retail investors are presented with (at least ostensibly) a homogeneous range of fund choices.

Managers may push the boundaries of what is acceptable in the search for improved performance, but the main outcome is that retail fund managers are concerned overwhelmingly about their performance relative to this limited group of competitors. Rarely is allowance made for the often sizeable differences in the risks funds within a sector may be taking, a comparison that portfolio theory in financial economics would suggest is fundamental.[9] This is in part because of the difficulties in assessing risk (Shah and Fernandes 2000). Measurement against peers can, however, also serve to limit the ability to take out-of-consensus positions and give rise to herding. One fund manager gave the example of Italian government bonds, a major component of the European government bond market, for a European bond fund:

> [P]eer pressure amongst investors will push everyone to still take some Italy into the portfolio. Especially for retail because retail in the end they will never ask what is in their portfolio . . . it's very difficult to go 'yeah, but in the long run Italy, it's a risky play, you should be defensive'; if everyone's in Italy at 22 per cent [of their portfolios] and you're in at 5 per cent you'll just be crushed [if Italy performs in line with or better than the market].

We can see here a possible reason behind the fixed income managers' reluctance to reduce their Greek positions discussed in Chapter 6. Fund managers often have to be careful not to take positions too radically different from their benchmarks, meaning that portfolios will also not vary too greatly from competitors'. This is one possible explanation of 'closet benchmarking'.

In explaining retail investor behaviour, fund manager interviewees recognized individuals' relative lack of knowledge regarding what 'their' fund managers are actually doing, a standard principal–agent problem. This is compounded by a lack of direct communication by fund managers to explain poor short-term performance and the outlook for improvement, or of investors exercising 'voice' in an attempt to improve performance (Hirschman 1970). Interviewees saw this as a lack of sophistication, but also equally an inevitable result of difficulties in information gathering. This gives potentially

---

[9] An analysis of risk-adjusted return simply calculates the likely returns on investment after allowing for the level of risk involved. A variety of measures of risk are used, some of which are discussed in Chapters 2 and 4.

greater freedom for retail fund managers when choosing what to invest in when compared to those managing institutional clients' money. They can be less 'index constrained' (less limited as to any deviation from the index against which they are measured), despite the observation above. Nor are they likely to face the same level of micro-management, including concern with the particular investments made, as those fund managers with institutional clients. Another fund manager told us that individual investors 'don't care about being short Greece or being long Greece.... They probably don't even know'. Interviewees viewed individual investors' informational disadvantages as giving them greater freedom, but also as making exit highly likely.

However, this widespread *perception* of retail investors as flighty needs qualification, as the data are not supportive. In the UK, for example, the average holding period for funds by retail investors was four years at the end of 2014, a fall from eight years in 1997 (Investment Management Association 2013: 60; Investment Association 2015: 68), but hardly indicative of retail 'churning'. Furthermore, on a net basis flows from retail investors into funds have increased 'on a relatively consistent basis year-on-year' since 1980. There were no net annual outflows even at the time of the global financial crisis (Investment Association 2015: 68), even if several months saw outflows (Investment Management Association 2009: 62).

Looking at the different types of investment shows greater volatility as a result of changing asset allocation decisions. However, even here the true level of 'flightiness' is questionable. The UK's Investment Association has seven of the broadest categories for funds.[10] Of these seven, only the smallest, money market funds, experienced net annual outflows from 2011 to 2014, and these were small negatives in two years. Where data are available for earlier years, the picture is the same: some monthly periods of outflows, but very few examples of annual net outflows (see Investment Management Association 2009, 2011). The next level down of analysis—different investment strategies within broad categories such as equity—shows more periods of outflows, but they clearly remain only small and account for a minority of cases. Even if they are painful for managers of certain funds, such as the interviewee discussing emerging market bonds earlier, there is no evidence of widespread retail exit in response to poor performance in particular market sectors. Instead, it is at the level of individual fund managers that significant volatility is seen. Net figures obscure sizeable buying and selling. In the UK in 2008, a period of high volatility, the positive net figure is made up of sales by individuals totalling £59.3 billion and purchases of £63 billion (Investment Management Association 2009: 62). In 2014, overall retail flows were positive

---

[10] Equity, fixed income, mixed asset, targeted absolute return, property, money markets, and other.

by over £21 billion, but across specific fund management companies, the flows ranged from inflows of almost £4 billion to outflows of nearly £2 billion (Investment Association 2015: 71). These are significant figures: the ten largest retail investment managers had total funds under management of between £21 and £43.9 billion. Previous years also show a wide diversity of experience: from 1992 to 2007, despite inflow in the aggregate, less than half (and as low as 20 per cent) of funds received inflows; most experienced net selling (Investment Management Association 2009: 53). Individual investor volatility and propensity to exit is experienced at the level of the fund management company, and therefore (though data are lacking) we must assume, at the level of the actual funds. The assessment of the performance of particular fund managers is far harder than that of particular investment sectors, yet this is where we see the greatest volatility.

Against this, as one interviewee pointed out, many sectors (the example given was UK income funds)[11] include very large numbers of similar funds that continue in existence despite performing relatively poorly over extended periods. Unlike in the case of hedge funds, poor performance does not lead to exit being sufficient to cause fund closures (see also Camara 2005: 230). Evidence from the period when direct investment in equities by individuals was high also does not support inherent flightiness amongst individuals. As the corporate governance literature highlights, non-financial companies' management enjoyed high levels of autonomy from shareholders, facing little pressure from either voice or exit by individual investors in the event of poor share price performance.

These are apparent contradictions in individual investors' behaviour that need explanation. The explanation, we argue, lies in the operation of the investment chain. Individuals are indeed deeply loyal to the next link in the investment chain. Even when advice to exit is available from external influences on the investment chain, there is a strong chance that individuals' responses will be slow or entirely absent. As these advisers gain more influence (and there is a continuum of influence between being totally ignored and fully delegated fund management), the likelihood of exit increases, with the highest likelihood occurring when an additional link in the investment chain is added, and decisions are fully delegated to wealth managers or other intermediaries. As the Investment Management Association (IMA) observed (2011: 52):

> The increasing intermediation of the industry that has taken place in recent years has brought a different kind of institutional investor to the fore: professional buyers, such as bank wealth management units or fund of fund managers . . . the

---

[11] Funds that invest in UK equities offering consistently high dividends.

growing presence of these intermediaries has already added, and is expected to add further, to the volatility of fund flows, particularly at the level of the individual fund houses.

Our interview evidence supports the IMA's conclusion, but the impact of this particular additional link in the chain requires further empirical research. This conclusion remains, for us, the only plausible explanation of the contradiction between retail investors' apparent loyalty to investment intermediaries and supposed flightiness when investing in funds.

Loyalty to Investment Intermediaries

Individuals' loyalty to intermediaries such as wealth managers and IFAs even surprises the intermediaries themselves, one of whom told us that 'it's amazing how sticky it is even in situations which you'd think they'd just be pouring out the doors'.

This 'stickiness' cannot necessarily be seen as the result of 'unconscious loyalty', because many of these intermediaries enjoy advantages in terms of their ability to communicate with their clients that the retail fund managers do not. This communication may enhance a relationship that is closer to that of fund managers with their institutional clients (see under heading 'Institutional Investors'). In difficult markets or times of underperformance, the wealth managers know that they have a chance to explain and reassure, so at least partially overcoming information problems.

Furthermore, individuals do not judge their wealth managers by focusing on quartile performance against peers, but rather a combination of absolute and relative performance, with the emphasis on absolute, as a wealth manager explained:

> The market's at twelve per cent and we're up ten, we'll be fine. Market's up twenty-two per cent and we're seventeen [i.e. a poorer relative performance], they're better than fine. Market is down twelve and we're down three and a half [an outstanding outperformance relative to the market], after some discussion, they're fine because they'll hear from people who are down fifteen at that point in time. But it is much more absolute return driven.

The interviewee quoted here worked at a relatively small wealth manager. However, many wealth managers are large and highly influential. In the UK, Rathbones has £28.3 billion under management for private clients (and 39,000 clients),[12] Brewin Dolphin £37.9 billion and 100,000

---

[12] <http://www.rathbones.com/about-us>, accessed 18 August 2014.

clients,[13] and St James Place £17.7 billion.[14] The Investment Association estimates that UK discretionary private client managers managed £395 billion at the end of 2014, compared to hedge funds managing £214 billion and private equity £202 billion (Investment Association 2015: 14). This is an influential (and under-researched) group of investors. To these figures must also be added the 'fund of funds' sector, which are funds that invest in other funds. The UK retail fund of funds sector totalled £98 billion (Investment Association 2015: 69).[15] Their decisions, either favouring one class of assets or particular funds, will result in sizeable flows, and they do not demonstrate the same level of loyalty as individuals investing directly. This is especially the case when a fund underperforms. Individuals investing directly are in a situation of 'unconscious loyalty' (Hirschman 1970) vis-à-vis the funds they buy, unaware of poor performance and changing rarely, but the intermediaries are more likely to utilize exit on their behalf.

There are also interdependencies between the intermediaries. For example, wealth managers also offer services to IFAs, often lone advisers who have small businesses advising individuals and face significant information problems themselves. There were around 20,000 advisers working at IFAs in the UK, as of summer 2012 (Financial Services Authority 2013: 3). This group was previously effectively a distributor of funds to their clients, and was incentivized by fee structures to move clients between funds. If clients follow their advice, these IFAs play a significant role in explaining retail flightiness, as an executive responsible for marketing funds recognizes: 'the IFAs are motivated to switch you around. So if you give them motivation to switch by having a couple of bad quarters, I think you're toast'. Fund platforms, described earlier, have empowered them to do this switching more easily, and this is thought to be one possible reason for a fall in retail fund holding periods (Investment Management Association 2014: 73).

Recent UK regulatory change represents an external actor having a significant impact on the investment chain, and potentially reducing intermediaries' influence on skittishness. National (or sometimes supranational) regulatory authorities are probably the most important external influence on this link in the investment chain (although interviewees thought them generally less constraining on retail investment). The UK Financial Services Authority's Retail Distribution Review (RDR) changed the fee structure for IFAs.[16] A specific aim was to 'remove the potential for commission

---

[13] <http://www.telegraph.co.uk/finance/newsbysector/banksandfinance/11374635/Brewin-Dolphin-brushes-off-a-drop-in-commission-to-increase-assets-under-management.html>; <https://www.brewin.co.uk/about-us>, accessed 18 August 2014.
[14] Investment Management Association (2014: 74).
[15] Some institutions that are primarily wealth managers also manage funds.
[16] Since 2013, the Financial Conduct Authority (FCA).

bias'.[17] IFAs are no longer rewarded by commissions on transactions, but now receive a fee for advice. Probably not coincidently, there has been a fall in investment in high fee funds (Investment Management Association 2014: 30). The fall in retail holding periods in mutual funds has also plateaued (although demonstrating causality is clearly difficult). The RDR also attempts to raise levels of IFA professionalism. The result is the concentration of asset allocation decisions. IFAs now look for more 'off the shelf' asset allocation suitable to the (often age-related) risk profile of their clients. Younger investors are deemed to need greater risk (usually more equities), older investors less risk (more bonds).

Fund management companies have responded to these developments, they told us, by offering their own 'asset allocation funds', a further chain link within a fund management company. These asset allocation funds received 22 per cent of retail investment flows in 2013 (Investment Management Association 2014: 57). However, the main asset allocation decisions still lie with wealth managers, who have their own set of indices, compiled by the Wealth Managers Association, against which they can be judged. At time of writing, it remains too early to understand fully the implications of these changes for the likelihood of exit from UK funds. However, it would appear likely that the concentration on a smaller number of larger actors will result in characteristics closer to those of institutional investors (see section entitled 'Institutional Investors'), and that in-house funds will be less likely to exit.

Fund managers are concerned about being on the lists of funds compiled by wealth managers. The situation is similar with bank distributors in continental Europe (although many have their own fund management companies). A senior fund manager described their evaluation criteria:

> They want to see consistency of product and performance, they want to understand what the strategy is trying to do, they want to know that you're going to be there. They like fund managers to be in one place for a reasonable amount of time.

A high rating from a fund evaluation company such as Morningstar is also seen by fund managers as helpful in being listed (see Chapter 1). These are not criteria associated with short-term, high turnover outlooks, but these minimum criteria only get funds onto the approved lists. Funds can be on such lists for a long time. However, flows really come from being on recommended lists, and fund managers see performance as key. As discussed earlier, the performance required is being in the first quartile of performance by similar funds.

---

[17] See <https://www.fca.org.uk/publications/guidance-consultations/gc13-5-supervising-retail-investment-advice-inducements-and>, accessed 9 January 2017.

These lists may also offer at least part of the explanation for the success of 'star managers' and herding into particular funds, as one interviewee responsible for marketing retail funds explained:

> They ... are so comfortable following each other ... 'no-one got sacked for buying IBM' ... no one really wants to take the risk. So they've got fund managers and that would include Neil Woodford[18] for example ... and he'll be on the panel [i.e. the list] for most of these guys and it's extraordinary really because you think active fund managers is about people who have skill ... there must be more people who are really good at it than the five or six who are being bought ... you get comparatively few funds that get bought in massive size because the asset allocators ... are all looking very closely at what each other are doing.

There are broadly similar accusations of herding addressed to institutional fund managers (e.g. Bikhchandani and Sharma 2001).

Individual investors demonstrate high levels of loyalty (often unconsciously) to the next link in the chain. The next link is most often to another professional intermediary, who decides which funds to buy. The result of this additional link is increased propensity to exit from those funds in the event of (almost always eventual) underperformance.

Institutional Investors

One link in the investment chain that is central to understanding modern financial markets is the link between institutional investors and those who manage money for them. How are investment decisions made in this part of the chain? For example, if a fund manager is investing on behalf of a pension fund, to what extent does the long-term nature of the pension fund's liabilities influence the time-frame of the fund manager? What role do intermediaries play?

With great increases in the amount of pension fund assets being managed by external managers, these are important questions. In the UK, for example, only a handful of pension funds do most of their fund management 'in-house'. In the US, the absolute numbers (and the assets they control) are larger, but the proportion is similar. Pension funds have been seen as a key driver of processes of financialization (Dixon 2008), so the broad political economic implications of questions regarding how much they influence those managing money on their behalf are clear.

Institutional investors cannot be considered a uniform group, though it is tempting to see institutional investors as all seeking to maximize returns.

---

[18] The highly successful UK equity fund manager at Invesco, the UK's largest fund manager, who left in 2014 to found his own company.

Institutional investing has highly varied investment targets, but we focus here on the distinction between investing targeted at meeting liabilities and investing to maximize returns. Investment targets influence what institutional investors require of their fund managers, and the likely loyalty investors demonstrate. This has very different implications for fund managers seeking to meet their investors' requirements.

Liability-Driven Investment

Liability-driven investment (LDI) represents arguably the most significant departure from a return-maximizing approach to investment. It involves instead an investment process that looks first at a given set of outgoings (liabilities) and invests to meet those liabilities. An obvious example of this would be found in insurance companies, across a range of different types of insurance. Insurance payouts are generally predictable, and investment can be aimed at meeting those payouts at the lowest level of risk. The insurance company then profits from the difference between investment income and liability payouts. Such insurance investment has existed for centuries, as has the hedging of annuities (which pay a fixed, often inflation-adjusted, amount to pensioners), but the most significant development in investment for this chapter is the increase in LDI in the provision of pensions, especially in the US and UK. This development changes the demands from investors on fund managers.

The focus here is corporate pension funds, the means by which companies provide their employees with future pensions. Historically, such pensions have been 'defined benefit' pensions: at retirement, employees receive a pension linked to their final or average salary while employed. To meet these pension payments, companies and employees set aside money each year to be invested. These investments into the pension fund came to be overwhelmingly invested according to a weighting of around 70 per cent equities and 30 per cent bonds. The aim was to combine the growth of equity markets with the greater safety of bonds.

However imprecise, this formula enjoyed considerable success. Equities performed well, despite the 1970s bear market and the 1987 crash, meaning investment returns at least kept pace with calculations of future liabilities. Some companies took 'payment holidays'—periods when they did not have to make annual payments into the pension fund—and others made pensions more generous as an alternative to pay rises. This Panglossian situation lasted for a surprisingly long time, and was even enhanced by equity market strength before the dot.com bubble burst in 2001. It was 2001 and its aftermath that moved pension issues from a relatively sleepy backwater within companies to an issue of concern to a company's Chief Financial Officer. Movements in the equity markets were not the sole reason for this. Ever-increasing longevity meant pensions had to be serviced for longer, and regulation meant that any deficits in the pension fund (i.e. where the value of the assets in the pension fund were deemed insufficient to meet future pension payments) had to be recognized and dealt with.

There are generally two separate regulatory influences in this regard. We use here the example of the UK. First, the Pensions Regulator is responsible for the viability of pension schemes. Second, the Financial Reporting Council (itself influenced by the International Accounting Standards Board) is responsible for the fair representation of pension costs in company accounts. Both (and their equivalents in other countries) are outside influences on the investment chain. For companies, substantial pension deficits require a 'recovery plan' to return the pension to a fully funded basis, with the Pension Regulator, fund trustees, and actuaries influencing this plan. All three are significant actors in or influences on the investment chain. This recovery plan could well include increased contributions from the employer. In addition, in a company's accounts, any pension deficit has to be valued at market rates and the cost of any liabilities appears in a company's profit and loss statement.[19] The result is that pensions could cause earnings and balance sheet volatility unrelated to developments which corporate management feel they control.

The differences between the two regulators and transnationally are beyond our concern here[20] but the outcome is the same: companies have substantial deficits in their pension funds, which must be recognized in their accounts and for which they are ultimately responsible.

Companies have reacted in two ways. First, defined benefit schemes have been closed to new entrants. This means that defined benefit schemes increasingly do not have payments coming in. They have become simply pools of assets aiming to meet future liabilities. The second, related, development is that companies became focused not on growing the scheme's assets, but on reducing the risk inherent in meeting these future liabilities (not least the risk of sizeable impact on a company's annual profits). This is the underlying

---

[19] Under the 2011 revisions to International Accounting Standard 19, the interest cost (which is also the discount rate used on future liabilities) of net liabilities appears in a company's profit and loss. Changes in the balance of assets and liabilities as a result of accounting period-to-period market movements appear only on the balance sheet as 'other comprehensive income', <http://www.ifrs.org/investor-resources/2011-perspectives/august-2011-perspectives/Pages/pension-accounting.aspx>, accessed 18 July 2016.

[20] In the US, the difference between accounting regulation's use of AA corporate bonds for discounting and the 1974 Employee Retirement Income Security Act's (ERISA) use of A to AAA for funding requirements is relatively minor (although interviewees noted some discretion in the choice of bonds in the A to AAA basket). In the UK, the difference is broader, with actuaries allowed discretion on discount rates for funding while requiring trustees to remain 'prudent'.

rationale for LDI. Also, as time goes by and its members retire, a closed defined benefit pension becomes increasingly irrelevant to current employees; companies simply wish 'to get the risk off the books'.

This is easier said than done, however. There are two options. An insurance company can be paid to take on the pension liabilities, or the company can itself construct a portfolio of assets which meet the future liabilities. Various risks also have to be hedged, most commonly longevity and inflation risk. This is expensive. Interviewees estimated that the assets of a pension fund would need to be worth around 115 per cent of the discounted value of future liabilities before those liabilities could be transferred to an insurance company at no cost to the transferring company. When equity markets bottomed out in 2003, most corporate pension funds in the US and UK were far from this point; they were in substantial deficit, with assets valued at far less than future liabilities. Companies' discomfort was compounded by more onerous requirements to make increased contributions to their pension funds to close this deficit. The time when LDI became more of a focus was the least propitious for its wholesale introduction.

The response from companies, aided by investment consultants and other advisers (further external influences on the investment chain), was the calculation of a 'glide' or 'flight path' for company pensions. As one fund management client service manager involved in such planning told us:

> Most companies have now created an explicit strategy where they're going to say 'Okay, as my funding improves [i.e. the amount the value of liabilities exceeds the value of assets reduces], if I go from 70 to 80 [i.e. assets are 80 per cent of liabilities] my asset allocation will switch from 60 per cent stocks to 50 per cent stocks, and if I go from 80 to 90 it'll go from 50 per cent stocks to 40 per cent stocks, and if I go from 90 to 100 it'll go to 30 per cent stocks. If I get to 110 I may take it down to no equities.'

The higher the deficit, the more the pension would choose to invest in 'growth' assets such as stocks, rather than 'fixed income' instruments such as bonds. As the performance of these growth assets closed the pension deficit, investment would be moved into LDI investments, predominantly bonds and bond-related instruments. The aim for many companies, over time, is to move entirely into LDI, or to pass the entire responsibility for the future pensions to insurance companies who follow the same strategy, removing all risk. The strategy is clearly dependent, however, on the performance of growth (or higher risk) assets. The financial crisis of 2007–8, and falling stock markets until March 2009, therefore substantially undermined these efforts. Nevertheless, the last fifteen years have seen pension liabilities become a risk to be managed. The move to having employees take the investment risk via defined contribution pension schemes achieves that for current employees, but the legacy defined benefits pensions require risk management.

For fund managers, LDI means greater investment in bonds, because of the greater certainty of cashflow, and greater constraint on risk and turnover. A focus on an investment strategy to meet cashflows, rather than maximizing returns, also means greater loyalty to the fund manager and the original investments made. At one extreme, the fund manager can be given a set of cashflows and will bid a (very low) fee to buy and hold securities (usually government bonds) that are certain to meet that cashflow, in what another fund management relationship manager called 'just an execution service'. The future payments to pensioners can be calculated for each year going forward, inflation and longevity risk can be hedged, and bonds can be purchased and held to meet the future payments.[21]

At the other extreme, LDI is little more than an argument for greater investment in bonds, with fund managers actively managing a bond portfolio. Even here, however, the nature of the investor for whom the fund manager is acting has a significant impact. First, the benchmark chosen is as close as possible to the investor's liabilities. The present value of the liabilities is discounted at a discount rate that becomes the yield that is required on the securities purchased as a hedge.[22] When liabilities are discounted using government bond yields such as UK gilts, the discount rate can very closely match liabilities through investment in gilts, making such investment very likely.

The discount rate used to calculate the net present value of future liabilities can be in a less liquid market than government bonds. This makes both the direct matching of future liabilities and a benchmark to judge any active management more difficult. In another example of regulation as an external influence on the investment chain, these problems occur in the US with the calculation of funding levels required by the 1974 Employee Retirement Income Security Act (ERISA). The discount rate had been the thirty-year US Treasury bond yield, but the reduced government borrowing of the William J. Clinton presidency saw issuance of the thirty-year cease. US companies successfully argued for the use of a basket of A to AAA corporate bond yields as the discount rate. An interviewee involved in the process observed: 'it wasn't because they thought corporate bond funds were objectively more pure as a discount [rate], it was because they were higher yield', meaning the present value of the future liabilities was lower. (International Accounting Standards have also adopted corporate bonds, but AA, or where such bonds

---

[21] Inflation-linked bonds could be part of the inflation hedge.

[22] The discount rate is the yield used to discount future payments to determine their present value. The basis of this calculation is a concept known as the 'time value of money'. Since money can earn interest over time, it is assumed the present value of money is less than its future value; conversely, a future value will be worth less in the present, and the discount rate is employed to calculate the present value of a future (forecast) sum of money, in this case the forecast liabilities of pension funds.

are not sufficiently liquid, government bonds plus a margin to reflect the yield spread for corporate bonds.) As the same interviewee pointed out, this solves a short-term problem, making the pension scheme appear better funded, but at the cost of creating another: the discount rate becomes the investment return the pension scheme must hit in order for assets to keep pace with the net present value of liabilities. This pushes the schemes into riskier investments, corporate rather than government bonds (Koenig and Keating 2015). An executive at a fund management firm believes that it also becomes an argument in favour of more active management:

> An LDI investor...want[s] less tracking error and less variance....We...dissuade them by saying 'look, it doesn't actually help very much because of those concentration issues [the risk of being heavily invested in the bonds of a small number of companies], even if you were passive you're still going to have volatility. So to give up the opportunity of alpha returns [returns above those of an overall market] on this illusory benefit doesn't seem to us to be a very good trade.... Passive just doesn't work, you're still going to lose money relative to the benchmark with passive, so if you don't have the alpha to generate performance you're going to be in a hole'.

The increased desire of companies to control the risks of defined benefit pension schemes pushes them in the direction of LDI. This in turn not only means increased investment in fixed income, but also towards putting greater constraints on the extent to which fund managers can actively manage their portfolios, and towards greater loyalty to the fund managers. The incentive to change managers is lower than with more active management. However, we can see national variation in the contrast between the US and the UK, caused by the choice of discount rate on future pension fund liabilities: in the US a corporate bond discount rate pushes towards more active management, while any pension funds in the UK still using gilts to calculate their funding position are likely to have a more passive approach to LDI.

The development of LDI within pension funds also represents a significant element of pension investment moving more in the direction of the investment strategy of insurance companies, with priority given to hedging risks rather than maximizing investment growth. As noted earlier, part of the process involves companies passing their defined benefit pension liabilities to insurance companies. These insurance companies then demonstrate a very different investment philosophy. The desire is to maximize yield within the portfolio, rather than generate alpha, outperformance of the market. As an interviewee who manages investments for an insurance company noted: 'they're interested in achieving the maximum book yield on their long term portfolios...and the intention to buy and hold'.[23] Insurance companies and

---

[23] The book yield is the overall yield on the insurance company's investments.

LDI more broadly therefore have very different requirements of fund managers to those looking to maximize returns. The focus is rather on the most effective matching of specific liabilities. Closer examination of the investment chain, in this case the particular requirements of the investors in funds, makes these issues clear.

Maximizing Returns

Even when institutional investors seek to maximize returns, they have significant influence on fund managers. As mentioned earlier, the principal–agent problem is a recognized issue between fund managers and their investors. The greater the potential freedom for the fund manager, the greater the principal–agent problem. Therefore, principal–agent issues are more important when investors seek to maximize returns rather than hedge liabilities: fund managers maximizing returns enjoy more freedom.

Investors' attempts to overcome agency problems by performance measurement exacerbate these problems. The overwhelming way in which performance is measured by institutional investors looking for returns is performance relative to a benchmark. A fund manager investing in UK equities, for example, will most often be charged by investors with outperforming the FTSE 350 index.

Multiple issues arise from this approach. 'Closet benchmarking', as mentioned earlier, is a concern raised to us by those who employ fund managers. If institutional investors are paying fund managers to be active, that is what they want to see. This can mean that the investors just cited seek fund managers that hold a concentrated portfolio with high conviction positions, rather than a highly diversified portfolio that more closely follows the index, thereby avoiding closet benchmarking. The conviction cannot be not to invest. As an executive responsible for marketing funds told us, 'we aren't hiring you to manage cash, we ask you to manage equities, we want you to be in the markets'.

The other issue is short-termism. Woolley and Vayanos (2012) blame short-termism on fund investors. Fund managers feel pressure to outperform in the short term, and expect to be closely scrutinized by institutional investors in the event that they underperform (see also earlier on other intermediaries for individual investors). The view as to how quickly underperformance will trigger uncomfortable levels of scrutiny varied, but eighteen months was the longest time-frame given by interviewees, and many expected even shorter periods. This is despite the fact that fund management mandates are generally awarded for three years. Even having to compete for the mandate again within three years is felt to be a constraint on investments where returns are expected after a three-year period. There can be little doubt that this has an impact on the behaviour of fund managers, even if this impact is less marked than for those managing for retail intermediaries. For fund managers, one possible response to this is an attempt to educate their investors into taking a longer-term perspective (see Chapter 2). Even in situations where the nature of the interaction between fund manager and investor is conducive to this, however, the investment chain raises significant obstacles (see Garratt and Hamilton 2017).

The argument that institutional investors into funds are entirely responsible for these issues of short-termism requires some qualification, however, in situations where those institutional investors enjoy a degree of control. Control varies depending on (the level of) standardization of the relationship between institutional investor and fund manager. Control over fund managers' activities does not really exist when institutional investors are investing into a pre-existing fund. This is a common situation, at least for the smaller institutional investors. The fund manager sets up a particular fund (a fund investing in UK equities, for example), determines the investment guidelines that are likely to make that fund popular with investors, and then seeks to sell it to those investors. Institutional investors, just as their retail counterparts, decide to invest on a 'take it or leave it' basis. In that circumstance, the choice for any investor is only to exit or remain invested.

Fund managers generally prefer investment into existing funds, because it is cheaper to manage. However, they will offer larger investors 'dedicated mandates', with terms agreed between the two parties. Under these circumstances, interviewees see an institutional investor as having far greater opportunities for voice, making exit less likely. Depending on the particular market and investor, the view given was that this is likely to be available when investments are above $40 to $200 million (£32 to £160 million). Such appointments are highly time-consuming for both the institutional investor and the fund manager. One initial questionnaire (sent to multiple potential fund managers) described to us had 187 questions, and another process involved visits to six to eight potential managers across a number of countries. We were told that the final agreement, the Investment Management Agreement (IMA), can run to fifty pages and requires extensive negotiations. This resource commitment is seen by interviewees on both sides of these negotiations as a significant disincentive to firing an existing manager.

Furthermore, the relationship between institutional investors and fund managers is often highly interactive, involving more than control and punishment. Institutional investor interviewees looked to their fund managers to discuss investment ideas, even potentially following their investment choices in a larger portfolio. Discussions about market developments frequently lead to changes in the investment mandate: interviewees noted changes regarding investment in the European periphery as a result of the Eurozone crisis, for example, but these changes can also come in reaction to market opportunities. Fund managers will discuss investment moves even if they are within the terms of the IMA; one interviewee who allocated investments to fund managers said that 'a lot of times they'll come to us and say "hey, we're about to make a shift in the portfolio, it's within the constraints and guidelines but we want you to be aware of it, and here's the reasoning for it. Is that okay?"' Such 'client sensitivity' enhances the relationship between fund managers and their institutional investors, but also recognizes that there is the potential for interpretation as to the meaning of the IMA. Although the speed of reaction of some pension funds makes it difficult to address such issues sufficiently quickly, this flexibility means institutional investors have the ability to utilize voice, reducing their incentive to exit.

Maximizing returns means something rather different to institutional investors from what it means to retail investors. This manifests itself in two connected ways. First, institutional investors look to maximize 'risk-adjusted returns', which involves calculating the volatility of returns or the 'tracking error', the amount the return deviates from the chosen benchmark. Even when looking for returns to reduce the deficit on their pension schemes, for example, companies tell their advisers that they want to 'smooth the flight path', avoiding the volatility that will have an impact on company profitability. A fund manager drew the distinction with retail investors that results from this situation:

> We manage [for a pension fund] . . . where their target out-performance every year will be fifty basis points or seventy five basis points [0.5 or 0.75 per cent] above the index, so if you're taking [big] positions . . . you might outperform by three per cent but you might under-perform by three per cent . . . that might be an unacceptable degree of risk whereas for [the retail client] base we rarely get questioned.

Particularly since the last financial crisis, the majority of clients emphasize risk management. Many clients agree on protection or a risk budget that should not be breached.[24] These issues impose serious additional constraints on investment managers' decision-making procedures. Clients can be particularly sensitive, as a fund management executive observed:

> We agree on the minimum value (floor value) with a client. We have to comply with it. It means: we agree with a client that 95 per cent of the value—as of the beginning of the year—will be preserved. This is our highest priority. Thus, even if the value is at the 95.01 per cent level, we cannot say: 'oh, the valuation is nicely low, we should go into the market'. No, we say: 'protection has the highest priority, we cannot go into the market'. What can we do then? We can talk to the client, ask him if he will give us a bigger risk budget; it might be a possibility. Otherwise, it's not possible for us to enter the market. If you get a bigger risk budget, that's a different case. You can

---

[24] This is a level of risk or losses the portfolio may not exceed.

use it, put your foot into the water, see if the water's any good. And if it works out, if the market goes in the right direction, performance goes up, you win a bigger risk budget and can increase exposure to the market.

A trade-off therefore exists between restrictions agreed with clients and the freedom to use the opportunities that the market offers spontaneously. Fund managers cannot react quickly to what happens in the market, a constraint that hinders performance because they need the client's approval to change the investment mandate, and we were told many pension funds can take months to take decisions. This is also an enabling factor, however, as it induces greater loyalty from investors.

Where return is the target, desire for a low tracking error in a particular fund can be the result of diversification strategies. In their pursuit of growth, investors look to reduce risks by a number of forms of diversification. Many are well recognized: diversifying by geography of investment, for example, or investment in 'real assets' such as commodities. It has been argued that much of this diversification is self-defeating, because the flow of funds from more to less correlated assets simply increases the correlations across all assets (e.g. Woolley and Vayanos 2012: 60). A further diversification strategy has, however, received less attention, namely institutional investors seeking to diversify across the investment strategies their fund managers employ. The result is an attitude to evaluating managers that is not solely focused on short-term performance. One interviewee summed up the views of a number:

> Are we looking for a defensive manager? . . . Are we looking for someone who has huge volatility but they also have a lot of alpha that they bring in? [S]ometimes we'll want to pick ones that don't really correlate to each other. So we'll have a manager that specializes in riskier loans and we'll have one that's a little bit more defensive. . . . We have one portfolio that's really defensive, they always lag a lot on their peers. But that's fine because in the times when the market is down they really outperform. So we allocate based on that.

The deliberate pursuit of diversification thus leads to investment in very different, including short-term, strategies. The overall portfolio of investments into funds may produce the relatively stable long-term returns many institutional investors seek, but in their pursuit of this stability the investors are supporting fund managers with strategies that may lead to short-term market volatility. The most obvious example is pension fund investment into hedge funds.

The Role of Investment Consultants

As we have noted at a number of points in this chapter, actors outside the direct links in the chain can have a significant impact on investment outcomes. The link between institutional money and fund managers is frequently influenced or even mediated, as with individual investors, and with potentially similar results in terms of greater likelihood of exit. As an important example, we focus here on investment consultants to pension funds. The importance of consultants has dramatically increased. As of 30 June 2015, the five largest consultants advised on investments worth US$22.2 trillion.[25] Goyal and Wahal (2008) estimate that 82 per cent of US public plan sponsors use investment consultants, as do 50 per cent of corporate sponsors (Jenkinson et al. 2016).

Consultants are similarly influential in the UK, though less so in continental Europe. The largest are global firms such as Mercer and Aon Hewitt. Investment consulting at these and similar firms has its roots in their actuarial practices, an outgrowth of their initial mathematical expertise in the calculation of pension liabilities, including, crucially, the discount rate applied to those liabilities. As discussed earlier, this is in itself a significant influence, but we concentrate here on the separate function of advising on overall investment strategy.

This discussion necessitates a more detailed breakdown of the chain. It highlights again that institutional investors are not homogeneous and do not fit neatly into one box. For example, a private company (the sponsor) may establish a pension fund (governed by trustees). The sponsor contributes money to the fund, while the fund is responsible for managing this money. Decision-making power as well as responsibility for the success of the pension scheme(s) is delegated to the trustees. Trustees often do not manage the money themselves but further delegate the investment management by appointing professional fund managers.

Trustees commission (and in a number of countries they are *required* to commission) consultants to help them determine investment goals and suitable investment structures as well as find the best fund managers for their purposes. Investment consultants function as 'gatekeepers' for the money that flows from institutional investors to fund managers and are supposed to ensure that this flow happens in the most efficient way. It is not in doubt that pension fund trustees as a whole need such advice. As interviewees consistently pointed out, many trustees, even at relatively large schemes, lack investment experience,[26] and can be appointments made for reasons (including, at public pension funds, political allegiance) unconnected to their role. Even for those with relevant experience, staying abreast of financial

---

[25] Source: Pensions and Investments., <http://www.pionline.com/gallery/20151130/SLIDESHOW2/113009999>, accessed 16 March 2017.
[26] Regulations in the UK, for example, prevent trustees from giving direct investment advice, but expertise is still important when assessing investment strategy.

innovation and acquiring the information to assess potential and existing fund managers in a part-time, often short-term, role is nigh on impossible. Consultants offer enormous economies of scale in information gathering and expertise.

The relationship between trustees and consultants is a relationship of the principal–agent kind, however, just as is that between investors and fund managers. Investment consultants are interested in generating as much business as possible; note that their fees are calculated according to time and effort, not the investment result. They thus have an incentive to innovate, or to recommend a change of manager, to create additional business. Innovation can certainly have a positive character, and even interviewees critical of some aspects of the consultants' role acknowledged their significant contribution in assisting and disseminating investment innovations that meet particular needs. Over time, the core competences of consultants have constantly increased and now include, besides the by now traditional selection of fund managers, the conceptualization of complex investment structures, permanent monitoring of fund managers' investment processes and asset allocations, and rating funds and fund managers. The extent to which consultants' advice is taken varies. We were told that the very largest pension funds, with extensive in-house competence that can include taking many of the actual investment decisions, may treat consultants as one of many advisers and may not follow their advice at all. Smaller funds may rarely question what they are being told.

The gradual extension of consultants' competences nevertheless contributes to the increasing influence consultants exert on fund managers' decision-making. Fund managers are aware that if consultants turn negative on them or their funds, significant money outflows will follow and/or no new money will flow in. In particular, consultants formulate criteria for identifying a successful fund manager. As Jenkinson et al. (2016) demonstrate, next to 'hard' factors such as past performance, 'soft investment factors' and 'service factors' play an important role in the selection process. Soft investment factors relate to the identification of the most capable portfolio managers with a consistent investment philosophy; indeed, Jenkinson et al. suggest that these factors dominate the initial choice of fund managers. Our fund manager interviewees agreed, and see many of these 'soft' factors as positively shaping investment practices, although interviewees also saw service factors related to the marketing efforts of the investment management company, including the abilities of sales personnel and the usefulness of their reports to clients, as crucial. Consultants may also (in theory) favour longer-term investment, but interviewees' perception was that it was relatively short-term performance that would subsequently determine whether they kept mandates, in a process similar to that initiated by wealth managers' 'approved lists'. Non-performance factors also necessitate constant impression management (as discussed throughout the book) on the part of fund managers. The latter adapt to increasing demands for seriousness, scientificity, and objectivity by generating the 'right signs'. For example, the head of the Quantitative Strategies and Risk Management group in the investment management arm of a big German investment bank justified the very formation of his group as an answer to the question: 'What do consultants want to hear?', implying that consultants are looking for formal investment processes and stringent risk management, the services officially provided by this group. Furthermore, individual fund managers and investment management companies know that consultants permanently monitor their work; therefore, fund managers prefer to make investment decisions which they can easily justify to consultants. Alongside the 'client gaze', there is an ever-present 'consultant gaze' from outside the investment chain.

At the same time, by delivering the 'right signs', fund managers not only try to comply with the consultants' formal requirements but also actively to build a relationship with them. Innovation, we were told, could be one consequence of such relationships. As well as demonstrating (they hoped) their ability to outperform, fund managers looked to foster trust, a 'confidence in the manager that is based on personal relationships, familiarity, persuasive advertising, connections to friends and colleagues, communication, and schmoozing' (Gennaioli et al. 2015: 92): fund managers are 'money doctors' for whom trust is the most crucial component of success (see also Chapter 2). Fund managers have to constantly perform a careful balancing act between seriousness and formality, on the one hand, and a familiarity and casualness that might become friendship, on the other. This problem is characteristic of many relationships within the investment chain covered in this book, wherever services are sold on an ongoing basis (see Ortiz 2014 on the relationship between fund managers and broker sales staff).

The constant push for more innovation is inevitably about change, and therefore must contribute to increased turnover of fund choices by pension funds. Assessment, while obviously difficult, must focus on whether this contributes to improved investment performance or not. The poor relative performance of hedge funds, recent recipients of large investment from pension schemes, is one example of where such innovation might be questioned. Interviewees with longer perspectives also noted cyclical shifts in where asset allocation decisions are taken (earlier by the pension fund itself, subsequently by a dedicated 'balanced'—the older term—or 'multi-asset'—the modern reincarnation—fund). One significant innovation made by investment consultants, especially in the context of the investment chain framework, is their push to offer their own investment management services. At its fullest extent, this involves 'fiduciary management', where investment consultants take responsibility for all aspects of the investment process. Effectively, they move to becoming a link in the investment chain.

The logic of this service is compelling. It offers both economies of scale and the ability to overcome the often slow response times of trustees to changing markets. A consultant whose company did not offer fiduciary management recognized that 'the great argument in favour of fiduciary management is the ability to trade instantaneously', and outlined the difficulties of effecting changes in pension fund investment strategy:

> One of my clients... [I've] been trying to persuade them that interest rates are going to rise and started persuading them of this nine months ago.... Your bond portfolios are hugely exposed, we need to adopt a strategy now to deal with this.... So my recommendation to the client was to switch to the absolute return bond fund. Which they agreed to. The members then had to have two rounds of training to understand, the trustees.... They then had two rounds of training... they had to go through a full procurement process with a prequalification questionnaire, scoring of that, shortlisting, invitation to tender for the shortlisted managers, scoring, tender clarification meetings... top four I think came in to present and then the manager is appointed. Then they have to have due diligence, legal agreement is drawn up.... They've still not started the strategy.

Fiduciary management therefore makes a lot of sense. The way it is justified, however, also implies that it is likely to lead to swifter exits from fund managers. Once again, a further link in the chain is likely to increase the short-termism of investment decision-making. Consultants might also find themselves in direct competition with the fund managers they are supposed to recommend impartially to trustees. This conflict of interests recently attracted attention from the UK's Financial Conduct Authority.

Trustees continue to employ consultants in one of their core functions, identifying the best fund managers, despite there being no evidence that the funds selected by consultants perform better than the rest (Jenkinson et al. 2016). A significant part of the explanation for this is regulation (see Chapter 1). Trustees still have discretion, however, as to how far they follow consultants' advice. The reason many choose to follow advice so closely (even to the extent, with fiduciary management, of effectively delegating almost all decision-making) relates to our suggestion in this book that it is not only money that flows through the investment chain. First of all, consultants help to redistribute responsibility (and the need for justification) between chain participants. Trustees are ultimately responsible for the performance of assets entrusted to them; thus, they are happy—and even feel obliged—to delegate key decisions, including the search for fund managers, to consultants. If the performance of the funds selected is not satisfactory, trustees are not solely responsible for this failure and can justify it by referring to consultants' mistakes. Consultants therefore provide a very important service within the investment chain: responsibility sharing. Second, as we have already demonstrated in our discussion of the fund manager—client and fund manager—consultant relationships, money flows are usually accompanied by the building (or loss) of mutual confidence and trust. Consultants, for their part, act as 'money doctors' who have to first earn (or deserve?) the right to reassure, make recommendations, and evaluate the results. Where trust is created, however, the relationship becomes 'sticky' and trustees become more confident. There is a vast quantity of research on trust and this would certainly go beyond the scope of this chapter. The point here, however, is that, in the investment chain, there exists a combination of formal principal–agent relationships with 'soft' (trusting) connections. This is nonetheless a fragile union as every participant in the investment chain may operate in various roles; for example, consultants might be simultaneously agents for trustees and principals for fund managers.

As previously highlighted, the roles and positions of players in the chain are not fixed, but nor is change unidirectional. Consultants are in the process of moving to become participants in the chain. At the same time, the relationships of trustees, investment consultants, and fund managers are in some situations also undergoing change because some trustees want more direct access to financial expertise, in a way not filtered through consultants. It means that fund managers are now brought into negotiations at the earlier stage and get a chance to convince trustees directly. '[G]ood consultants will have sufficient confidence to pave the way for this closer dialogue' (Harrison 2007), even as they continue to function as 'gatekeepers'.

This chapter fleshes out further how investment chain incentives and constraints shape fund management, by examining the importance to fund managers of the different types of investors in their funds and the impact of additional links in the chain. Fund managers often manage differently depending on whose behalf they are managing. Ultimately, the needs of the final investors will nearly always have a determining role in fund managers' actions. The issues involved go far beyond those of the principal–agent problem. In many cases, a genuine and many-sided affective relationship exists between fund manager and institutional investor.

We cannot, however, assume that the wishes of even large institutional investors, let alone individual investors, will flow smoothly down the investment chain. At each stage, further intermediaries in, and other influences on, the investment chain shape the final investment decision. This chapter only scratches the surface of the relationship between fund managers and the investors who provide their investment. This remains one of the most important, but least studied, issues in financial markets.

4

Quantitative Asset Managers and Their Chains

The idea of this book is to show how the positioning of investment managers in the investment chain influences their behaviour. On the one hand, links to other market players such as clients, regulators, and competitors determine how investment managers 'see' the market, which information they collect and process, and how they value assets and make investment decisions. On the other hand, those links require self-presentation. As we have stressed throughout the book, this self-staging is not just about numbers; it can also be understood as a sequence of impression-management performances, where investment managers present themselves to the other members of the investment chain (Figure 1.1). At the same time, self-dramatization takes place internally, within the asset management company, for example, as part of the processes of communication and cooperation, but also competition with colleagues (Figure 4.1). In this chapter, we will argue that there is interdependence between the chains. In particular, the *external* chain influences how investment managers behave *internally*, that is to say how they position themselves within an organization, develop their relationships with their colleagues, and demonstrate to others, through their performance of self, that their professional role is a necessary one. The chapter is focused on this tension between 'outside' and 'inside'.

Above all this chapter stresses that many promises staged in performances for an external audience (clients, consultants, and regulators) cannot be lived up to in practice within the organizations. 'Hard' promises of professionalism, scientificity, and objectivity are softened in the process of internal implementation and the lived experience of investment processes.

This chapter is based on an open qualitative research method approach, and draws on two sets of primary empirical data. The first set contains thirty-six semi-structured, in-depth interviews conducted in a number of German and Swiss investment management companies and banks from 2007 to 2009

```
          ┌─────────────────────────────────────────┐
          │  Client Service Managers/Marketing Staff │
          └─────────────────────────────────────────┘
```

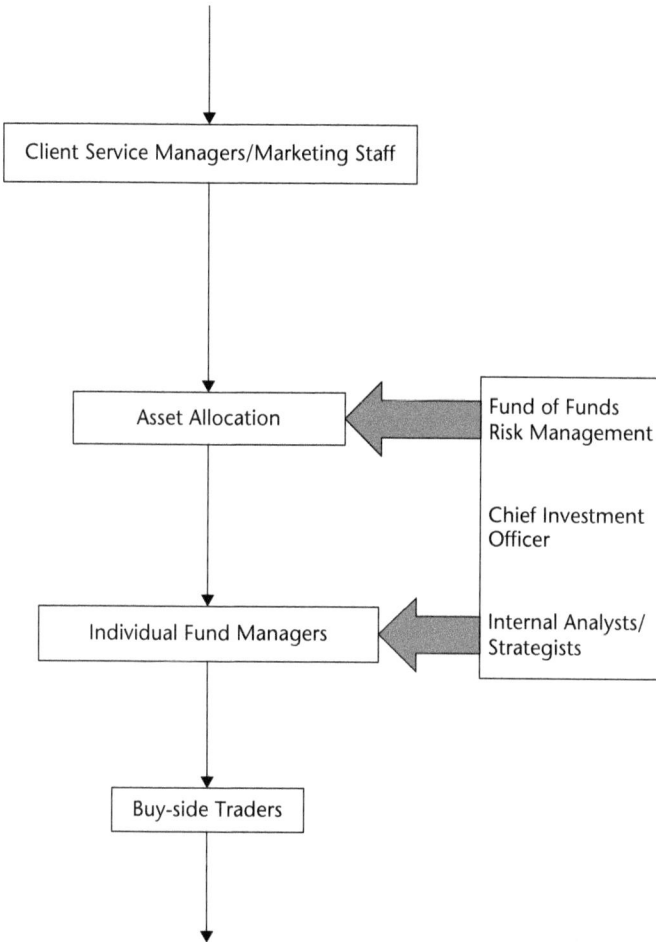

Figure 4.1 The investment chain within the investment management firm

and 2013 to 2014. Interviewees worked as fund managers in Frankfurt and in Zurich and predominantly pursued an active investment strategy (see Chapter 1). The interviews were complemented by three months of participant observation that one of us (Svetlova) conducted in the portfolio management department of a private Swiss investment bank in Zurich and the quantitative department of the investment branch of a big German bank in Frankfurt. The extensive field notes made during those stays form the second set of data.[1]

---

[1] In the ethnographic materials that follow, 'I' therefore refers to Svetlova.

Setting the Stage

On a foggy morning in March 2008, I found myself among the skyscrapers of Frankfurt-am-Main. As a participant in an ethnographic project on fund management, I was going to join a series of presentations given by representatives of the Quantitative Strategies and Risk Management group within the investment arm of a big German bank. The audience was made up of in-house trainees, and the event was part of a standard trainee programme that usually involves trainees visiting various departments of the bank.

The first presentation was given by the group head, a dynamic man in his early thirties, who was supposed to introduce the group to the audience. From the very beginning of his presentation, I was puzzled—and this puzzlement did not subside throughout the day—by the strong urge for justification that dominated his narrative. He and other group members also giving talks that day were keen to explain why their group existed, why colleagues within the department (might) need their work, and how the firm as a whole benefited from their achievements. It was clear they did not consider these truths to be self-evident. But why?

The first words the group head uttered, and the first slides of his presentation, already contained a clear message of success. He told us that he had arrived at the 'house' roughly three years ago in order to build up this new group within the portfolio management department; at that time, there were five of them involved in quantitative tasks; now, they were fourteen. This tripling of staff numbers was not a coincidence but rather the result of the house's targeted strategy—the management board had decided to develop quantitative investment strategies and risk management in the aftermath of the 'new economy' market turmoil at the beginning of the millennium. He said that, at that time, both areas—quantitative investments and portfolio risk management—had been in the process of being slowly 'discovered and developed' in fund management worldwide; they had not yet clearly come into focus in the 1990s. The house decided to join this trend even though its overall investment philosophy had not been at all quantitative up to this point. As the group head said, 'at a particular moment, the top management realized "We don't have anything in that area"'. After the bank had decided they needed 'somebody who can calculate', it also immediately provided a clear signal as to the strategic importance of quantitative techniques in the organizational set-up, as it separated and bundled all quantitative activities into one group within the portfolio management department and started to hire people.

From the very beginning of the introductory presentation, the active development of the Quantitative Strategies and Risk Management group was presented to the audience as an important step in the house's 'modernization', a way of keeping up with the times. Follow-up interviews with group members supported this first impression: the top-down decision to establish a new group had been taken to signal seriousness and competence to related members of the investment chain: clients, consultants, competitors, and regulators.

The development of the group was rapid and successful (some well-performing strategies and funds were mentioned in the presentations). Why then this urge to justify their own existence, an urge I observed from the very first minute of the meeting? During the course of the day, the answer to the question started to emerge: successful self-presentation to external partners in the investment chain comes at a cost internally, since it causes difficulties and frictions in dealing with internal colleagues. As discussed in Chapter 2, the chain enables in one place but constrains in another.

Alvesson (2013) claims that making things 'look good' has become an important—if not the most important—activity of modern organizations. He summarizes under the notion of 'grandiosity' 'attempts to give yourself, your occupational group/organization, or even the society in which you live, a positive—if somewhat superficial—well-polished and status-enhancing image. As much as possible is targeted and becomes symbolically upgraded and made remarkable and impressive, adding to status and self-esteem' (Alvesson 2013: 8). Quantitative strategies and risk management played a significant role in the generation of grandiosity, of an impression of consistent excellence, in the portfolio management arm of the observed bank—they signalled putative emotionlessness, number-based scientificity and objectivity, and contribute to an effective *staging* of the quality of decision-making. Referring to Power (2003), Alvesson (2013: 15) writes that 'in an "audit society" it is important to exhibit the correct indicators to be ticked off when mass media or authorities pay a visit'; in the case under discussion, this occurred when external partners in the chain came into play. For an investment management company, it is important to demonstrate that its investment process is based on serious, rule-based (and thus disciplined) practices, that decision-making is scientifically justified, and does not rely on gut feeling and guesswork. This is what external stakeholders such as clients, consultants, and regulators want to see.

At the same time, the development of quantitative expertise—which, as mentioned earlier, is clearly a response to the requirements of the external chain—cannot remain a phantom, a castle in the air, just 'an illusion trick' (Alvesson 2013). The quantitative group was established as an organizational unit and had to demonstrate constantly that it was a valuable part of a department which had not paid serious attention to quantitative work before. All promises made to the 'outside' therefore had to take the form of concrete activities such as constructing new products and strategies, and helping 'fundamental' managers with asset selection, portfolio construction, and risk assessment. Those activities could not just be boiled down to illusions and empty signalling; they had to happen and to be integrated into the life of the portfolio management department as a whole.

This process created tensions. The quantitative analysts' (often known in the industry as 'quants') promises of rigour and objectivity could not simply be imposed upon colleagues who had happily worked without their quant colleagues so far. These colleagues were mostly fundamental portfolio managers. Fundamental investors (who are also the main actors in Chapter 2) analyse various 'fundamental' data, for example companies' financial statements, information about their market position, and quality of management, to find promising securities. Usually, their decisions do not rely heavily on modelling and calculations but are rather based on judgement calls, partly because many fundamental factors are not quantifiable, partly because those that are (including valuation) are nonetheless open to conflicting interpretations. The quants had to overcome these major differences in investment approaches.

It is important to note that follow-up interviews conducted two years later in the same department demonstrated that the investment philosophy remained driven by fundamental investing. During these years, therefore, the quants went through the difficult process of organizing their collaboration with fundamental portfolio managers and adjusting their own practices to the fundamentally driven investment process. On the surface, the modality of this collaboration (discussed in the following) suggests a strenuous balancing act between the 'loose', rule-free culture of fundamental investing and the 'rigorous', disciplined culture of quantitative investing. We would like to stress, however, that the need to 'balance' was also driven by organizational factors, as the quants were set up as a separate group inside the department and had to struggle to gain legitimacy within it.

The way in which the quantitative group was 'dropped in' from above into the department created a very fragile situation internally: satisfying the requirements of external marketing led to a permanent need for internal marketing. Quants found themselves obliged to demonstrate the added value of their own work to fundamental portfolio managers and other colleagues.

This explains why a form of defensive self-portrayal came to the fore in the presentation series for the in-house trainees: the quantitative group was eager to convey an image of itself as a competent and indispensable part of the organization to future colleagues.

It is worth considering in more detail how the quantitative 'intruders' solved the problem of working together with people who were often convinced they did not need them. To do this, we will focus on the first of the group's two core tasks, namely the development, packaging, and selling of quantitative investment strategies. The second function—risk management—will be briefly discussed afterwards.[2]

Internal Battles

It was the responsibility of one set of group employees to develop all kinds of quantitative or rule-based strategies. In other words, they developed methods for identifying and exploiting market inefficiencies ('mispricings'). They used quantitative techniques such as filter systems, (statistical) trend extrapolation, and screening models to identify potentially outperforming securities and to assess future market movements.[3] For example, when selecting equities, they screened a particular investment universe according to price/equity, book/value, and other multiples to find overpriced or underpriced shares.[4] Prior to screening, rules were usually set defining over- and underpriced securities and their weightings in the portfolio. Quants also evaluated historic data series to identify patterns in the markets that had been profitable so far and which might deliver a reliable forecasting signal. In particular they focused on seeking out factors that are used to positively influence performance of given securities. Strategies developed in this way were back-tested (simulated using historic data) and then 'packaged' into products (e.g. investment certificates)[5] that were distributed to clients.

The fact that these quantitative strategies are *rule-bound* was particularly stressed in the introductory presentation by the group head, as well as in all following talks and interviews. Mathematical rigour was presented as an

---

[2] For discussion of a case that offers both arresting parallels and striking differences, see the discussion in Chapter 6 of the divergent evaluation practices of equity and fixed income fund managers at a French firm.

[3] Filter systems and screening models are computerized tools that allow companies in a given investment universe to be ranked according to particular parameters (e.g. valuation, size, past performance). Statistical trend extrapolation is a forecasting method that aims to predict future price movements based on historical data.

[4] Multiples, or investment valuation ratios, are used to assess the attractiveness of a company as a potential investment. They are usually constructed by dividing one number (e.g. share price, net asset or 'book' [accounting] value etc.) by another (e.g. cash flow, forecast earnings, etc.). Multiples are simple and effective tools of company valuation. For example, the price to earnings ratio (P/E) gives an indication of how much at any given time purchasers of a given share (aggregated as 'the market') will pay for $1 of earnings. These measures do have their detractors, however, often for reasons to do with the large number of perfectly legal and conventional, but contestable, accounting decisions that have to be taken for any large company and its auditors to arrive at a figure like 'earnings', as well as the uncertainty inherent in forecasting these numbers; it is ultimately the future that most market participants are interested in.

[5] The German *Investmentzertifikat* has no exact equivalent in English-speaking jurisdictions. They are 'structured products', that is to say designed by and therefore specific to the firm that issues them, and usually have a derivative component, i.e. the investor who purchases them receives payouts whose amount depends on the movements in the price of an 'underlying', which could be an equity, an index, a commodity, etc.

advantage the quants had over 'gut-oriented' fundamental colleagues, one which allowed the quants to distance themselves from the latter. Fundamental investors' reliance on gut feeling was considered by quants to be rather dangerous ('we saw what happened during the TMT [the technology, media, and telecommunications sector] crisis', the group head said) and something that should and could be avoided.

Due to these 'official' differences in investment philosophy, fundamental (qualitative) and quantitative portfolio managers attached different importance to the various links of the chain.

For fundamental portfolio managers, contacts with securities analysts (buy-side and sell-side), brokers, and securities issuers (companies) were essential. They followed earnings guidance provided by companies and paid attention to related assessments issued by analysts.[6] Fundamental investors visited companies or met with their management, and frequently talked to analysts and brokers in order to find divergences between what company management expected and what 'the market' (in the form of current share prices) expected. Communication, processing, and interpretation of fundamental information (news about a company, management comments and outlook, accounting numbers, etc.) are central to this part of the investment chain. Communication flow is crucial: in personal and telephone conversations, and through email exchange, numbers and pieces of analysis were disseminated and commented on, rumours spread, and discussions about the mood of the market and fund flows evolved. After digesting this information, fundamental portfolio managers made investment decisions (to buy or to sell) and initiated trades (placed orders).

In contrast to fundamental managers (and this contrast is a part of their investment philosophy and marketing strategy) quants officially maintained a distance from this communicative chain and its emotional charge. They claimed to be focused on numbers. Group members stressed that associations between factors influencing share price movements and their effects on future security returns were determined with the help of objective statistical procedures.

The idea behind the quants' procedures is that they should become an 'emotionless' part of the investment chain. Decisions in this area (ideally, at least) are objective, disciplined, and consistent with rules defined in advance. Quantitative portfolio managers claimed to be at a distance from the market—from its fluctuations, gossip, and excitement. This distance allowed them to exploit the emotions of their fundamentally driven peers as well as anomalies arising from those emotions.

---

[6] Listed companies regularly issue their expected results (sales, earnings, etc.) to the market. These official company forecasts are referred to as 'guidance'.

These putative advantages of a quantitative investment process—objectivity, reliance on mathematics and statistics (and thus the scientificity of the approach), resistance to emotion—are, however, primarily ingredients of *a selling strategy* for quantitative products. Calculations and rules lead to superior returns, they claimed. They are a part of the 'Quant Story', a meta-narrative that celebrates 'rationality', 'calmness', and a 'systematic approach to security valuation against the irrational market and market participants' (Tuckett and Taffler 2012: 64–5).

Scholars have noted that external clients (especially institutional investors) and consultants generate a 'demand pull' for quantitative products and reinforce the implementation of structured investment processes with quantitative elements (Fabozzi et al. 2008). This demand could not be ignored in the fund management industry. The investment arm of the bank in Frankfurt where the ethnographic work took place was one of the first in Germany to recognize the importance of the trend and reacted by establishing the new quantitative group. The idea behind it was to tap into the seriousness and objectivity that numbers signified and in this way to enhance sales. Reliance on quantitative strategies seemed to be an effective marketing hook. The question of *how clients perceive us*—the clients' gaze—was crucial.

For example, at the investment manager Svetlova observed in Frankfurt, there was a Dividend Fund (name changed) which was developed on the basis of the extensive quantitative work, as a quantitative fund manager explained:

> This fund was created on the basis of a lot of back-testing. We did not just say 'we simply buy equities with high dividend yields'; we looked at what *makes sense*. There is a model portfolio for this fund and the fund manager has to keep the weightings close to it because it is *tightly linked to marketing*.

In this context, back-testing ('we looked at what makes sense') is not just a quantitative technique but a part of the sales pitch. The manager continued, explaining that 'back-testing is persuasive. [It tells us] the thing has functioned well for ten years. There is no guarantee that it will continue but it is a confidence building measure'.

Here, again, the issue of marketability comes into play. Throughout the development of new quantitative products, *efforts to calculate* go hand in hand with *efforts to sell*. It is not just about, 'how do we generate the best performance?', but also 'how can a financial product be successfully marketed?' This issue has attracted increasing attention in research in the social studies of finance, which applies wider social science disciplines, and not just economics, to the study of financial markets (McFall 2011a, 2011b; Vargha 2011; Lépinay 2011). According to this emerging literature, it is crucial not just to discover a mathematically interesting and promising product, but rather the one that can be most convincingly marketed. Quantitative strategies are strong candidates here.

Enemies or Friends?

Though clear demarcation of quantitative approaches from fundamental portfolio management was necessary for marketing purposes, it was not so rigorous in practice. On the one hand, fundamental managers integrated formal methods, such as scorings and rankings based on statistical and econometric analysis, into their investment processes as one possible but not determinant decision-making factor. On the other hand, quantitative managers could not completely ignore or exclude human judgement and emotions from their decision-making due to the fallibility and blind spots of formal models. Quants everywhere are aware that human asset managers are able to provide knowledge that cannot be delivered by purely formal methods. Two surveys by Fabozzi et al. (2007, 2008) show that the investment management industry is still in search of the optimal balance between judgemental and quantitative approaches, and that in practice hybrid variants of these approaches are adopted. Indeed, in active fund management it is impossible to find a single instance where judgement is completely excluded; at the same time, in contemporary investment management there is hardly a fundamental investment process that operates completely without rules. The process of collaboration observed at the German bank provides a good illustration of how such hybrid approaches are actually practised.

I observed various modes of collaboration. First, there were funds that are managed purely quantitatively; in this case, the development and implementation of the strategy as well as responsibility for the performance clearly lay with the quantitative group. Second, some funds were partly managed according to a quantitative model and partly 'traditionally', according to a qualitative fundamental approach (the so-called 'multi-manager' concept). However, the division of labour and thus of contribution to fund performance was not straightforward. Rather the predominant model was one of 'advisory overlay', under which quants provided advice for their part of the fund (e.g. in the form of a model portfolio) but did not have the power to make a final decision; their advice could be adopted, or could be overridden by the fund manager responsible for the fund as a whole. Third, the quantitative group provided research accessible to all members of the department who were able to use or ignore it as they saw fit.

Consistent with this classification, there were also three ways in which quantitative research and services were used in fundamental portfolio management in-house. The head of the Quantitative Strategies and Risk Research group explained it thus:

> We have three basic approaches.... First of all, we have a strong *research supply* for all fund managers. We send an email with a model suggestion. Some portfolio managers (I would say three out of ten) delete the email immediately without opening it. A further three on the other hand are waiting for this email, and implement the model recommendations; or, at least model recommendations are important for their decisions. The other four managers are still to be convinced. Then we have funds which are managed according to a strictly structured investment process with a significant quantitative element. This process is particularly relevant for the funds with a large investment universe (for example, small caps or high dividends). The larger universe is filtered, we prepare a list of the most interesting equities, sometimes we allocate weightings to them; this is then a model portfolio. These lists with their weightings are checked by fund managers. This is the so-called 'overlay'. Finally, we have products that are managed strictly quantitatively. No overlay is allowed here.

Notably, in the first two cases (research supply and advisory overlay), responsibility for funds' performance lies with the fundamental managers; the quantitative group supports them by providing investment suggestions and weighting recommendations, but there is no obligation for the managers responsible to accept and implement the quants' ideas.

Here, quants place themselves in an ambiguous situation. In these cases, they are not responsible for the performance of the end product, and this fact allows the fundamental managers not to take them or their suggestions seriously. Fund managers' opinions are decisive (and can override all the quants' recommendations) because they bear responsibility for fund performance. Somewhat ironically, the *measurement* of quants' contribution to fund performance is difficult if not impossible. 'This is a tough story', one member of the quant group told me. How should the performance contribution of advice that might not have been followed be measured? This difficulty clearly stemmed from the freedom which fundamental managers enjoyed to use or ignore this quantitative input.

Finding themselves in this situation, quants sought to reconcile the parties and position themselves, within an internal chain, as people 'doing a consulting job'. They claimed that their task was not to force everyone to use their services, but to persuade, to offer help and support, and to let colleagues implement quantitative suggestions at their discretion. Their goal as they articulated it was to strengthen this *informal interplay* between themselves and the fund managers. For the quantitative group, fundamental managers were above all *internal clients* who must be wooed, convinced, and retained. Quants considered it important to convince the 'non-believers' among the fundamental managers of the quality of their services, that is to say to reduce the number of managers who deleted their emails without reading them, or who simply ignored their advice. Demand for their services had to be slowly created and sustained. At the same time, quants did not completely distance themselves from the end results in terms of fund performance. 'We are in one boat', said a quant in one of the presentations to trainees. He stressed that this cooperative consulting stance helped to smooth out internal conflicts.

On the other hand, this conflict avoidance strategy apparently did not succeed all the time. The presentations and interviews gave a picture of the rather insecure position the quantitative group found itself in. The fact that quants did not assume responsibility in most cases (as in case of the advisory overlay mandates, for example) provoked the question: 'Do we really need these guys who do not have "their skin in the game"?' Fundamental managers responsible for funds knew that if performance was bad, they could not lay the blame on a model or a ranked list. In these cases, quantitative managers were not generally under fire, and it was thus not a big surprise that their advice was often not taken seriously. There is a well-attested difference in the effectiveness of recommendations or forecasts made in a situation where one bears the consequences and those made where one does not (Taleb 2007).

On the other hand, the services the quants provided were not without consequence, not simply ignored and forgotten. Indeed, they might create additional tensions. In one of the presentations to the trainees, a case was explicitly discussed where a fund manager ignored the recommendations of the model portfolio, was wrong in his opinion, and, as a result, the fund performance suffered. Because this happened in one of the flagship funds,[7] the fund manager was asked by senior management to justify his decisions and to explain his performance; in other words, he was asked to justify deviating from a quantitative tool he was not obliged to use! This case became very prominent in the portfolio management department and was discussed in every corner. In this way, all the fundamental managers became aware that a non-compulsory quantitative tool could become an instrument of observation and control even where it was supposed it should merely be a means of help and support.

It was of course imperative that these tensions not leak outside, to partners in the external chain. An imaginative marketing solution was developed to sweep these advisory overlay and responsibility issues under the carpet. Describing a large multi-manager fund, the investment bank's website praised its *strict team approach*. It pictured quantitative research as an integral part of the investment process and remarked that:

---

[7] A flagship fund is (one of) an investment management firm's best-known and most important fund(s), central to the firm's marketing efforts.

Even if the portfolio manager responsible decides autonomously, each investment decision is the result of teamwork. To make this approach work, close communication within the portfolio management department is necessary.

In this way, the whole issue was presented to clients and consultants as an advantage rather than as a source of conflict and internal disagreement.

To sum up: the simple idea presented to external chain partners—the advantages of rigorous, rule-bound quantitative strategies—turned out to be considerably more flexible when actually implemented. In particular, strict reliance on rules was diluted when these rules were applied in a hybrid (quantitative and fundamental) environment. In other words, the need to market financial products to clients and consultants as 'serious' or 'rigorous' led to messiness and internal battles within the organization; this mess was in its turn presented as an advantage (a 'team approach') to the outside world. This example clearly shows how the self-staging of fund managers to other elements of the investment chain influences their status and actions as part of the internal chain, that is to say within the fund management company.

Living in the Markets

In this part of the chapter, we argue that not only the 'rule-boundedness' of quantitative strategies but also their alleged 'emotionless character' are descriptions whose reality is not supported by our observations of the investment management industry.

In contrast to fundamental managers (and, as already discussed, this contrast is a part of their marketing strategy), quants officially maintain a distance from the communicative emotional chain of markets. They supposedly concentrate calmly on numbers alone. At the same time, there are various investment chain partners involved in the quantitative investment process (Figure 4.2), and human relationships usually involve emotions, (mis)communication, and liking or disliking of each other.

At the beginning of the quantitative process, quants usually have an idea of which factor might be significant for the future outperformance of given securities. Associations between the factors of influence and their effects on future returns are determined with the help of statistical procedures. Then, computers are used to analyse historic data and determine if a given factor was indeed significant in the past (back-testing). These analyses are based on data sets provided by specialized data providers (IBES, Bloomberg, Reuters, etc.). If the results of the analysis are satisfactory (particular criteria are set, e.g. the

Acquisition of investment ideas (internal, talks to brokers and competitors)	→	Data feeding/ Back-testing (data providers, fundamental colleagues)	→	Development of new strategies (internal; broker's quant team)	→	Implementation/ Execution (brokers/traders) Selling Efforts (clients)

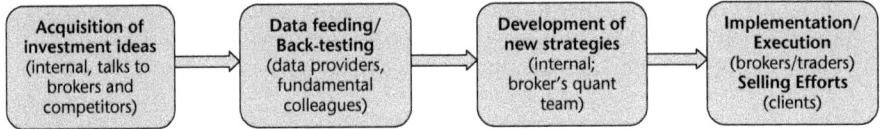

Figure 4.2 The development of the quantitative investment product and the relevant chain partners

Information Ratio threshold),[8] quantitative portfolio managers develop and implement new strategies in the form either of a model portfolio or of a product for clients (e.g. an investment certificate). The implementation of these strategies is the final and crucial phase (also discussed in Chapter 5).

As Figure 4.2 illustrates, at different stages of product development, various links in the chain are activated: links to competitors, data providers, fundamental colleagues, clients, brokers, and traders. These groups essentially shape the work and decisions of quantitative portfolio managers and draw them into the tumults of markets and emotions. The idea of the emotionless chain is not a lived reality. The next section provides arguments in support of this statement through analysis of the main phases of the quants' investment process.

Getting Investment Ideas

The first part of the process is the creation of investment ideas, one necessarily according an important role to communication. Quantitative managers do in part generate ideas internally, within their group. The internal development of ideas is often considered by the quantitative department to be inefficient, however. The head of the group commented to us that 'only every sixth or seventh idea we develop ourselves is good. As far as effort and workload go, it is a major waste of resources'.

It seems to be more efficient by far to adopt and modify the products that are already circulating in the market. Indeed, quantitative portfolio managers use external sources and arrive at new ideas during the process of observation of and communication with the market in the broad sense (see Kellard et al. 2016).

---

[8] In quantitative portfolio management, the Information Ratio (IR) is used to assess the quality of a strategy or a structured product. The IR is defined as the excess return (of a product) above the relevant benchmark divided by the tracking error (the standard deviation of the excess returns, or volatility). As the tracking error is frequently interpreted as the risk related to the deviation from the benchmark, the IR is supposed to tell if this risk taking is rewarded by positive excess return and, if so, how consistently this excess return is generated: in other words, how adequately the risk is under control. In their presentations quantitative managers stated that they issued only those products to the market having an IR of at least 0.5. This was their internal quality criterion.

First, they communicate with brokers. There are brokerage houses who specialize in quantitative research and have analysts as well as dedicated sell-side teams which develop and distribute this research (e.g. Morgan Stanley, Credit Suisse, First Boston). When their ideas are implemented, brokers and analysts are rewarded with commission on trades directed to their banks (a process discussed in Chapter 5).

Second, quantitative managers observe and actively talk to their competitors. Kellard et al. (2016: 9) describe information sharing among hedge funds thus: 'in almost all of these exchanges, whether face-to-face, by phone or email, the goal of the conversations was not to discover a new trading opportunity but to scrutinize existing or contemplated investment ideas'. This exchange is of mutual benefit. Our empirical materials also suggest that quants loosely 'borrow' ideas circulating in the markets. One quantitative expert, while presenting tools developed in his division, used the word 'steal' several times, commenting that 'we stole this model from such and such bank', and this seems to be a common practice.

Finally, finance academics also participate in the dissemination of quantitative research through publishing papers on promising factors that might positively influence investment returns.

The handling of strategies discovered in the process of market communication is loose. Quantitative portfolio managers do not copy existing strategies and models as they find them; they do not blindly apply them. As one quantitative portfolio manager put it:

> We are at [a] level which is high enough for us to know what we are dealing with here, [to know] whether it [the model or strategy] works or not.... We can take them and look at what they do in detail, [see] if it is possible to recalculate ... only half of them actually work.

Though the waste of resources in this case is high (as half of the circulating strategies 'do not work'), recalculation of others' strategies is still cheaper and less time-consuming than the development of ideas from scratch.

The question then arises which strategy should be considered for further development. There are some interrelated considerations at play. First, it is important that the strategy can be recalculated and its results verified. Second, there are considerations of practicality. For example, if the strategy requires too frequent restructuring of portfolios (reallocation), this strategy is not considered to be practical, because it would incur excessively high trading costs. Finally, as already mentioned, sales considerations are crucial: can the potential product be successfully marketed? From this point of view, 'stealing' the products has an advantage when it comes to tapping into established marketing strategies and their well-recognized 'keywords' or 'buzzwords'. The Frankfurt quantitative group head put it as follows: 'for example, if we do the volatility short gamma strategy[9].... In the broker research, this keyword is always present. This is good. We can tag along behind...'. This 'tagging along' allowed them to classify the product successfully, making it recognizable and attractive for analysts (Zuckerman 1999) and clients; it was made marketable.

If, at the end of this preliminary analysis, the strategy was considered promising, that is to say that it could be recalculated, was practical, and marketable, development of a distinct in-house model or product began.

Developing Products

At this stage, the outstanding role of data providers becomes particularly prominent. Quantitative portfolio managers draw on the information provided by IBES, FactSet, Thomson Reuters, Bloomberg, and other databases.

The quality of the data is key. The high standards required by quants are not always satisfied by these databases. Their data are not always up-to-date or correct; the ways in which updates are incorporated vary from provider to provider. Thus, quantitative portfolio managers do not always know if the data are accurate. This represents a major challenge for their work.

Some mistakes are obvious: they can be easily noticed as outliers in the results of analysis. For example, if there is an outlier because of a change in capital (e.g. a capital increase),[10] a portfolio manager can find this out very quickly ('we see the news or one simply sees the chart').

In some other cases, the data are obviously wrong, as one Frankfurt quantitative fund manager put it:

> Or there is an earnings estimate which is zero; it stands in the data bank as 0.000000001. We get an enormous PE.[11] But we know there is a zero; we eliminate the company.... We cannot divide by zero; we do not have data in this case.

In some cases, however, quant managers do not have an easy method for noticing or evaluating an outlier. In these cases their relationship to fundamental managers within the same investment house becomes crucial.

---

[9] To be 'short gamma', an investor sells options that have a non-zero gamma. Gamma is the second order option Greek parameter that tells how much the option's delta changes if the underlying price moves, while delta for its part measures how strongly the option's value changes if the underlying price moves. The short gamma strategy is a bet on low volatility and mainly allows money to be made from collecting the time premium as options decay.

[10] That is to say that a company has raised more capital, either in the form of additional debt or in the form of new shares (equity). New capital affects common calculations such as price/earnings (because in the case of an equity issue there is now a larger number of shares by which the company's earnings need to be divided in order to arrive at the earnings per share [EPS] figure by which the share price is divided to arrive at the P/E ratio).

[11] The price/earnings multiple (see note 4).

Fundamental managers are essential for checking the plausibility of data, because they are aware of the latest news about the company, rumours, and flows of funds. Here, it is not the quants providing a service; on the contrary, they receive help from their fundamental colleagues. These exchanges highlight once more the hybrid character of contemporary fund management.

One example is the following: a quantitative portfolio manager screened an investment universe and discovered a new equity he was not familiar with.

> Then I asked myself 'What kind of security is that?' It looks interesting: an unusual name; I have a look and see that it promises me a more than 70 per cent return; I see drops in price . . . a strong price movement in January. . . . And at that point, I sit there and ask myself, 'Is this a data error? Or have the analysts just not discovered it? Should I bet on it?'

In this situation, the quantitative manager called his fundamental colleague:

> I call the fundamental analyst; he is not familiar with the security either; however, he can check the plausibility and give me feedback. Eventually he said 'this thing seems to be OK, seems to be realistic. There is no justification for the price drop, they even gained new business'. And in the end, he implemented the idea himself.

Relationships to fundamental colleagues allow for quality management of the data. Data series provided by the databases naturally relate to the past. Even in the case of analysts' consensus estimates of future earnings, these are forecasts which are products of history; they rely on past or recently available information. There is always a time lag between news announcements and database updates. For example, a company releases a profit warning. Analysts need first to incorporate new numbers into their estimates; the new estimates must then be fed into the databases, and only then can a new consensus estimate be calculated and published. Until this physically happens, the consensus data for this company in the database are out of date.

Portfolio managers, however, need the data in real time. Databases cannot ensure this timeliness. Thus quantitative portfolio managers use their position in the internal investment chain (within the investment management firm) to close this gap. They move between data providers and fundamental colleagues to constantly check the plausibility and timeliness of data.

Execution of Quantitative Strategies

At the implementation stage, brokers become central figures again. It is crucial to understand that to implement a strategy usually does not mean just to sell or to buy stocks, bonds, or futures. Often, it is about a joint search for solutions in difficult situations.

For example, one quantitative manager told me a story about the implementation of the department's first portable alpha product,[12] for which it was necessary to replicate the complete MSCI World index[13] as well as particular country indices. Initially, futures were used; however, they were expensive. Furthermore, it was essential for the replication of this strategy to go short;[14] however, German investment companies faced regulatory restrictions on going short. Thus the twin challenges were to find cheaper alternatives to futures and to create a means to go short. The solution was the application of swaps.[15] This solution could not have been found and implemented without brokers. The quantitative portfolio manager explained how brokers help in such situations:

> Today, we use swaps. This week, we entered [new markets]: Canada and Denmark. I just called a broker: '200 MSCI Canada [index] with particular maturities; executed next day'—and I have it. The broker arranges everything for me in this transaction. The broker hedges himself while he buys single securities and replicates the MSCI Canada or MSCI Denmark and swaps them to me. In a similar way, I can go also short of MSCI World. And this is a nice thing. Actually, we are not allowed to go short. We are not really allowed to say for our funds 'In this ETF or in this share, we go short.' We have to do it indirectly, that is, the broker goes short for us and transfers the returns to us.[16]

Of course, brokers are paid for their services. The execution of quantitative strategies is usually quite lucrative for them: it means a lot of work, and substantial fees. These fees are subject to negotiation. Quantitative managers

[12] Portable alpha products were developed as an alternative to traditional long-only products where securities are bought with the aim of outperforming a benchmark. Traditional long-only investment simultaneously moves with the market (producing beta but also keeping the investment exposed to the market risk) and (hopefully) generates an excess return above the market return (alpha). The idea of the portable alpha is to separate the production of alpha and beta. This is achieved through a series of investments. First, beta is guaranteed through selling a fixed income or money market portfolio (the benchmark) and simultaneously replicating it by means of futures and other derivatives. Second, the majority of the funds raised from selling the portfolio are invested in various alpha strategies, for example, in the equity market (without taking the risk of the equity market as a whole because the equity benchmark is simultaneously shorted by using futures). As a result, an investor receives the return on the fixed income or money market benchmark (beta) plus some additional return from equity investments (alpha). The returns of the portable alpha product are thus independent of capital market movements.

[13] The MSCI World index is an instrument to measure the value of the stock markets worldwide. It includes the most important stocks from the so-called 'developed' markets.

[14] To 'go short' means to sell stocks or bonds which one does not own in the hope of buying them back later at a lower price, thus netting a profit.

[15] Swaps are derivative contracts that allow two parties to exchange financial instruments or income flows (e.g. commodities, currencies, interest payments, etc.) under particular pre-agreed conditions; they are so-called 'over the counter' contracts because they are usually arranged on an ad hoc basis by banks for their clients.

[16] ETFs (exchange-traded funds) are a kind of fund that usually track a stock market index and can be traded like a share on the stock market on which they are listed.

claim to have significant power in these negotiations because they 'give a lot of business'.

However, relationships with brokers are not simply reducible to the monetary element. The 'soft-dollar' agreements discussed in Chapter 5 are in full force here. Brokers and their teams constantly interact with quantitative investors while they generate investment ideas, share market rumours, and provide information about flows of funds, (discreetly) informing them about what the competitors are doing, helping to solve implementation problems, and so on. There is a whole package of services paid for when fund managers 'give business'. There is no tariff that regulates how much the 'package' costs; this is at the sole discretion of the fund manager. At this point, personal relationships come to the fore.

We should not underestimate how intensive contact in these official and unofficial situations over a long period of time (usually years) binds people together. Often broker–fund manager contact is about 'reciprocity', 'relationship value' (see Chapter 5), trust, and even 'friendship'; business partners become well informed about each other's private lives, hobbies, and so on. Here it is a question of 'embedded ties', 'close or special relationships' which enable 'fine-grained information transfer' as well as efficient joint problem solving (Uzzi 1997). These close connections feed into decisions about 'giving business' in the form of non-regular payments for services.

At the same time, as we pointed out in Chapter 3, because this relationship is simultaneously about business and friendship, participants find themselves in a fragile, conflict-laden situation. In this situation, judgements about people and feelings of liking and disliking become crucial, opening the way for the expression of personal preferences as to the shape of people's noses or the cut of their clothes, and more generally for sexism and racism. In other words, instead of friendship, the relationship between clients and brokers can develop into a hidden or open antagonism involving insults and abuse. For example, one of us observed how a broker (female) was made to cry on two occasions by a male fund manager who was unhappy about the price he had received for his order (a quarrel over the second decimal place) and abused her over the phone. The investment chain is very much about people, with all that entails.

In our eyes, those issues are highly under-researched.[17] At the same time, they are important because of the impact they exert on the transaction costs of

---

[17] Both within financial economics and the social studies of finance. In the industry itself, there are now important voices trying to understand these issues and effect change. We interviewed a consultant to the investment industry based in New York, a former salesperson for a large investment bank. She emphasized both relationships between brokers and fund managers and the benefits to investment management firms of having diverse teams (from the perspective of ethnicity as well as gender). She pointed out that many women fund managers were alienated by

funds (and thus their overall performance), and more fundamentally on the structure of the investment banking, management, and brokerage industry: questions of who effectively gets most business and power.

Risk Management

Now we will briefly discuss the second strand of the group's activities, namely risk management. The Quantitative Strategies and Risk Management group was launched at a time (beginning of the 2000s) when it had become common to set up a dedicated risk management unit within investment management departments (or firms). However, even a couple of years after its launch, at the time participant observation was being conducted, there was still a clear need for justification of the group's existence. In his presentation, the head of the group stressed that the group 'had been installed with much ballyhoo' exactly because the need for the internal risk management unit had not been self-evident. This was particularly so because the asset management company already had a centralized department of risk control and performance measurement. Why, then, set up another organizational unit dedicated to risk management while provoking internal competition?

The head of the quantitative group emphasized that the character of the relationship the group maintained with the fundamental fund managers was what made the difference. While the centralized department observed, controlled, and sanctioned, the internal risk management *collaborated* with the fund managers, offering support in the form of various services. 'Our mission is risk research', he said.

His colleague explained in another presentation what *risk research* meant. Group members adapted specific tools available in the market to analyse portfolios (UBS Delta, FactSet). They would enter the existing funds into these tools' spreadsheets, verify that the symbols and quotes for live securities' prices were correct, and manually incorporate some non-standardized derivatives. Regularly (once a week), they ran the program and produced a report which they sent to the portfolio managers responsible for the funds.

The goals of reporting were mainly to draw fund managers' attention to the most significant risks in their portfolios (in terms of overweight or underweight

the highly gendered character of the 'soft-dollar' arrangements we discuss in Chapter 5: rounds of golf and trips to sporting events or strip clubs. She also argued that having large numbers of women working alongside men as fund managers would enable investment management firms to avoid the kinds of cognitive biases that had contributed to the 2007–9 financial crisis.

positions, currency, duration, etc.)[18] and to ask if, in each case, risk taking was deliberate, that is to say that it reflected the fund manager's fundamental view, or whether it had happened accidentally, meaning that the fund manager was not conscious of the risks taken. In other words, fund managers were asked if all risks in the portfolio were intended. As the head of the group highlighted:

> In our philosophy, risk management is not risk avoidance. For us, risk management means taking risks selectively, only when we have a research opinion, and eliminating all other risks. Somebody who doesn't want to have currency risks in an equity fund should hedge them away. Or when I believe that a particular bond is an attractive investment, then I certainly can buy it for my bond fund but I should ask myself: do I want the duration risk, yes or no? I can take the duration risk only when I have a clear opinion about interest rates.

The goal of the risk managers was to make risks transparent to the fund managers. This function was considered to be an important contribution made by the group to the success of the portfolio management department as a whole (again: 'we are in one boat'). At the same time, the head of the group stressed later in his presentation that 'opinions about interest rates' were clearly the subjective opinions of fund managers, and therefore responsibility for duration risk lay with them. As with the quantitative model portfolio, the fund managers received information on risks from the quants as a support service, but retained the final decision as to whether they should act upon it or not. The fund manager became an internal client, a recipient of services, while risk managers were officially concerned only with technicalities (spreadsheet maintenance and reporting). This positioning of the quant group within the department represented an adjustment strategy to an environment which continued to be dominated by fundamental investing. The penetration of quantitative techniques happened slowly, and, in order to survive, risk managers wisely decided not to force the pace.

At the same time, as already mentioned, risk managers possessed, alongside their support function, an implied (or hidden, or unofficial) control function in keeping under surveillance the colleagues with whom they were supposed to cooperate. The risk managers' gaze was as present as the gaze of clients and consultants discussed in Chapter 2. By making risks transparent, risk managers issued warnings which fund managers received as soon as they read the

---

[18] Duration denotes the period of time that is required to 'recover' the full cost of the bond from coupon and other payments. As coupon payments are received in the future, their net present value (NPV) is decisive for calculation of the duration. The standard definition specifies that duration depends on the bond maturity, coupon payments, and interest rates. Note that duration risk is related to changes in interest rates: if interest rates fall, duration increases, and vice versa. A bond portfolio has duration, too. The duration risk of a portfolio is commonly understood as the deviation of the portfolio duration from the benchmark duration.

risk report. In cases of bad performance, the question could always be raised as to why warnings had been ignored, implying a need for (often unpleasant) justification. Internal risk managers produced a hidden pressure on fund managers.

Finally, we would like to highlight that the difficult—ambiguous, semi-official—internal positioning of risk managers within the department was clearly offset by their importance for external marketing and communication with clients, for perceptions of the company as a whole in the market. While discussing the failed implementation of the proprietary risk management tool, the head of the group stressed that:

> As for external communication, we are well known for [our efforts to build up professional risk management]. We are the company that invests the most in the field, is the most ambitious, and there are many in the market who stay there and watch with huge interest to see whether we manage it or not. It would be good to make some progress here.

Thus the 'ballyhoo' around internal risk management was necessary not only at the moment of the launch of the risk group, but has been a persistent effort and an important element of self-impression management towards the external investment chain ever since. Interestingly, in communication with clients, demonstrable efforts to introduce efficient risk management can, to some extent, even offset poor performance. A member of the quantitative group reported that:

> What frequently happens is that when colleagues want to go to see clients they come to us and say 'you know, the fund has done quite poorly.... Could you maybe provide us with some screenshots from the UBS Delta so that we could tell clients about our excellent risk management here?' This kind of request is a part of our job.

This statement illustrates once again the issues we have discussed throughout the chapter: demands and pressures from the external chain for (staged) professionalism and scientificity influence the way fund managers think and act, generating internal demand for concrete evidence of this same professionalism in the form of spreadsheets and screenshots, but also in the very existence of the risk management group itself.

Quantitative Investing as Emotional Finance

The case study of the Quantitative Strategies and Risk Management group in this chapter illustrates how a particular organizational unit within the investment management department (and the bank as a whole) plays a double role. Having been installed 'from above' in order to fulfil demands from along the external investment chain (clients, consultants, competitors) for professionalization of the investment business, group members found themselves in a difficult position internally. They faced a constant requirement to justify their own existence, particularly to their fundamental manager colleagues, but also to the central risk monitoring department. While their value for external communication was clear, namely to signal the seriousness and objectivity of investment processes, their role within the department had to be worked out. Internally, the group invented itself as a service provider for the fundamental fund managers; however, their services were often not appreciated or simply ignored, and their position remained fragile.

It was fascinating to observe how the entire organizational unit was (mis) used as a marketing hook, as a tool for impression management—successfully, indeed. The launch of the group allowed the investment management division to retain its leading position in the German fund management market. At the same time, promises of objective, number-based, emotionless investing could not be kept in practice.

In this chapter we have argued that quantitative fund management is neither less emotional nor less communicative than the activities of fundamental managers; quantitative portfolio management is part of 'emotional finance' (Tuckett and Taffler 2012). We demonstrated how the very process of quantitative investing means that group members had to become involved with an always emotional market. Contacts with brokers and competitors, being based on personal relationships that vary from friendship to animosity, facilitated reciprocal information exchange concerning capital flows, price movements, and investment ideas.

We also showed that relationships with fundamental colleagues in the same department involved emotive and often conflict-laden forms of cooperation. Quants provided services to fundamental managers in the form of model portfolios, investment universe screenings, and risk reports; in turn, fundamental fund managers carried out sense checks on data on behalf of their quantitative colleagues. At the same time, these forms of cooperation were complicated by asymmetries of responsibility. Numbers are emotionally charged; investment ideas are not only statistically tested, but also judged; emotional attachments to particular investment methods are strong. These findings suggest that the clear division of fund managers into fundamental and quantitative is possible only organizationally (where formally they belong to different groups), but is difficult to maintain in practice. What we find instead are hybrid investment managers who are simultaneously quantitative and fundamental because they have to combine numbers and fundamental information and to take on associated responsibilities. A clear division between quants and their fundamental colleagues was possible only in the organogram of the department, a situation that led to important tensions and misunderstandings.

5

Entangled Trading

Fund Managers and Dark Pools

When fund managers decide to buy or to sell shares or bonds, their orders pass through links in the investment chain that are different from those that tie savers to fund managers, but are no less entangling. The nature of those links differs according to whether the order is for shares or bonds, and we return to the differences at the end of the chapter. Our focus in the chapter is on shares. We discuss the links in the chain through which an order to buy or sell shares is executed, examining it historically, focusing on developments in it over the past three decades, especially developments in the US, which have had a huge influence on how shares are bought and sold in Europe, East Asia, and beyond.

The changes since the 1980s in how shares are traded are, of course, far too large a topic to be covered comprehensively here. We therefore concentrate on a particular aspect of those changes: the emergence and evolution of 'dark pools'. As noted in Chapter 1, these are private share-trading venues in which subscribers can bid to buy shares or offer to sell them, without those bids or offers being visible to the market at large, as they usually are on a registered stock exchange. The reason we focus on dark pools in a book on investment management is that, at least originally, they were intended to provide a mechanism by which investment management firms could trade with each other at low cost and without alerting the wider market. The latter aspect of dark pools was, and is, attractive to fund managers because they often want to buy or sell on a large scale, for example to buy or to sell a block of shares (in a particular company) that might be worth millions or tens of millions of dollars. To do that in a 'lit' trading venue—one in which orders that have not yet been executed are visible to all subscribers—causes what participants call 'market impact'. If, say, professional traders or their algorithms infer the presence of a big buyer, they may themselves try to buy the shares in question in the hope of then selling them profitably to the big buyer, a process that will drive the price up. Hence the attraction of trading in the 'dark', on venues in which orders that have not yet been executed are private.

Dark pools are an example of what Muniesa et al. (2007: 2–4) call 'market device[s]...the material and discursive assemblages that intervene in the construction of markets...[f]rom analytical techniques to pricing models, from purchase settings to merchandising tools, from trading protocols to aggregate indicators...devices do things...detach things from other things and attach them to other things'. Over the past decade, there has been a sharp increase in social scientists' focus on market devices as 'sites at which questions of worth, value, valuation and measurement [are] raised' (McFall 2015: 4).

Dark pools are market devices in a literal sense. None of the dark pools discussed here was or is operated manually: all were or are computer systems. (The single most important physical location of those systems in the US is NJ2, a relatively old but, as an interviewee told us, not hugely expensive computer data centre in Weehawken, a township in New Jersey just across the Hudson River from Manhattan).[1] Dark pools are also sites of the kind referred to by McFall: they raise questions of worth and of measurement. However, unlike many of the sites on which the literature on market devices has focused, they are not primarily sites at which the objects being traded are ascribed a value. Indeed, shares are often bought and sold on dark pools at prices that are taken directly from more public trading venues, instead of being set in the pool itself. Rather, one striking issue of 'worth' that dark pools raise is that of the value of particular classes of market participant. As we will describe, the emergence of dark pools falls into two broad phases. First-generation dark pools, set up from 1986 onwards, often involved drawing a boundary between fund managers and all other classes of market participant, especially professional traders. These dark pools were designed to promote trading among 'naturals', as they are often called in the US. 'Naturals' are fund managers (or traders acting on their behalf) who wish simply to add a block of shares to a portfolio they manage, or to liquidate part of that portfolio. The implicit contrast is with a trader looking to make a profit by very short-term buying and selling.

Access to first-generation dark pools was often restricted to 'naturals'. Since 2004, however, a second generation of dark pools has emerged. These involve the labelling of participants by the dark pool's operators, rather than their exclusion. In particular, some participants are labelled 'opportunist' or 'aggressive' (or, sometimes even 'predatory' or 'toxic'), but are allowed to continue to trade in the dark pool. Other participants, however, are given the option of

---

[1] For example, Credit Suisse's Crossfinder and Barclays' LX are both located in NJ2.

having their orders never interact with those electronically stigmatized in this way. A crucial criterion employed in this classification is the short-term profitability of participants' trading: the higher the profit rate, the greater the risk of stigmatization.

At the very heart of financial capitalism—second-generation dark pools were set up by, and are managed by, the world's leading investment banks—market devices have thus emerged that deploy a measure of participants' 'worth' that stigmatizes excessive profit making! Fascinating though this is, however, a certain scepticism is in order. If you come to the study of market devices as one of us (MacKenzie) does, from the social studies of science, it is easy to focus too much on their cognitive aspects—on the way in which devices produce valuations and other forms of knowledge—and too little on their place in economic relations in a down-to-earth, grubby, monetary sense.[2] (For a critique of insufficient attention to the relations in which market devices are embedded, see Mennicken and Miller [2014], though even they seem to mean something more intellectual—'the interrelations between such instruments and the historically varying ideas or rationalities that require and inspire them' [Mennicken and Miller 2014: 18]—than we do here.) Financial markets, after all, are not simply places in which 'facts' are constructed and the objects being traded are valued, but also places in which money passes from hand to hand, especially along the investment chain. Attention to market devices thus needs to involve attention to apparently mundane, monetary, distributional matters such as who is paying how much, to whom, for what, attention of the kind that makes—for instance—Godechot's work on investment banking (especially Godechot 2007) exemplary. In studying trading's entanglements in the chains of finance we need to 'follow the money', not just follow the operation of devices, the construction of facts, and the relations among traders—although all these aspects remain of central importance too.

This theoretical and methodological issue has two manifestations in this chapter. The first concerns a particular link in the chain in which the management of portfolios of shares is embedded: the link connecting fund managers to brokers or broker-dealers, including the big investment banks

---

[2] Competition in science can be fierce, sometimes even vicious, but the reward directly at stake was traditionally recognition by one's peers, not money, as Hagstrom (1965) emphasized half a century ago. It was his background in the social studies of science that led MacKenzie (2007, 2008) to see the importance of Libor (London Interbank Offered Rate) to the financial markets, and therefore grasp the extent to which doubts about its status as a set of facts could unsettle markets. That background also, however, led him to underestimate the likelihood of groups of dealers conspiring to manipulate Libor. He could see that obviously manipulative inputs into the calculation of Libor would be visible to London's interdealer brokers, with the intimate knowledge of their market that comes from their role of facilitating trades between dealers. He underestimated the simple fact that brokers' incomes come from fees paid by dealers, and there was thus an incentive for them to keep quiet about, or even participate actively in, manipulative inputs.

such as Credit Suisse, Goldman Sachs, and Morgan Stanley.[3] As noted in Chapter 1, investment management firms are referred to by participants as 'the buy side'; the firms, such as investment banks, that act as their brokers and/or sell other investment services to them are 'the sell side'. The terminology of 'buy side' and 'sell side' suggests arm's-length commercial transactions, but—as we shall see—the link in the chain connecting investment managers to their brokers and broker-dealers was much more entangling than it appeared, and part (though not all) of that entanglement was monetary.

The second manifestation of why we have to attend to monetary, distributional matters is that, in interpreting the fact that second-generation dark pools classify and label traders and their algorithms, we must not forget that dark pools are business enterprises. In June 2014, Eric T. Schneiderman, Attorney General of the State of New York, filed a securities fraud complaint against Barclays Bank, which runs a second-generation dark pool. At his press conference, Schneiderman said that these pools were supposed to protect 'institutional investors such as mutual funds and pension funds holding the savings of millions of New Yorkers' from 'the predatory high-frequency trading tactics that are seen on public exchanges'.[4] In actuality, Schneiderman alleged, protections in Barclays' dark pool were much weaker than its users might have expected.[5] The Securities and Exchange Commission (SEC) joined Schneiderman's action against Barclays, and also took action against Credit Suisse concerning both the latter's dark pool, Crossfinder, and its 'lit' market, Light Pool.

In 2016, the two banks reached settlements with the SEC and the New York Attorney General's office. Barclays admitted wrongdoing and paid $70 million in penalties. Credit Suisse agreed to penalties of $60 million, but neither admitted nor denied the accusations against it.[6] Central to both cases was the allegation that the monitoring and classification of participants in the two banks' pools was not always as rigorous as was suggested to users of them. This allegation highlights the fact that the policing of participants in dark pools is not a straightforward moral impulse. It also serves a crucial business purpose: to reassure actual and potential clients, and perhaps also regulators, that—despite the sometimes negative connotations of their name—nothing nefarious is going on in dark pools.

---

[3] A broker transacts on behalf of clients; a broker-dealer also transacts on its own behalf.

[4] As described in Chapter 1, high frequency trading, or HFT, is the fast, automated trading of large numbers of shares or other financial instruments, and Schneiderman is an outspoken critic of it.

[5] A video recording of the news conference at which Schneiderman announced his complaint can be found on his website, <http://www.ag.ny.gov/>, accessed 30 June 2014.

[6] For details of the settlement, see <https://www.sec.gov/news/pressrelease/2016-16.html> accessed 1 February 2016.

Table 5.1 The additional set of interviews drawn on in Chapter 5

High frequency traders	51
Exchange- and trading-venue members and staff	54
Dealers, brokers, and broker-dealers	20
Practitioners of other forms of algorithmic trading	13
Manual traders	6
Suppliers of technology and telecommunications links to HFT	18
Researchers/market analysts	14
Regulators	5
Total	181

The research reported in this chapter draws on our interviews in investment management firms but, as noted in Chapter 1, also on our interview-based study of the emergence of high-frequency trading and the development of the markets in which it is practised. (See Table 5.1 for these additional interviews.) Particularly pertinent here are seven of the fifty-four interviews with exchange and trading venue members and staff. Those seven interviewees were all employed by firms that manage dark pools; by good fortune, they were all interviewed before Schneiderman's lawsuit, which has made the detailed operations of dark pools a sensitive topic. This subsample is clearly small, and oral history interviewees' recollection of past events can be faulty. As far as possible, we also therefore cross-check interview evidence against documentary sources. By the late 1980s (the start of the period we examine), the new discipline of financial economics was in full swing, and its literature contains what are now historical data, for example on the typical sizes of brokers' fees. Particularly useful to us is a survey conducted in 1994 by two financial economists, Nicholas Economides and Robert A. Schwartz, of 150 personnel at US investment management firms who traded shares on behalf of those firms.[7] The firms for which respondents to the survey worked managed shares worth around $1.5 trillion, about half of what was then the total shareholdings of US investment management firms (Economides and Schwartz 1994: 31). The survey is, again, now historical evidence: it throws light on the reception of the first-generation dark pools by their intended clientele at investment management firms.

First-Generation Dark Pools

Although the term 'dark' was not employed to describe private share-trading venues until the early 2000s—it was first used in a marketing campaign for a

---

[7] While the larger firms employed designated traders, at the smaller firms in Economides and Schwartz's survey the trader was often simply a fund manager (Economides and Schwartz 1994: 31).

particular pool[8]—what are now regarded as the first dark pools were set up in the US in 1986–7. To understand why, it is helpful briefly to review how US shares were traded in the 1980s. The dominant trading venue was the NYSE, the New York Stock Exchange. Its leading role was signalled by its location in the heart of Manhattan's financial district and by the imposing Corinthian columns and pediment of its main building, at the corner of Wall Street and Broad Street. To buy or sell shares on the NYSE, a fund manager had to use a broker-dealer or other firm that was a NYSE member. That firm could send the order to the NYSE's five large trading rooms, or it could be handled by one of its 'sales traders' or 'upstairs brokers' (they were called the latter because their offices were often on the higher floors of the NYSE's buildings). The job of sales traders or upstairs brokers was to keep in regular touch with fund managers and other big market participants who might wish to buy or sell the shares for which they were responsible. When they received a buy order for a block of shares, for example, they would discreetly seek out a fund manager or other market participant who might be prepared to sell the shares in question.

Trading via the NYSE was expensive. The exchange's origins were in the 1792 Buttonwood Agreement, in which twenty-four brokers agreed not to charge commissions of less than 0.25 per cent of the value of stock transactions.[9] After pressure from Congress and the stock market regulator (the Securities and Exchange Commission), the system of fixed NYSE commissions was finally ended in 1975. Commissions remained substantial, however, averaging 0.18 per cent—nearly 7 cents per share for an averagely priced NYSE stock—in 1985 (Berkowitz et al. 1988: 104). In the early 1990s, they ranged from around 4 cents to as much as 15 cents per share (Keim and Madhavan 1998: 51; see also Edwards and Wagner 1993). Nor was trading on the main alternative to NYSE, Nasdaq (the National Association of Securities Dealers' Automated Quotation system), necessarily any cheaper. Nasdaq had no trading floor—its broker-dealers circulated price quotations electronically and traded primarily over the telephone—but a tacit agreement among many of those broker-dealers kept the typical minimum difference between the prices at which they would buy and sell shares to 25 cents per share.[10]

As we shall shortly discuss, fund managers were happier to pay NYSE brokers' high commissions than might be imagined. There was, however, also a degree of distrust of brokers' behaviour: 'many institutions, even though

---

[8] See Weisberger (2015), who reports that he advised use of the term 'quiet', rather than 'dark'.

[9] A facsimile of the Buttonwood Agreement manuscript is available at <http://en.wikipedia.org/wiki/Buttonwood_Agreement>, accessed 18 April 2015.

[10] In the 1980s and most of the 1990s, US shares were still priced in the traditional eighths of a dollar. The tacit agreement took the form of avoiding price quotations in odd-eighths, so keeping the minimum difference between broker-dealers' buy and sell quotes to two eighths of a dollar, or 0.25 cents. See Christie and Schultz (1994).

they dealt with brokers, they didn't trust them . . . they felt they got screwed', an interviewee told us. '[S]ell-side block traders . . . had more information than the buy-side institutions', says stock market veteran Steve Wunsch, 'and were constantly accused of abuses of that privileged position' (Wunsch 2014). As already noted, broker-dealers traded on their own account as well as acting on behalf of clients such as fund managers, and one fear was that their own-account trading profited from knowledge of what clients were trying to do. Even 'agency brokers', who did not trade on their own account, might leak information: they '[would] frequently tip off one institutional client about another's trading interest, hoping to win more commission business as a reward', reported Schwartz and Steil (2002: 42).

Even if there was no deliberate abuse, a sales trader's or upstairs broker's need to 'call around other institutions to try and find a match [was] prone to information leakage', as another interviewee put it. Economides and Schwartz found that 37 per cent of the investment management firms' traders they surveyed cited fears of being 'front run' (meaning an agent such as a broker profiting by trading on its own behalf before executing a client's order) as the most important or second most important factor leading them to want to execute their trades quickly. Forty-five per cent reported being concerned—and two-thirds of those were 'very concerned'—about information leaking when they called a broker (Economides and Schwartz 1994: 15, 17). Such fears seem to have been justified: economists Donald Keim and Ananth Madhavan (1996: 1) found price movements 'consistent with information leakage as the block is "shopped" upstairs'.

The most important alternative in the 1980s to telephoning a broker was for fund managers or traders employed by their firms to use the Institutional Networks Corporation's 'Instinet', which was an electronic system, set up in 1969, to 'enable . . . institutional investors [to] deal directly with each other without going through an intermediary . . . [and] be assured of confidential treatment' (Adams et al. 1971: 1). At least initially, use of Instinet was restricted to investment management firms; broker-dealers and professional traders were excluded. Users entered bids to buy shares or offers to sell them via terminals linked to Instinet's central computer system in Watertown, MA. The bids and offers that could not be executed immediately were entered into an anonymous, aggregate order book visible to all subscribers on their terminals' screens.

Because the order book was visible, the original Instinet system was what would now be called a 'lit' market. As suggested earlier, its visibility had the disadvantage of likely 'market impact'. A visible, big buy order, for example, would typically push prices up, even though it was anonymous and could be seen only by other Instinet subscribers; a big sell order would cause prices to fall. In 1986, however, Instinet launched what would now be called a 'dark pool', its new Crossing Network, which it described as 'an equities trading service that eliminates market impact' (Instinet 1989: 1). After the NYSE had closed, users of the Crossing Network could submit anonymous bids to buy a corporation's shares or offers to sell them. These bids and offers were not displayed to other subscribers. Users simply entered, via their Instinet terminal, the number of shares they wished to buy or sell: the price was always that day's closing price of the shares at the end of public trading. At around 5 p.m. Eastern time, Instinet's computer system would 'cross' those orders, matching as many bids and offers as possible. Instinet charged a firm whose orders were successfully crossed in this way only 1 cent per share traded (Blume 1993: 39), far less than the 4 cents or more that they would have had to pay a traditional broker.

A similar attractively priced, anonymous crossing service for investment management firms called Posit (the 'Portfolio System for Institutional Trading') was launched in 1987 by the Investment Technology Group, a division of Jefferies & Company, a 'third market' brokerage firm and critic of the NYSE's alleged monopolistic dominance, along with investment management consultancy BARRA (Barr Rosenberg Associates).[11] Like Instinet's Crossing Service, Posit's four daily crosses matched buy and sell orders at the price at which shares were trading on the public markets, in its case at a randomly chosen moment during the seven-minute interval during which users could enter orders into its system.[12]

A later first-generation dark pool was Liquidnet, set up in 2001 by Seth Merrin, who, as two interviewees reported, was well known to US fund managers because his original firm, Merrin Financial, had pioneered order management systems. (These cut out the need to use the telephone to transmit orders, a process vulnerable to misunderstandings and mistakes: fund managers could simply type into the system details of the shares they wanted to buy or sell. The system would then pass the order electronically to the firm's traders, who could also use it to send the orders on to a broker-dealer.) While the Instinet and Posit 'crosses' took place only at set times, and relied on fund managers or their traders taking an active decision to use them, Liquidnet enjoyed—and still enjoys—continuous electronic access to the digital 'blotters' of fund managers' order management systems; these blotters contain lists of the orders for shares that have not yet been executed. '[B]ecause [Merrin] invented [order management systems], he had recognition and credibility with the

---

[11] The 'third market' was the collective name for the trading of listed shares outwith Nasdaq, NYSE, and other exchanges.

[12] Although it was an auction-based exchange, not a dark pool, the Arizona Stock Exchange (for which see Muniesa 2011) seems in practice to have operated as a crossing network similar to Instinet's and Posit's, as an interviewee told us; see also Domowitz and Steil (1999: 64, n. 46).

institutional investors', many of whom already used Merrin Financial's products, an interviewee who managed a dark pool told us. Merrin was thus able to persuade increasing numbers of investment management firms to grant Liquidnet's system access to the highly sensitive contents of the blotters.

Whenever Liquidnet's system discovers that one fund manager's blotter contains an order to buy IBM shares, for instance, and another's blotter an order to sell them, it invites the two managers or their traders to begin an anonymous, computerized negotiation over the price. Each of those orders also has to meet the minimum size of trade that the other trader will countenance, but neither trader is told anything about the size of deal the other is seeking, other than that it is at least as large as his or her minimum. A window opens on each of the two traders' computer screens, with a range of possible prices between the price of the highest bid on the public markets and that of the lowest offer. If, using these windows, the two traders reach agreement over the price, Liquidnet's system tells them how many shares they have bought and sold (that number is simply the smaller of the sizes of transaction each trader was seeking). If both parties are genuinely keen on a deal, no real haggling over price is usually required. '[M]ost veterans that have been on the system for a while don't even negotiate, they just offer the mid [the midpoint of the range of prices in the window]', and typically that is accepted straight away, said the interviewee quoted at the end of the previous paragraph.

Why Not Trade for a Cent? The Role of Soft Dollars

As noted in the previous section, Instinet's Crossing Network offered its investment manager users the opportunity to trade for a cent per share, and other first-generation dark pools also sharply undercut the commissions of around 4–15 cents per share charged by traditional brokers and broker-dealers. Yet these new, anonymous, computerized market devices did not sweep away traditional human intermediaries, even though the latter were not only far more expensive but, as noted, also distrusted as possible conduits of information leakage. While a third of the traders for institutional investment firms surveyed in 1994 by Economides and Schwartz had tried Instinet's Crossing Network or POSIT, only 5 per cent of their sample had gone on to become frequent users of them (1994: 24, table 20). Nor has that situation subsequently changed radically: see Table 5.2. First-generation dark pools remain relatively marginal to US share trading. Why?

Economides and Schwartz's 1994 survey suggests some reasons. They asked their investment management firm respondents what would get them to use systems such as Instinet's Crossing Network and POSIT more often. The most common answer (given by 55 per cent of respondents) was if 'they gave higher execution rates' (1994: 29, table 25). A frequent experience, in other words, was that sometimes you just couldn't find via a crossing network another 'natural' who wanted to buy when you wanted to sell, or vice versa.[13] It was a complaint that persisted: Carrie (2008: 53) reported an estimate that 'only 6 of every 100 trades that enter into a Dark Pool actually get executed'.

There is, of course, a certain circularity to this complaint. Trading venues such as dark pools manifest network effects akin to those of telephone systems: the more users a trading venue has, the easier it is to find a human user or algorithm that wants to buy when you want to sell (or vice versa), and the more attractive the venue becomes. However, a number of factors made it harder for first-generation dark pools to reach the tipping point at which they would have become real rivals to traditional venues. One factor was simply that, by design, they restricted their users, typically excluding professional traders. Another factor is that—because of fears of missing an opportunity, and perhaps also concerns about front running and information leakage— fund managers often wanted their trades completed as quickly as possible, and they might therefore not be happy with their traders waiting until a match could be found on Instinet, Posit, or Liquidnet. As a trader for an investment management firm put it in our interview with him:

> You know what the problem . . . is, and Liquidnet had this trouble . . . [in] the early days, is they wanted to paint it as 'we're the only thing you need. You can do all your trading in Liquidnet'. No I can't because I have this order and I can expose it to Liquidnet or I can expose it to Posit or I can expose it to any other crossing network, but if I don't get a match I can't wait forever.

From the viewpoint of the entangling nature of the investment chain, however, the most interesting barrier to the adoption of first-generation dark pools was what in the US are called 'soft-dollar' arrangements (sometimes called 'soft-commission' arrangements in the UK). Soft dollars were, for example, the second most commonly cited barrier among Economides and Schwartz's 1994 respondents. In a soft-dollar arrangement, an investment management firm receives payments or 'free' services (especially research reports on the companies whose shares they may invest in) from a broker, and in return executes trades via, and pays trading commissions to,

---

[13] Although it is not clear that this was known in the early 1990s (its possibility seems not to have been incorporated into Economides and Schwartz's questionnaire), there is evidence that the use of crossing networks—precisely because it does not directly affect prices in public markets—is attractive to those who have private information relevant to the value of a stock. There is therefore a degree of adverse selection in the probability of matching on crossing networks: the probability of a buy order being matched is higher if there is an informed seller, and vice versa for a sell order. This effect was, however, not large enough to offset the cost advantages of crossing networks (see Næs and Ødegaard 2006: 91).

the broker. These arrangements were a major reason to keep using expensive brokers rather than cheaper crossing networks. Typically, a soft-dollar arrangement involves an investment management firm formally or informally guaranteeing a broker-dealer an annual minimum total of commission payments. A large investment management firm will normally use multiple broker-dealers, and if it has soft dollar commitments to each of them, its traders could be left with little discretion to direct their trades anywhere other than to those broker-dealers.

Soft-dollar arrangements first emerged as US investment management firms grew in scale in the 1950s (Blume 1993). Because their orders for shares were much larger than those of most individual investors, these firms were attractive customers for brokers and broker-dealers. The rules of the NYSE, however, prevented brokers competing for business from investment managers by offering discounted commissions on large trades. Accordingly, they began to provide investment managers with research reports, other free services (such as, in later years, computer software and hardware), and direct payments, including, for example, expenses for trips to Europe with only a tangential research rationale. By 1983, for example, these 'soft-dollar' arrangements totalled around $600 million annually (Smith 1984). Brokers thus handed back to investment management firms—sometimes as payments, but mostly as 'free' services—part of the high commissions the firms paid them. Sometimes, too, investment management firms arranged with brokers that part of their commission payments be redirected to other brokerages that marketed the firms' saving products.

The economic rationale for these apparently odd arrangements, and the reason why the dollars involved were 'soft' from the viewpoint of a firm managing a mutual fund or a pension fund, was (and is) that commissions and other trading costs are charged to those funds, while if research, computers, hotel bills, etc. had to be paid for explicitly it would have to be by using the investment management firm's 'hard dollars' (i.e. its own money). Of course, the higher the commissions paid out of the stock market funds a firm manages, the poorer the performance of those funds. Share price movements, however, are very 'noisy'. The effects of high commissions do not stand out among the inherently large fluctuations in the returns from portfolios of shares, while soft-dollar arrangements can directly and substantially increase the profits of investment management firms by eliminating costs (especially payments for research) they would otherwise have incurred. An interviewee pointed out that they also enabled firms to portray themselves as efficient, low-cost investment managers, who incur only modest expenses. As economists Robert Schwartz and Benn Steil put it, investment managers 'have a clear incentive to hide costs in returns', via high commissions and soft dollars, 'rather than reveal them in expenses' (2002: 40).

Soft-dollar arrangements survived the 1975 end of their original motivation, the NYSE's fixed commissions. Fearing that fund managers who paid more than they needed to in order to trade would be charged with breaching their fiduciary responsibilities, what Blume (1993: 36) calls 'the soft dollar industry' successfully sought from Congress a 'safe harbor'—Section 28(e) of the Securities Exchange Act, added in 1975—legally protecting the practice. In the early 2000s, more than 70 per cent of US investment management firms still engaged in soft-dollar arrangements (Schwartz and Steil 2002: 41). Although modified and increasingly constrained over the subsequent decade—and structured and regulated somewhat differently in Europe[14]— soft dollars remained, and still remain, important to the economics of fund management in the US. Above all, the stock market research reports and other services provided by top broker-dealers such as Goldman Sachs would be dauntingly expensive if they had to be purchased explicitly, and fund managers without access to reports and services available to their counter- parts in competing firms could easily feel badly handicapped. Maintaining that access took priority over the costs of trading. As a former Instinet employee told us in interview:

> Within a buy-side institution, for the most part, the portfolio manager is king; the trader is the low man in the organization. And so the portfolio manager says: 'look, if I get the right research, or if I get the right colour on a stock [see the next section], or the right access to [corporate] management, road shows [in which a corpor- ation's senior managers present the case for investing in it face-to-face], IPOs [initial public offerings of stock], whatever, that makes a huge difference in my performance and a few basis points [hundredths of a percentage point extra costs] on the execution is all rounding error'. So I'll trade with people [brokers] who give me bad execution because I'm getting other things from them.

Hence the continuing attractiveness—even necessity, especially for smaller investment management firms—of 'free' access to sell-side research and other benefits and services provided by investment banks and other brokers. 'We always used soft dollars. We still use soft dollars', said a trader who worked for

---

[14] It originally seemed as if the European Union's MIFID (Market in Financial Instruments Directive) II, which comes into force in 2018, would entirely separate the mechanisms by which the costs of trading and of research are charged to investment management firms' clients, but at the time of writing (September 2016) it looks as if the two, even though they need to be separately identifiable, can be collected simultaneously even after 2018 (Ganatra 2016). A trader for a UK investment management firm explained to us in 2013 the typical arrangement as it stood in the UK prior to MIFID II (which may, of course, come into force only temporarily in the UK following the vote to leave the European Union). Trading commissions were still charged not to the investment management firm but to the funds it manages, but were explicitly split into an 'execution' and a 'research' portion. The firm's fund managers periodically voted on the relative usefulness of each broker's research, 'and if the amount we've paid to them is more than the value of what they provided, then we claw that back'.

a medium-sized firm. 'It would be hard to stay in business if we didn't use them. [Y]ou'd put a lot of these smaller [investment management] companies out of business if they couldn't use soft dollars.'

Second-Generation Dark Pools

First-generation dark pools challenged, but thus ultimately failed to under-mine, the relationships between fund managers and brokers, especially the biggest broker-dealers, the global investment banks. Soft dollars were an important component of those relationships, but not their entirety. One of the authors recalls that, in her time as an investment manager, if she wanted to go to the ballet, a telephone call to a broker would get her a couple of tickets; another of the authors recalls gifts from brokers of fine wines (meticulously shared with back office staff rather than all kept by fund managers and analysts). To well-paid fund managers, the monetary value of such gifts was not an important inducement, but they signalled the importance—especially to the sales staff of investment banks and other brokers—of developing per-sonal relationships, indeed friendships, with fund managers. A big bank might also offer favourable prices to a valued investment manager client who wanted to trade immediately and directly with it rather than simply using it as a broker, or—as the interviewee quoted in the previous paragraph said—might offer useful market 'colour' (informal accounts, usually over the telephone, of market conditions such as the presence or otherwise of big buyers or sellers) or the potentially highly profitable opportunity to buy shares in an 'initial public offering' in which a promising new business first makes those shares available to the market, typically via an investment bank. An investment bank might, furthermore, reward a buy-side firm for trading with it by being more active in marketing the firm's savings products to its customers (Schwartz and Steil 2002: 41). As a trader for an investment management firm put it to us, using a first-generation dark pool could feel as if it did nothing to reinforce ties of reciprocity, such as these, that bound such firms to their investment bank broker-dealers: 'you couldn't get credit. The feeling was, this is business that I'm throwing out the window or dropping in a black hole because I get no relationship value from it'.

The second generation of dark pools, however, ran with, not against, the grain of the relationships between investment management firms and investment banks, because they were set up by the latter.[15] These new pools

---

[15] For reasons of space, we do not discuss a third type of dark pool, sometimes called a 'ping destination' (see Zhu 2014: online appendix). These were typically set up by firms, such as Knight and Getco (see Table 5.2), that had expertise in applying the techniques of high frequency trading

emerged from the procedures used by investment banks to 'internalize' the execution of orders from investment management firms and other customers. It is quite common for a big broker-dealer such as an investment bank to have a buy order from one customer and a corresponding sell order from another, so the broker-dealer can 'match' the two orders without incurring the costs of sending them out to the NYSE, Nasdaq, or other markets. Although 'internalization', as this is called, thus offered cost savings, it had—as an interviewee told us—'a nasty connotation in the US, because there was always a lot of gamesmanship...."did I get a fair price?", "did I not get a fair price?"' In addition, the Securities and Exchange Commission's 2005 Regulation National Market System (Reg NMS) increased the complexity of internalization, and also that of 'upstairs' block trading. Reg NMS—the centrepiece of the current regulation of share trading in the US—prohibits executing trades at a price lower than the highest bid to buy, or higher than the lowest offer to sell, on any of the registered exchanges in the US. Since these 'national best bid and offer' prices can change from second to second, and often more frequently than that, manually 'internalizing' orders, while ensuring compliance with Reg NMS, was becoming too difficult by the mid-2000s: 'it's just not possible for a person to do', said the interviewee quoted above.

First Credit Suisse (in 2004, with its new 'Crossfinder' dark pool) and then the other big investment banks reached for the same solution to the complexity and lack of legitimacy of internalization. They turned the internal, sometimes manual matching of orders into an entirely automated dark pool registered under the Securities and Exchange Commission's (SEC's) Regulation ATS (Alternative Trading Systems), the relatively loose regulatory framework governing dark pools. As an interviewee heavily involved in the new investment bank dark pools put it, 'we could create an execution venue, a proper execution venue with a blessing of the SEC, and all of a sudden it wasn't internalization anymore, it was crossing, right? It's identical process, identical flows; everything was the same except we had a machine do it instead of having people do it'.

Usually, first-generation dark pools simply matched buy and sell orders in the middle of the price range prevailing on exchanges such as the NYSE (as noted earlier, this was in practice what usually happened even on Liquidnet). Second-generation US dark pools more closely mimicked electronic exchanges:

(especially very short-term price prediction) in automated market-making: i.e. in constantly posting, and frequently adjusting the prices of, bids to buy and slightly high priced offers to sell shares. If an order to buy or sell shares is sent by a broker-dealer, investment manager, or other firm to a 'ping destination', then the algorithms of the firm running the latter rapidly decide whether or not to fulfil that order. If they decide not to do so, the order is cancelled. In other words, ping destinations accept only 'immediate or cancel' orders, and the order 'pings' the pool (as market participants would put it), discovering near immediately whether it can be executed there. If an incoming order is executed, the counterparty in the trade is the firm that owns the pool.

although orders are in practice frequently matched at the midpoint between the highest bid price and lowest offer price, subscribers do not have to use them in this way. Just as they can on a registered exchange, subscribers can enter into the dark pool's order book a bid to buy shares or an offer to sell them at a specific price, and those orders are executed by the pool's computer system only when there is a matching order at the same price or better. However, unlike on registered exchanges or other 'lit' markets, the electronic order books of these dark pools are not visible to the traders and computerized trading systems that buy and sell shares on them.

The new investment bank dark pools also differed from first-generation dark pools in that the former reflected the more automated forms of trading that were becoming available. As stock markets became more entirely electronic from the mid-1990s onwards, 'algorithmic' trading began to be possible. This involves entering a big order from a fund manager into software that splits it up into small parts ('child orders', as they are called) in the hope of reducing its market impact (as noted earlier, this means its adverse effects on prices), and computerizing the execution of those small orders. Alongside what began to be called the 'high touch' execution of orders by human brokers, investment banks started also to offer their investment manager clients somewhat less expensive, 'low touch', algorithmic execution, for example via Credit Suisse's Advanced Execution Services department, set up in 2001. Credit Suisse's algorithms didn't demand any technical knowledge on the part of fund managers or their traders, who were provided with a simple computer interface. As an interviewee explained, you would select the shares you wanted to trade, 'just type in "buy 100,000" ... and it all gets worked on by the computer behind the scenes. You don't need to be a programmer'.

As well as an investment bank's or other broker's computer systems splitting a fund manager's big order into many little 'child orders', those systems also typically decide where to send those orders. In the US from the late 1990s onwards (and in Europe from around 2007), established share-trading venues faced increasing competition from new lit markets and dark pools, so there were and are multiple venues to which child orders can be sent. Investment banks' systems thus employ programs known as 'smart order routers' to determine where clients' orders are sent. Although we know of no publicly available systematic data on the routers' choices of destination, our impression from industry discussions is that it is very common for a child order to be sent first to an investment bank's own dark pool; if it is not filled there, it is then sent on to other dark pools and/or public markets.

Although analogues of earlier 'upstairs' block trading remain common in Europe, such trading has been eclipsed in the US by execution algorithms and smart order routers. While traders working for investment management firms quite often split up orders using their own execution algorithms (or algorithms provided by third parties), responsibility for order routing and order execution is typically handed over to an investment bank's or other broker's system. So these sell-side intermediaries remain central to trading, and the commissions that buy-side firms continue to pay them thus enable those firms to continue to fulfil their 'soft-dollar' obligations.

The new investment bank dark pools fitted well into these 'lower touch', more algorithmic, trading relations between investment managers and broker-dealers. While the original dark pools aimed to match limited numbers of big, human-generated orders, for tens of thousands of shares or more, second-generation dark pools typically handle larger flows (from smart order routers) of much smaller, algorithmically generated child orders, each for as few as a couple of hundred shares (or even fewer). Another crucial difference between the two generations of dark pools is that while first-generation pools typically excluded professional traders, the second-generation pools set up by investment banks allow professional traders to participate—including those who employ computerized high frequency trading (HFT)—and, at least until very recently, a bank's own trading desks would also often trade in its dark pool. HFTs, which specialize in handling large numbers of small orders, were the perfect counterparties to the high volume flow of little 'child' orders from investment management firms. By allowing HFTs to participate in its dark pool, an investment bank could therefore make trading in that pool more liquid—and increased liquidity meant a higher market share (making the pool more attractive to buy-side clients) and increased revenues. It also enabled the bank's smart order routers to execute more of its investment manager clients' orders in its own dark pool, thus avoiding the costs that would be incurred if the bank had to pay execution fees to other trading venues.

As suggested earlier, the second-generation dark pools were thus consistent with close relations and reciprocity between investment management firms and investment banks, and fitted well into algorithmic share trading and automated order routing. It was a recipe that generated substantially larger volumes of trading than on the first-generation pools. By September 2009, for example, Credit Suisse's Crossfinder was trading an average of around 155 million shares a day, and Goldman Sachs's Sigma X about 112 million, compared to around 28 million traded on Liquidnet, the highest-volume first-generation pool (see Table 5.2). Dark pools as a whole gained market share. In 2008, only just over 4 per cent of share trading in the US was in dark pools (Angel et al. 2013: 29, table 2.19). By December 2014, that had climbed to 17 per cent (D'Antona 2014).

Despite this success, dark pools—especially second-generation pools—had to contend with a persistent fear: that they aren't entirely dark. As *Traders Magazine* noted in 2012, there was and is 'concern on the buy-side that trades done in dark pools can result in information leakage that negatively impacts

Table 5.2 Approximate average daily transaction volumes on leading US dark pools (September 2009), in millions of shares and as a percentage of overall US share trading

Credit Suisse Crossfinder	155	2.2%
Knight Link	128	1.8%
Goldman Sachs Sigma X	112	1.6%
Getco Execution Services	90	1.3%
Level	52	0.7%
Citi Match	44	0.6%
MS-Pool	36	0.5%
UBS PIN	32	0.5%
Liquidnet	28	0.4%
Barclays LX	24	0.3%
ITG Posit	22	0.3%
Instinet CBX	21	0.3%

Sources: Mackenzie and Thomas (2009); Angel et al. (2013).

the final price at which they trade. The buy-side often blames its problems in dark pools on professional traders, particularly the high frequency variety' (Chapman 2012). 'A lot of dark pools are different shades of grey' was how one trader for an investment management firm put it to us: information leaks out of them that can be used to infer a firm's future trading activity, making that future trading more difficult and more expensive. That makes some pools 'toxic', as a trader for a hedge fund put it. Asked what he meant, he replied: 'I mean that there's high frequency trading dudes in there.'

For example, as suggested earlier, a typical way an investment bank's smart order router executes a large order from an investment manager is to make as many purchases or sales as possible in its own dark pool, then in other dark pools, before finally executing the remainder in lit markets. A particular fear, therefore, is that if an HFT algorithm can infer the likely existence of a big order from activity in a dark pool, it can position itself to profit when the purchases or sales in lit markets begin. The extent to which that fear is justified is uncertain—the best documented mechanism by which investment management firms lose money trading in dark pools is different, and is a consequence of the fact that in many dark pools the 'matching engine' (the system that manages orders and consummates trades) is slow by the standards of 'lit' markets[16]—but the managers of dark pools take such fears seriously and seek to provide credible reassurances to investment management clients.

---

[16] The issue arises from the widespread use in US dark pools of 'midpoint peg' orders, which are orders that should be filled at the midpoint between the national best bid and national best offer. Research by the consultancy TABB Metrics and the Boston Company Asset Management found that, in many dark pools, the matching engine—the software that maintains order books, finds matching bids and offers, and executes trades—was sufficiently slow that its calculation of the midpoint was frequently based on 'stale' (out-of-date) prices, giving trading firms that were aware of this lag the opportunity to profit. (HFT firms told TABB Metrics that they did indeed monitor dark pools to find such conditions.) Note that this effect is different from—and, according to TABB Metrics, the delays involved can be as much as fifty times larger than—the well-publicized issue of

That a dark pool might be exploited by unscrupulous actors was an issue even with the first-generation pools. For example, the reason that the precise times of Posit's crosses were randomized was to make it more difficult to profit by trading or placing orders in public markets in such a way as temporarily to move the prices that were used to set the price on Posit. However, the openness of second-generation pools to HFTs, and widespread negative media coverage of HFT (culminating in 2014 in Michael Lewis's best-seller, *Flash Boys*), have meant that assuaging investment managers' fears of predatory trading by HFTs has become a central aspect of successfully managing a dark pool.

Monitoring and Classifying Participants in Dark Pools

Simply excluding high frequency trading algorithms was, however, not an attractive option for the second-generation dark pools. There was fierce competition among them for market share, and (as suggested earlier) the presence of HFTs was helpful—perhaps even necessary—to the pools' capacity to handle the large numbers of small orders generated by the algorithms executing investment management firms' orders. So, as far as we can tell, rather than barring HFTs, all the second-generation investment bank dark pools sought to reassure their investment manager clients by monitoring and categorizing the behaviour of HFTs and other participants in the pools. Thus a leading figure in Barclays' LX dark pool told *Traders Magazine*: '[w]e want our clients to know we really understand what is going on inside LX and that we are watching on their behalf'. As the magazine itself put it:

> By using a sophisticated new surveillance system, Barclays is able to evaluate the trading practices of the participants in its pool and create precise profiles of those traders. Armed with that information, it can confront the bad actors and ask them to change their behavior. If they don't, they may be asked to stop trading in the pool. (Chapman 2012)

How the monitoring system at Barclays worked is in the public domain because of the lawsuit between the bank and Attorney General Schneiderman,

---

delays in the SIP (the Securities Information Processor data-feed, which aggregates price quotations from the various stock exchanges in the US) relative to the direct data-feeds from those exchanges. Indeed, some of the pools were using the direct feeds in their calculations of the national best bid and offer, but their matching engines were still slow enough to lead to exploitable delays. See Alexander et al. (2015). Although, to our knowledge, no similar analysis has been done of European dark pools, the same effect could very well be present there too, because deals in European dark pools are typically consummated at the midpoint between the best bid and offer on a lit venue such as the London Stock Exchange, and a slow matching engine could indeed lead to exploitably stale midpoint prices.

so let us focus on that pool. (The systems employed in the other pools were broadly similar in structure, but cannot be discussed in detail, because the details of such systems would make the pools at which we conducted interviews identifiable.)

Barclays' surveillance system, called 'Liquidity Profiling', was launched in 2011, with (as the bank put it) the goal of distinguishing between 'beneficial liquidity that should be accessed by all clients' and more '"aggressive" order flow' (Barclays' 2011 marketing materials, quoted in Barclays 2014: 8). The system classified the order flow from firms using the pool on two dimensions. The first was 'one-second take alpha', which involved calculating the average change in the price of a stock in the second after a firm's human traders or algorithms had 'taken liquidity': that is, had consummated a trade by sending in a buy order that was matched against an existing sell order in the invisible order book (or a sell order that was matched against an existing bid to buy). 'Alpha' is a common financial market term for profit.[17] Here, a positive value of 'alpha' implied that prices tend to change in a firm's favour immediately after its liquidity-taking trades. 'This could indicate that the trader is trying to benefit from short-term price changes' (Barclays 2014: 9).

The second dimension on which participants in Barclays' dark pool were ranked was 'normalized order size', measured by calculating the ratio of the average size of a firm's algorithmic or human-generated orders for each stock to the overall average size of executed trades in that stock. 'Lower values indicate that the trader places small orders', said Barclays (2014: 9), 'which may be an indication that the trader is using an aggressive trading strategy'. For example, a firm whose algorithms 'pinged the book'—repeatedly sent in very small orders in the hope of detecting large orders that had not yet been filled—would have a low 'normalized order size'.

Drawing upon its measurements of firms' alpha and 'normalized order size', Barclays assigned participants in its dark pool a score from 0 to 5. A score of '4' or '5' indicated the 'safest, most passive, long-term investor-like trading activity', while 'neutral traders were rated "2" or "3"' (Barclays 2014: 9). A score of '0' or '1' indicated the 'most aggressive, predatory trading activity' (Barclays 2014: 9).[18] Those who used Barclays' dark pool were given the option of never having their orders interact with those of participants in this electronically stigmatized category.

As noted earlier, other second-generation investment bank dark pools employ similar surveillance and categorization schemes, typically also involving

---

[17] In many uses, but not here, 'alpha' is a firm's (or trader's) performance relative to that of the overall market in which it is operating.

[18] In other places, Barclays described such activity as 'very toxic' (Barclays' analysis of 16 January 2014, quoted by Schneiderman 2014: 18).

measurement of the short-term profitability of a firm's trading. As we have already suggested, however, it would be naïve to take such classifications—even if conducted entirely rigorously, which seems not always to have been the case—as simple moral impulses. Only two of the seven interviewees whose trading venues engaged in surveillance and classification of this kind said they viewed it as moral in nature. The view that 'this is business', as one interviewee put it, was more common. Other motivations for surveillance and classification that were cited by interviewees were simply that 'clients do want it'; that it was important to be able to demonstrate that when an investment bank's own trading desks traded in its dark pool—which, as noted, has not been uncommon—their trading was nonetheless benign; and that in a situation in which dark pools were being heavily criticized by the leaders of 'lit' markets such as the NYSE, it was vital to be able to show regulators that behaviour in dark pools is under 'full control'.

Nevertheless, the labelling of participants employed by Barclays and the other second-generation dark pools was value-laden in its use of terms such as 'predatory' and 'toxic'. Even if there was no moral motivation for this label-ling, it is striking in its invocation of a moral order in which the short-term profitability of trading is seen not just as evidence of superior skill or of a sophisticated capacity to predict price movements, but as an indicator of a participant of dubious worth that others—especially investment management firms whose benign trading merited a rating of '4' or '5'—might wish to (and perhaps should) avoid.

Lit and other Markets

The picture we have drawn is thus one of the entanglement of trading: both in the relationships between investment management firms and broker-dealers and also—at least sporadically—in a moral order in which trading for very short-term profit is stigmatized either implicitly (as in the exclusion of such traders from first-generation dark pools) or explicitly, as in the electronic labelling of participants. It should be emphasized that the entangled nature of trading in dark pools is in no way exceptional. Indeed, what is historically noteworthy is not dark pools but the 'lit' markets (in which there is a central order book that is accessible to and visible to all participants) against which they are judged dark.

Prior to the 1990s, there were only a small number of lit markets, and they were all peripheral.[19] All the world's main financial markets either had no

---

[19] See, for example, the detailed early history of electronic markets in Gorham and Singh (2009).

central order books, or such books existed but were private. The latter, for example, was the situation of the most important market with central order books, the NYSE. There was an NYSE order book for each stock, but its contents were private to one specified market maker, the 'specialist', and the specialist's clerks. However, in the case of shares (and also that of futures), 'lit' markets with central order books visible to all participants have become dominant over the last two decades; it is only because this has happened that 'dark pools' are thought of as a distinctive, unusual, and perhaps glamorous but also sometimes alarming category of market. The processes by which lit markets have come to dominate in shares and futures are complex, involving competitive and conflictual processes within the ecologies of trading, of trading venues, and—at least in the case of shares—of regulation.[20] Constraints of space, however, prevent us discussing these processes here: see MacKenzie (forthcoming).

Here, rather, we would emphasize that shares and futures, with their lit markets in which investment management firms' orders can participate directly, are actually unusual. None of the other markets in which investment managers operate (foreign exchange, sovereign bonds, corporate bonds, swaps, property, etc.) are dominated to the same extent by that form of market. Take bonds, for example. Human intermediaries—dealers and brokers—remain hugely important in bond trading; much trading is still done by direct person-to-person contact, for example by telephone; where there are lit markets analogous to those in shares, buy-side investment managers are often excluded from them; the electronic trading venues that are open to buy-side firms are usually structured quite differently from the electronic order-book markets in shares.

How investment management firms trade in these other markets largely remains to be researched in detail. One of the few studies of this is Montazemi et al. (2008), which gave an insightful account of fund manager/dealer entanglements in bond trading and of how those entanglements were a barrier to full adoption of electronic trading. Their study suggests that the chains of finance via which trading takes place in bond markets are, if anything, even more entangling than those in the markets for shares that we have examined in this chapter; our own preliminary research on bond trading supports that conclusion. The main way in which an investment management firm trading bonds pays dealers is not via commissions, as in share trading. Rather, those payments take the form of the 'spread': the difference between the price at which dealers will buy a bond and the price at which they will sell it. In fixed income (bonds and bond-like investments), there are in effect two markets—between dealers and clients, and among dealers—with a

---

[20] 'Ecology' here is used in the sense of Abbott (2005).

carefully policed boundary between the two and no guarantee that the prices available to clients such as investment management firms are as good as those that dealers themselves can access. There are as yet only very limited opportunities in fixed income markets for investment management firms to trade more cheaply by dealing directly with each other.

As in the case of shares, dealers in bonds and other 'fixed income' products provide their fund manager clients with 'free' research (that is, research that is in effect paid for by the beneficiaries of the funds being managed). Dealers also reward prized, loyal clients by giving them favourable prices, and by being prepared to buy bonds from them or sell bonds to them even when the dealer thus has to take on a trading position that may be difficult to unwind.[21] As with shares, the relationship between a fund manager and a dealer's 'sales trader' quite often becomes long term, indeed becomes a friendship.

The links of fund managers to dealers in fixed income trading therefore have consequences similar to those of their links to broker-dealers in share trading: what the interviewee quoted earlier called 'relationship value' can outweigh price as a determinant of how and where an investment management firm chooses to trade. Another interviewee reported to us an investment management firm's fixed income fund managers saying they would rather trade with Goldman Sachs than with a fixed income trading arm that the firm itself was considering establishing, even if their own firm's trading arm offered better prices, because of the wider benefits of trading with Goldman.[22] When the bonds being traded are government bonds, these entanglements also involve states. Sovereign bond dealers, for example, are often granted a privileged status (for example, the role of the 'primary dealer' in the US government bond market or 'gilt-edged market maker' in the UK) in return for a commitment always to participate in auctions of these bonds and continually to facilitate their subsequent trading. The detailed dynamics of these investment manager/dealer/state relationships cannot, however, be discussed here: they will be one of the topics of our future research.

---

[21] Since the 2007–8 financial crisis, tighter bank capital requirements seem to have reduced dealers' willingness (and perhaps their capacity) to do this.

[22] The firm's investment management business told the person considering setting up a fixed income trading arm of the firm: ' "If I send an RFQ [request for quotation] to you and Goldman and Goldman showed a worse price I would call Goldman and tell them to improve their price before I would trade with you." They [wouldn't] always trade on the best price and the reason why is today...Goldman provides them all these other services that they depend on, the mortgages [mortgage-backed securities], the new issue credit [newly issued bonds], the financing. There's a bundling of services in the investment banking world where [the investment management firm] is still incentivized to...pay the dealers.' Even the apparently minor matter of the fear of errors can be a reason for investment management firms to be loyal to dealers. As this interviewee put it, 'people are like "what if I had an error trade, what if I bought and I meant to sell?" Over the phone you can call the dealer and say, "look I'm sorry, I really went the wrong way" and for a good client you [the dealer] do that [cancel the trade].'

6

Bringing Society Back into the Investment Chain

Responsible Investing during the Financial Crisis

The 2008 financial crisis made history as it involved simultaneous problems in money, credit, banking, property, equities, and sovereign and corporate bonds. Several catalysts of the crisis have been identified (Pezzuto 2012; Stiglitz 2009; US Financial Crisis Inquiry Commission 2011; Wade 2008). First and foremost was the US subprime mortgage problem: a housing bubble in the form of complex structured credit securities that allowed banks to transform risky assets into apparent non-risky ones, while transferring the risk of borrowers' default to the buyers. The consequent anxiety about the high default risk of some financial assets and the reluctance of lending organizations to extend more credit set the liquidity and confidence crisis in motion, leading to the collapse of some of the largest banks in the world. Faced with this turmoil, governments and central banks responded with unprecedented monetary policy expansion and institutional bailouts to help restore investor confidence and restart financial investment. Despite these moves, a sovereign debt crisis unfolded in the European Union, especially following the wave of downgrades of the government debt of various European states, and culminating in speculation about the possible break-up of the Eurozone. The crisis had significant adverse economic and societal effects in various countries, especially in Greece, where the unemployment rate reached 27.5 per cent and the level of child extreme poverty increased to 16.3 per cent (Matsaganis 2013).

Reflecting on the crisis, the US Financial Crisis Inquiry Commission concluded that it could have been avoided had it not been for 'widespread failures in financial regulation; dramatic breakdowns in corporate governance; excessive borrowing and risk taking by households and Wall Street; policy makers who were ill prepared for the crisis; and systemic breaches in accountability and ethics at all levels' (US Financial Crisis Inquiry Commission 2011). A limited number of financial actors were actually aware of the fact that the US housing market was speculative and would most likely break down. Few in the industry, however, thought they were right: it was impossible to believe that US real estate prices could collapse (Lewis 2010).

This chapter accounts for a similar pattern, although at an ethnographic level. It describes how fixed income managers inside a French asset management company refused to consider repeated alerts from Responsible Investing (RI) analysts regarding the solvency problems of Greece and Italy. By comparing the reaction of fixed income managers to that of equity managers, the chapter identifies the form of connection that linked fixed income managers to society beyond financial markets[1] as the main explanatory factor for their refusal to listen to RI analysts. While RI analysts focused on the environmental, social, and governance (ESG) aspects of these countries—e.g. governance structures, property rights, healthcare systems, etc.—fixed income managers looked at their financial models. Since the financial models used by fixed income managers assessed countries on a different set of evaluation criteria—mainly financial and market-based—they were unable to take into consideration the information provided by RI analysts. In addition, and because of their lack of perceived technical expertise, fixed income managers lacked confidence in RI analysts and deemed them of little relevance when it came to financial decisions.

In explaining this process, the chapter contributes to understanding how 'clusters of evaluation practices' associated with different asset classes sustain but also are based on different ontologies: 'distinctive presuppositions about the nature and properties of the features and processes of the economic world' (MacKenzie 2011: 1783). RI analysts and equity managers portrayed financial markets as one element of broader society—thereby implying that what happened in society at large would eventually be reflected in the financial markets and conversely. Further, by investing 'responsibly', they explicitly sought to put financial markets at the service of the wider society, incorporating this goal into their job descriptions. In contrast, fixed income managers perceived the wider society and financial markets as being two different realms that obeyed separate logics. They believed that their duty was not to serve society at large but to provide good financial returns for their clients. In other words, the chapter shows that what constitutes the investment chain differs depending on which financial actors are asked. In particular, it argues that the way investment managers and analysts integrate 'society' into the investment

---

[1] What is meant by 'society' will be developed later in the chapter.

chain depends largely on the 'epistemic cultures' (Knorr Cetina 1999) of each group of actors.[2]

Before the Storm

'May 2006: I have just started at the Z company. Everybody seems happy. The CAC 40[3] went up by more than 20% last year and everybody got good bonuses' (Field Notes, May 2006). My PhD had started well.[4] I had succeeded in being recruited as an RI analyst at the asset management subsidiary of one of the largest French mutual insurance companies. A three-year contract between my doctoral school, the Z company, and me was signed,[5] allowing me to gather all the data I needed for my dissertation in exchange of my work as an RI analyst. I had no research topic besides a broad interest in the integration of non-financial concerns by the asset management industry. I planned to follow the research methods of William Foot Whyte in *Street Corner Society* (1943)—a classic of sociological research and a model for urban ethnography. Harvard fellow Whyte decided to live for three and a half years in a poor Italian American neighbourhood, including eighteen months with an Italian family to be as close as possible to the street gangs he was studying. Like Whyte, I was entering a world I actually knew little about.

The Z company was a small asset management company, managing around €2.5 billion, mainly the parent company's assets. Not dissimilar to the situation described in Chapter 2, the company hierarchy was clear. The investment managers were at the top. The financial analysts were just below—especially since many investment managers started as financial analysts. The sales managers followed: although they were key in attracting new assets—which gave them a central role in the company—they were nevertheless criticized by the investment managers and the analysts for their lack of technical background. 'They sell funds like they would sell ties.' At the bottom of the hierarchy were the support functions whose job was mainly administrative and operational but nonetheless essential to the unfolding of investment decisions. 'We are nothing, really. Nobody looks at us', one of them commented to me.

---

[2] 'Epistemic cultures' are the 'aggregate patterns and dynamics that are on display in expert practice and that vary in different settings of expertise' (Knorr Cetina 1999: 8).

[3] The CAC 40 index represents a capitalization-weighted measure of the forty most significant shares among the one hundred largest companies listed on the Euronext Paris stock exchange.

[4] As elsewhere in our book, references in this chapter to the first-person singular indicate we are drawing on ethnographic research conducted by one of us, in this case, Arjaliès.

[5] Known as a CIFRE—Convention Industrielle de Formation par la Recherche en Entreprise.

Although investment management companies vary, the pyramidal organizational structure often dominates (Ortiz 2014). However, there was in the Z company a group of analysts that escaped the usual categories: the RI analysts. Since the parent company belonged to the social economy sector—a sector that aimed to put 'people before profits',[6] the Z company decided to manage their assets in a socially responsible way. The goal of RI was to put money at the service of the public interest, in a very broad sense of the term.[7] Due to France's secular tradition, and contrary to Anglo-Saxon and Scandinavian countries where socially responsible and ethical investing were pioneered by churches, French RI did not consist of excluding companies belonging to the 'sin stocks' (e.g. tobacco, alcohol, arm manufacturers, etc.), but instead of selecting the best socially responsible and financially performing companies, whatever the industry (Arjaliès 2010; Gond and Boxenbaum 2013). In the world of French RI analysts, there were actually as many socially responsible arms manufacturers as socially responsible firms in other industry sectors—rather surprisingly to many overseas ethical investors.

In practice, RI consisted of integrating ESG criteria into investment processes; this could take place at the level of the analysis of the issuers, as well as at the level of portfolio construction, or at both levels. No issuer was excluded from the portfolios based on normative ethical criteria, such as is often the case with ethical investing. Abortion, animal testing, and alcohol were not considered to be socially irresponsible per se. The goal of RI analysts was to assess the quality of the 'sustainable development' of the issuers, i.e. their ability to meet the needs of the present without compromising the ability of future generations to meet their own needs (Brundtland 1987).[8]

Analytical criteria for the bond issues of the OECD countries in which the fixed income managers of the Z company were investing included: (1) environmental criteria, such as per capita CO_2 emissions, energy mix, ecological footprint, percentage of arable land; (2) social criteria, such as the level of obesity, the Global Peace index,[9] murder rates, the Gini index,[10] university graduation rates; and (3) governance criteria, such as the Corruption Perceptions

---

[6] The social economy sector includes cooperatives, non-profit organizations, social enterprises, and charities.

[7] RI 'is a form of investment that aims to reconcile economic performance and social and environmental impact through financing companies and public organizations that contribute to sustainable development, whatever their activity sector. By influencing the governance and the behavior of actors, RI should favour a responsible economy' (Association Française de Gestion/ French SIF Press Release, 2 July 2013). RI represented €746 billion of assets under management in France in 2015.

[8] 'Sustainability' involves environmental, social, and governance-related elements.

[9] The Global Peace index (GPI) ranks independent states and territories according to their level of peacefulness and is generated by the Institute for Economics and Peace (IEP).

[10] The index measures the degree of inequality in the distribution of income in a country.

index,[11] political stability, and public debt. RI analysts believed that integrating these elements into more standard credit analysis would help them identify countries that were more sustainable than others from both ESG and financial perspectives. RI analysts indeed expected countries with a good ESG rating to be more likely to serve the public interest and the long-term development of the nation, which would consequently help them repay their debt.

The same type of analysis was applied to corporate bonds and equities although the type of ESG criteria used for private issuers differed. These criteria included carbon footprint, board diversity, stakeholder relationships, sustainable product innovation, and public controversies, among many others. Just as with state issuers, RI analysts believed that companies that shielded themselves from ESG risks would be more likely to be financially successful and socially responsible in the long term.

RI analysts at the Z company assessed companies and state borrowers on these ESG criteria and made recommendations to investment managers based on this analysis. To do so, RI analysts mainly relied on information provided by social rating agencies and brokerage companies. Contrary to financial analysts, RI analysts had never been trained to conduct these evaluations: it was a new job, supported by little academic expertise, which was just emerging in the industry. RI analysts were Parisian *bobos*—a French expression for 'bourgeois-bohemian', referring to 'highly educated folk who have one foot in the bohemian world of creativity and another foot in the bourgeois realm of ambition and worldly success' (Brooks 2010: 10–11).

The educational background of RI analysts confused most equity and fixed income investment managers. It made little sense to them that a graduate—someone like themselves—would prefer a low-paid job[12] requiring little technical expertise to a high-paid financial one. Many investment managers seemed to believe that RI analysts were either tree-huggers or bad at maths. In either case, investment managers often seemed to think that RI analysts could not be relied upon when it came to investment. RI analysts were tolerated only because the parent company wanted to integrate ESG criteria into investment processes, but as one investment manager explained to me, 'they don't get to decide, they work for us'.

The hierarchy was reflected in the offices themselves. There were three open-plan offices. The first one was occupied by the investment managers and the financial analysts; it was situated between the office of the chief executive and those of the Director of Sales and sales managers. Because the

---

[11] Based on the opinion of relevant experts, the Corruption Perceptions index measures the perceived levels of public sector corruption worldwide. It is published by the NGO Transparency International.

[12] Salary is a significant point in hierarchy.

Z company was a small company, financial analysts were also assistant invest-ment managers, which meant that they had little time to conduct in-depth analysis of the issuers. They therefore relied heavily on suggestions made by sell-side analysts, analysts working for brokerage companies (see Chapters 1, 4, and 5). The second open-plan office contained the support functions: it was located in front of the investment managers. The smallest office belonged to the RI analysts, and was situated farther away from the investment managers, at the end of a small corridor. While there were many exchanges between the first and the second offices, the RI office was more isolated. On the other hand, it was a place for gossip and confidences: RI analysts were easy-going and nobody could see who was in their office unless they were in the corridor. Despite the hierarchy, the atmosphere at the Z company was very friendly, people from different offices ate together, and everybody seemed to benefit from this organization: 'we are lucky', one employee told me, 'especially when we compare ourselves to other industries; money is easy to make in finance'.

Opening the Black Box of Investment Processes

After one year spent at the Z company, I felt that I had been adopted by most of my colleagues. I was a strange, underpaid, over-educated RI analyst who was carrying out some kind of research on them. Everybody agreed to answer my questions, spending hours explaining to me in great detail the workings of their job, their joys and frustrations. Everybody but the fixed income man-agers. Despite numerous demands, they always refused to talk to me about their job: 'too complicated', 'no time', 'later'. While the equity investment processes broadly made sense to me and the rest of the company, I realized that nobody seemed to understand what fixed income managers did on a day-to-day basis.

My basic understanding at this time was that fixed income managers lent money to borrowers—mainly corporates and states—in exchange for interest payments (coupons), and that they used credit ratings to assess the solvency of these issuers. This job looked pretty simple to me—simpler than equity invest-ment where managers had to identify those companies whose share prices and dividends were most likely to appreciate in the future. Fixed income managers were for me like 'super financial advisers', lending a lot of money to large organizations. I therefore had some difficulty understanding why each man-ager's desk had on average six screens full of graphics and numbers. I asked the new chief executive, a former equity manager, as well as political science graduate, for more explanation. He answered, 'it is very complicated; basically, it is complex econometrics'. Faced with these elusive answers, I started won-dering whether he himself knew what he was doing.

It was the summer of 2007 and the atmosphere of the company had dramatically changed. The parent company complained about Z company's lack of commercial success. The investment management subsidiary was not able to attract new assets from external clients (see Chapter 3 for more on the sources of assets of investment management companies). In particular, the parent company did not understand why, although the number of requests for proposals for RI was increasing at the industry level, the Z company was never selected by trustees (see Chapter 7 for further explanations on the role of trustees). The new chief executive, who had some forty years of experience in mainstream investment management, had been given one year to conduct a strategic review. According to him, this strategic transformation would be his 'last challenge before retiring'.

At first, the chief executive considered stopping RI and firing everybody—me included—to start afresh with new people, but the parent company advised him against it. His second choice was then to launch two working groups—one on equity investment and the other on fixed income investment—to see what could be done to convince trustees to buy the Z company's RI funds. The chief executive believed that it would also be a good opportunity for him to discover what RI meant in practice. 'I arrived here and I had no clue about what RI was. For me, finance is about financial performance', he told me. Each working group was composed of investment managers, RI analysts, financial analysts, and sales managers: everybody was supposed to meet once a week, for a few weeks. The redesign of the investment processes eventually took one year and the working groups met twenty-nine times.

It was September 2007 when the first meeting officially convened. It was the first time that everybody had met to speak openly about the investment practices themselves. Seizing the opportunity to be at the forefront of the redesign, the RI analysts complained about the fact that they had no idea how the ESG ratings they provided were used by investment managers. The truth was that investment managers perceived these ESG ratings as constraints that made little sense financially. In practice, investment managers made investment decisions based on financial criteria. It was only at the end of the investment process that they adjusted the portfolio so that the average ESG rating of the portfolio—based on the average of the ESG ratings of the issuers inside the portfolio—would be above 50 out of 100. Why 50 out of 100? Nobody could really answer: 'that was the process decided by the previous CEO, we just implemented it', said an equity manager. How were portfolios adjusted? 'It depends.' To say the least, RI analysts found the integration of ESG criteria into the investment processes mysterious.

To elucidate these mechanisms, an equity manager stood up and started sketching on the white board of the meeting room the different steps he (like all his fund manager colleagues, a man) followed when selecting companies for the portfolio. After thirty minutes, the fixed income manager responsible for the redesign showed his impatience: 'I don't have time for these things. I understand that RI makes sense for equity investment but fixed income is a complicated form of investment, that is the reason why I am paid to manage these funds. It is not my job to do RI and I have nothing to do with equities, so when you all agree, just come and tell me about the new RI constraint. Now I have more important liquidity issues to deal with.' The fixed income manager left the room and did not come back for months. The black box of fixed income investment was not yet ready to be opened.

Trouble Comes

There were good reasons for the fixed income manager to be busy. British bank Northern Rock had just collapsed. The subprime crisis was beginning to be a source of public concern. Every day I took notes, and every day brought new rumours of a financial crisis. I did not know what to think. Some investment managers reassured me that 'the stock markets are fine, it's just an adjustment', while others were more alarmed, saying that 'there is a fundamental problem in the industry'. However, as the weeks unfolded, it became apparent that the subprime crisis might need some state intervention and could potentially lead to a plunge in equity indices.

The brewing crisis spurred many discussions within the company. While RI analysts and equity managers were working together on the new investment process, they started rethinking the value of RI. 'Do you believe that ESG ratings could help us identify those companies which are over-valued?', an equity manager asked. 'In theory, yes. I mean the principle of RI is to work on the fundamentals of the company. We look at the sustainability of their strategies, their relationships with their stakeholders, their long-term prospects, the quality of the management, all these things',[13] an RI analyst answered. The more the equity working group feared that a crisis might happen, the more they thought that there was a major problem with the valuation of some companies. After several weeks of work, they concluded that they needed to comprehend what was behind the ratings they were using—both financial and ESG—to get a better understanding of the real value of the companies they were investing in.

On 21 January 2008, the Société Générale bank closed out positions, opened without authorization by a trader named Jérome Kerviel, totalling as much as €49.9 billion, following which equity indices fell precipitously.

---

[13] Like financial analysts, RI analysts based their decisions on the information provided by the social rating agencies as well as on their own views of the issuers.

Losses attributed were estimated at €4.9 billion. The actions of this 'rogue trader', although not directly related to the financial crisis, meant that in France the workings of financial markets were called seriously into question. Politicians and intellectuals agreed on the need for stronger regulation of financial markets. For the Z company, meanwhile, the Kerviel affair had two direct consequences.

First, it was clear to the chief executive that these events would hardly encourage trustees to invest in equity funds, and therefore redesigning the fixed income funds became a matter of urgency. Second, the board members and the top management team of the parent company were worried that a Kerviel affair would happen at their firm too. Société Générale was a very well-known and respected organization and most actors believed that if it had failed, anybody could fail. Clients also asked for more monitoring: they wanted to be reassured about the security of their assets. As a consequence, new internal control procedures were swiftly put in place and it was decided that investment managers' positions had to be carefully scrutinized.

RI analysts made the most of this situation to impose RI constraints on the fixed income managers. They convinced the chief executive of the need to control the content of portfolios and to prove to clients that RI fixed income funds were not simply 'greenwashing'.[14] The chief executive approved: it was agreed that investments in the worst 25 per cent of issuers based on the ESG ratings should be excluded from portfolios and that RI analysts should monitor the funds' constituents on a monthly basis. The RI analysts were thrilled.

The fixed income manager responsible for the redesign immediately complained: this would mean that he could not invest in Greece and Italy, two countries poorly rated on ESG ratings because of their low performance on various social and governance criteria, but financially very interesting. The investment manager openly doubted the ability of RI analysts to provide better analysis than credit ratings agencies. According to him, this choice would clearly threaten the funds' financial performance. Disturbed, the chief executive asked RI analysts to find a solution. RI analysts agreed to loosen the RI constraints by authorizing that 10 per cent of the assets be invested in these ESG low-performing countries, meaning that Italy and Greece could represent 10 per cent of the portfolio. Because it was not based on statistical analysis, the decision not to invest more than 10 per cent of assets in Greece and Italy was judged to be arbitrary by fixed income managers, as well as dangerous financially.

---

[14] That is to say, the misleading use of marketing to promote the perception that an organization's products, aims, or policies are environmentally friendly across the board, when in fact they are not.

Meanwhile, and paradoxically energized by the huge crisis that was unfolding, the equity working group was analysing in great detail all the ESG ratings they worked with. The group's commitment level was high: they spent days and nights working on the new investment process. A young team with great hopes, they believed that they could do a better job than these 'US folks'. They analysed competitors, interviewed brokerage companies and social rating agencies, ran statistical analyses to compare financial and ESG ratings, and tested investment decisions on fictitious portfolios. As a result of this work, and in contrast to their fixed income counterparts, the equity managers believed that the new equity investment process was informed by extensive research.

Over a few months of intensive collaboration, the equity managers and RI analysts gradually formed the belief that adding ESG ratings to financial analysis was a way to recouple the financial markets with the 'real economy', hence avoiding speculative behaviour and overvaluation of assets. ESG ratings were believed to help investment managers select the companies more likely to succeed in the long term by focusing on the 'fundamentals' of their corporate strategy. For instance, equity managers and RI analysts believed that ESG criteria could be used to assess whether the product that was sold by a company would still exist in ten years given the scarcity of natural resources, or to evaluate whether its board was diverse enough to reflect the diversity of its customers. According to the group, RI was a way to enrich the equity investment process by providing information which was not factored into either financial analyses or market prices. It was also a way of putting financial markets at the service of society by channelling money to socially responsible companies.

Alerting the Fixed Income Managers

Intrigued by the discrepancy between the ESG and credit ratings regarding Greece and Italy the fixed income manager had identified when implementing the new RI constraints, RI analysts decided to conduct further analysis of these countries. In doing so, they discovered that, although the credit ratings for these countries were good, they were rated extremely poorly by social rating agencies and brokerage companies specializing in ESG analysis. For instance, RI analysts could not understand why Greece was rated A/A–[15] whereas the more they investigated the ESG analysis, the more problems they found. Governance in these countries was poor; sometimes property rights barely existed; there was a high level of corruption;

---

[15] The Fitch credit rating from 2007 to 2009. Further information on credit rating agencies is provided later in the chapter.

healthcare and retirement systems functioned ineffectively—and these were just the major issues. The RI analysts believed that these countries had to be excluded from the portfolios: they were convinced that money should not be lent to governments that did not support the sustainable development of their country.

They warned the fixed income manager responsible for the redesign, who politely and firmly rejected their suggestions. Both yields and credit ratings were good. He was already very unhappy to be limited to investing only 10 per cent of the assets he managed in bonds issued by these countries. The RI analysts went to the chief executive, who also refused to exclude such countries: the 10 per cent limit was already constraining enough. The RI analysts insisted at various meetings over the course of several weeks that 'it does not make sense. The [ESG] fundamentals of the countries are bad'. The fixed income manager's riposte, however, was that 'nobody cares. We are in Europe, nobody will fail. It is not because the Greeks are indeed a bit weak when it comes to transparency that the bonds will behave badly. Come on guys, fixed income is more complicated than equity investment, so how about you just let me do my job?' Fixed income managers did not believe that RI analysts could know something that the credit rating agencies and financial markets did not know, especially given their lack of perceived technical expertise (Larminat 2013; Ortiz 2014). As discussed in Chapters 2 and 4, in investment management it is often important not merely to be qualified, but especially to be able to demonstrate to one's interlocutors that having these qualifications means they should trust you.[16]

I was persuaded that RI analysts were right. Thinking about the Kerviel affair, I felt obliged to alert my bosses, and decided to step into the discussion; I was an RI analyst myself after all. I first talked to the fixed income manager: 'Why don't you care about RI? I mean don't you see the problems that are coming, with the crisis?' Then I went to the chief executive. 'This does not make sense', I told him, 'something is wrong'. Both gave me the same answer: 'This is a complicated investment process. Much more than equity investment.' I became suspicious: making things out to be complicated and opaque was for me the best way to prevent people from looking at them.

---

[16] Spreads between Greek and German debt were low over the 2005–9 period, and at the same time, a raft of ESG reports highlighting significant differences in the non-financial performances of Greece and Germany were published, drawing attention to governance issues in the former (exposure to the risk of corruption, the weight of the informal economy, etc.), without especially attracting the interest of financial market participants until the beginning of 2010, a few exceptions notwithstanding (Desmartin et al. 2014: 5).

The Real Problem with Fixed Income Investment

I admit it: I was angry.[17] I could not understand why nobody was taking action, since it seemed obvious to me that there was a problem. Once again I went to my supervisors: 'This manager is completely stupid. He does not see what is happening.' One of my supervisors asked, 'Is the chief executive OK with this?' I answered: 'Yes, this is insane, isn't it?' My supervisor continued: 'OK, then, there must be another reason. People don't do things inside organizations just because they want to. Organizations enable them to do so. You haven't looked far enough.' I was exhausted. I had already spent two years full-time in the field and my supervisors told me that I had not looked far enough. This was too much; I needed a break. A winter visiting in Sweden seemed perfect: I could access all the documents of the Z company on the company intranet while standing back from life at the company. I wondered: 'Is there something about fixed income investment I have missed?'

I went to the library and started reading portfolio management books. I realized that I had never closely looked at what fixed income management consisted of. I believed that when fixed income managers bought €200,000 of a five-year Spanish government bond yielding 4.5 per cent on Day D, that meant they were lending €200,000 to Spain on Day D, would receive a coupon twice a year, and eventually be repaid €200,000 by the Spanish government on Day D+5 years.[18] In my world, then, if Spain was not sustainable, it was very likely that it could not repay the bond, just as home-owners in the US could not repay their mortgages. RI made a lot of sense. What I discovered, however, was much more complex.

---

[17] Although I had always been an RI analyst at the Z company, I constantly tried not to make value judgements about what I witnessed, in order to build relationships of trust with my fellow employees, as well as to foster the view that I was first and foremost a researcher. However, there were several weeks during which I openly voiced my concerns about the ESG aspects of the fixed income investment processes because of the worries I had. I became at this moment a native ethnographer—i.e. a member of the community I studied. 'Going native' is a common experience for ethnographers who spend a long time in the field (Whyte 1943). I nonetheless decided to leave the company for a few months after this episode to be able to stand back from the data I was gathering. With hindsight, ethnographic work inside investment management firms could afford an excellent opportunity for collaborative ethnography of the type that scholars have in recent years attempted to develop as a technology for the shared generation of knowledge about the contemporary world (Rabinow 2003), with ethnographers taking their interlocutors as their 'epistemic partners' (Holmes and Marcus 2005), recognizing that academics are far from unique in wanting to systematically analyse social relations, even if the stakes and interests of academic ethnographers, and, in our case, fund managers, are often quite divergent (Rabinow et al. 2008; Rees 2007).

[18] The yield of a bond is the rate of return it offers over its lifetime at its current market price, normally measured by finding the rate of interest at which a bond's coupons and principal have to be discounted so their total present value is the bond's current price.

131

Inside the Z company,[19] fixed income managers indeed bought Spanish bonds on Day D, but did not keep them for five years and patiently wait for the coupons to come. In fact they did not hold the bonds for a very long period at all. Instead they were constantly buying, exchanging, and selling the bonds they held in their portfolios. I had thought that fixed income investment was a long-term affair, but I came to realize that it was actually extremely short term. Much to my surprise, they regularly dealt in derivatives, convertible bonds, and various forms of swaps and other complex financial products; indeed, these instruments were at the heart of their daily practices. They also regularly sold the bonds they bought to other investment managers a few weeks or months after the purchase, because they could buy a similar security with a higher interest rate. Additionally they often switched one bond for another because they believed that the market had temporarily mispriced the two bonds, a discrepancy that represented a profit opportunity.

Why did they do this? The answer is at once simple and complicated. Complicated because this form of investment practice is the result of decades of financial education, regulatory guidance, and institutional reproduction, which is beyond the focus of the chapter (see Zaloom 2009 for further explanation). Simple because fixed income managers do not make money only from the money they lend to issuers, in the way a bank might. They also make money from their ability to 'exploit minor inefficiencies arising from market frictions' (Fridson 2013).[20]

How is this possible? First, thanks to the credit rating agencies. A credit rating agency is a private company that assigns a credit rating to an issuer based on its assessment of the latter's ability to pay back the debt. When a private or a public issuer—a company, a state, or a municipality, for example—wants to borrow money on the financial markets, it pays the credit rating agency to be rated. If the rating is BBB– or higher,[21] the bond is considered 'investment grade', which means that most institutional investors—like the Z company's parent company—can buy them. Because the likelihood of a European country going bankrupt was perceived at the time to be almost nil—because of a putative Eurozone solidarity—the credit ratings of Greece and Italy were good (see Pénet 2015 for further explanation).

Second, because fixed income managers believe these credit ratings. At a given moment in time in a given market, there is a pool of 'investment grade' bonds available, from which investment managers may choose. While equity

---

[19] The practice of fixed income investment does, however, vary significantly between firms.

[20] Fixed income managers make money mainly from lending money to issuers. However, their performance relative to other managers operating in the same fixed income market often depends on how well they exploit these minor efficiencies.

[21] A security is considered to be investment-grade if it has an S&P rating of BBB– or higher, a Moody's rating of Baa3 or higher, or a Fitch rating of BBB– or higher.

managers at the Z company tended to look at the 'fundamentals' of the company to see which one was the most likely to succeed, the fixed income managers seemed not to care; they mostly outsourced this judgement to credit rating agencies. Yet these credit ratings determined the outcome in advance: issuers that were 'investment grade' were deemed almost riskless. According to the Z company's fixed income managers, there was indeed no risk in lending money to Greece and Italy.

Third, because fixed income managers' financial performance is compared to a 'benchmark'.[22] The benchmark is often an index based on bonds with maturity ranging from five to seven years, whose returns are usually higher than bonds with short-term maturities because of the increased risk associated with longer time periods. To 'beat the market', fixed income managers must construct a portfolio whose overall financial performance exceeds the benchmark, which is in practice very difficult. Indeed, the only way to do it is to generate better yields than the yields of medium maturity bonds (five to seven years) which themselves tend to outperform short-term bonds. Moreover, fixed income managers are highly constrained when investing. Unlike equity managers who can choose from a large pool of issuers, fixed income managers must invest in a pool of bonds whose maturity and yields are fixed (whence the appellation 'fixed income investment'). The only way for a fixed income manager to beat the market is therefore to buy and sell bonds with different maturities and risk profiles in order to outperform their benchmarks over time.

Fourth, because of the associated propensity of their peers to lend money to borrowers. When bonds are issued, their yield and credit ratings already embody these predictions. For instance, the yield at issuance of an issuer's bonds is higher if there is little willingness to lend to it or if its credit rating is poor, factors which in turn shape its yield curve. In other words, the evaluation practices of fixed income managers are based on a circular reference system—a series of references where the last object refers back to the first, resulting in a closed loop (Ortiz 2015). Indeed, credit ratings are used by investment managers to judge issuers and these judgements are then used by credit rating agencies to set their ratings. As Zaloom (2009: 247) explains, 'financial participants are knitted in a loosely entangled economic public through recursive loops of feeling, reading, interpreting, and acting around this tool. . . . But the curve does not merely indicate; like all indicators, it also produces its own uncertainties'.

After several months of study, I realized that there was a large disconnect between the investment rationale used by fixed income managers and the

---

[22] This aspect is also relevant to equity investment. Benchmarks are part of the enabling and constraining apparatus of investment management—they both subject managers to scrutiny and give them a means of justifying their expertise, as discussed in Chapter 2.

reality of these countries. Fixed income managers had little understanding of the day-to-day experience of the countries they invested in since they observed them through the lens of credit ratings, interest rates, and yield curves. RI analysts knew almost nothing about the investment rationale of fixed income managers but were much more knowledgeable about what was happening inside these countries. The fixed income manager was factually correct, I concluded: nobody in the financial markets cared about the sustainability of the issuers themselves. The financial performance of fixed income investment funds did not result from the sustainable behaviour of lending countries but from the ability of fixed income managers to take advantage of small pricing differences at the aggregate level of the market. It became obvious to me that even if Greece and Italy paid no attention to ESG issues, their bonds would not be impacted unless the solvency of the countries was threatened and their credit ratings downgraded, which seemed impossible. I closed my books and returned to the Z company, wondering how this asset class had become so complicated.

When Society Comes Back

From then on the situation became much clearer. Both fixed income managers and RI analysts were right. In the world of financial markets, the investment managers were right: market participants seemed not to worry much about what Italy and Greece did, provided credit ratings were good. Beyond the world of financial markets, however, RI analysts were right: these countries were not governed sustainably and from this perspective their credit ratings made little sense.

One element remained to be elucidated: why did it appear to me that fixed income managers did not feel much responsibility for the financial crisis? Everybody inside the Z company talked about the financial turmoil; people lost their jobs; French citizens accused 'greedy traders' of 'playing with their money like at the casino'. I almost apologized to all my friends and relatives for working in financial markets, but fixed income managers never looked guilty. Equity managers believed that they were connected to wider society through the flow of capital they were investing in companies. They somehow felt responsible for what happened. I did not understand why the fixed income managers who lent money to the very countries caught up in solvency crises did not look remorseful. Had they not encouraged the debt crisis by sustaining such behaviour, all the more dangerously given that fixed income investment was the largest asset class worldwide (Responsible Investor Insight 2014)?

I later asked a fixed income manager about this, and he replied: 'When I invest, the interest rate is known. The maturity of the bond is known. The credit risk is known. I am not a shareholder. Nothing I would do would impact this issuer.' I discovered that fixed income managers did not think that their decisions affected society or economy. Equity managers perceived themselves as being one element of the investment chain: a chain they could influence and for which they were partly responsible. Fixed income managers, in contrast, appeared to me like external observers, data processors facing a market 'out there' they wanted to profit from. It was as if they were paradoxically not active in the markets their activities created.

Wider society eventually came back into the world of fixed income managers too, however. The debt of several European nations kept growing as they rescued their banks and their economies. Iceland, Ireland, and Spain were among the first to be downgraded by the credit rating agencies. By the end of 2009, the credit rating agencies reduced their confidence in Greece. Greece was again downgraded, this time to junk level,[23] in April 2010, and further downgrades followed to the debt of Spain, Portugal, and Ireland. Pressure continued on Greece as rumours of bankruptcy increased. Portugal and Ireland followed. By the following year, the pressure had also extended to Italy. The European Central Bank bought Spanish and Italian debt in order to reduce the market pressure on the two countries. What nobody believed could happen had happened: the European debt crisis was upon us.

What is particularly striking is the time fixed income managers took to realize that they were also hit hard by the financial crisis. Previous research has suggested that one of the main reasons for such a late response was the perception that fixed income investment in the Eurozone was riskless because of the disappearance of the risk of currency fluctuations (Brunnermeier et al. 2011). The above findings complement this view by showing that the decoupling of wider society and the investment practices of fixed income investment have certainly contributed to the belief that a debt crisis could not occur. Fixed income managers were immersed in an 'epistemic culture' (Knorr Cetina 1999) that differed from equity investment, a culture whose elements acted as a lens which prevented them from seeing what the ESG fundamentals of these issuers looked like. As already discussed in Chapter 4, these epistemic divergences can make communication between different teams or departments of investment management firms very difficult.

'Society' is not an object to which any of us have unmediated access. RI analysts and fixed income managers both relied on condensed indicators to gain their own knowledge of 'society'—each set of indicators focusing on different elements (ESG measures for the former, financial measures for the latter). All securities do indeed have a connection to the 'reality' of companies

---

[23] 'Junk' means 'below investment grade' as defined in note 21.

and governments and so on, a connection which is always mediated in one way or another (Mosley 2003). In this sense, RI analysts and fixed income managers were actually epistemologically close to each other. What we mean here by 'bringing society back into the investment chain' is that RI analysts and equity managers explicitly aimed to connect their work to the wider society, to put financial markets at the service of the general public. They aimed to render something they called 'society' visible in their evaluation practices through supplementing financial measures with ESG criteria.

Fixed income managers, on the other hand, did not believe that this societal role was part of their duties. They instead perceived themselves as experts whose professional role was to focus on the financial aspects of investment decisions alone (Eyal 2013). The difference in terms of their relationships to the concept of 'society' is worth mentioning, especially in the context of the European crisis during which critiques of how financial markets were 'decoupled from the real world' abounded (Gitlin 2012). Previous research shows that evaluation practices sustain different ontologies (MacKenzie 2011). This chapter points to the fact that different perceptions of the world and one's role in it also contribute to fashioning different evaluation practices. Because these ontologies and evaluation practices are deeply consequential, not only for financial markets in the strict sense but also for the rest of society, this chapter is additional evidence of the need to better understand the connections that link different actors along the investment chain.

Examining the US subprime mortgage crisis, Pozner et al. (2010) explain that micro-mechanisms at the organizational level, such as learning processes and strong competitive pressures to conform to shared practices, underpin the persistence of structures and practices despite contra-indications of their effectiveness. These micro-mechanisms, they argue, contribute to self-reinforcing cycles and biases in decision-making and lead to maladaptive changes at the institutional level. Insights into these types of micro-mechanisms may help explain why, despite repeated alerts, fixed income managers were not able to foresee the shortcomings of their investment processes. It may also explain why they were so resistant to RI analysts whose evaluation practices appeared to them to be so arbitrary and unscientific. In unravelling these mechanisms, the chapter provides additional evidence that financial markets are not, as financial economists have long contended, objective efficient information processors, but social constructions that function as 'collective calculative devices' (Callon and Muniesa 2005; MacKenzie 2006) wherein market behaviour is guided and constrained by prevailing institutional logics and theories (Ferraro et al. 2005; Lounsbury and Hirsch 2010; Zajac and Westphal 2004).

The Same As It Ever Was?

At my PhD defence, I asked the chief executive whether he felt responsible for what happened in the debt market.

> No, why should I?...The main problem was the credit rating agencies: they gave us bad information and we had to work with that....Our models are robust. We just need good data, a good assessment of risks, and that's where RI could help, I believe, by helping us assessing the bankruptcy risk.

When I asked this question, I was hoping for a different answer, such as 'Yes, let's invest in socially responsible issuers only, whose societal and economic projects make sense in the long term.' I was dreaming. Questioning the models and the investment decisions processes used in fixed income investment was like questioning the whole profession, its education, its identity, and therefore almost the entire institutional infrastructure of the financial markets and of the societies that relied on these markets.

A few years later, however, I discovered that a new market in this asset class had emerged: 'green bonds'. Green bonds were created to fund projects that have positive environmental benefits. Investor interest in these bonds is rising. According to the Climate Bonds Initiatives (CBI),[24] $11 billion in green bonds was issued in 2013, nearly $37 billion was issued in 2014 and $41.8 billion in 2015, with $100 billion predicted in the coming years. Green bonds are a potential way of reconnecting the bond market with societal interests, by focusing the investment decision on the sustainability of the project funded rather than on the yield curve or the credit rating. However, these bonds remain marginal and some investment managers already try to apply their evaluation practices based on yield curves and credit ratings to this pool of assets, simply transposing one market technology to another market. Other investment managers have suggested abandoning benchmarks, but no one seems actually ready to do it, since it is how funds are evaluated against their peers. If it took decades to build fixed income investment processes, it seems as if it might well take decades to take them down again.

---

[24] Source: <http://www.climatebonds.net>, accessed 1 June 2016.

7

Trapped in Resistance

Collective Struggles through the Investment Chain

The investment chain is at once a highly contextualized and humanized network—tied to particular physical spaces and specific actors (Beunza and Stark 2004, 2012)—and a worldwide technology-driven system from which human beings tend to disappear (Borch and Lange 2016). Thus Chapters 2 and 3 demonstrate the immense importance of relationships between individuals, such as fund managers and client service managers (Chapter 2), or financial advisers and their clients (Chapter 3). In sharp contrast, Chapter 5 describes how dark pools were instead developed as complex technical systems whose aim was to transform investors into anonymous orders. As a 'global microstructure' (Knorr Cetina and Bruegger 2002), the investment chain thus both connects and separates people from each other, making global issues such as tax evasion or climate change very difficult to address (Hanlon et al. 2015; Zindler and Locklin 2016).

This chapter is an account of a unique moment when a number of actors linked through the investment chain decided to reconnect in a deliberate and informed way to address a specific social issue. It describes how a group of French pension fund trustees sought to mobilize investment managers, service providers, and board members of a company to help workers unionize in some automotive plants in the US state of Mississippi. Despite their efforts, all actors appeared to be trapped in the web of their connections to each other: the more individuals aimed to grasp the chain, the more the chain seemed to escape their grasp. What first appeared to be a major advantage of their working together—being able to mobilize the entire investment chain thanks to the tight relationships existing between people—eventually revealed itself to be what prevented the chain from moving. This chapter explains why.

Trustees' Role in the Investment Chain

On 23 November 2012, I (Arjaliès) was participating in the Seventh International Meeting of Trade Union Pension Trustees at the OECD in Paris. As a faculty member of one of the best-known French business schools, I had been invited to give a presentation about Responsible Investing (RI) in France. The conference was organized by the Trade Union Advisory Committee (TUAC) to the OECD, which brings together fifty-eight national trade unions from the thirty OECD 'industrialized' countries, and the Global Union Committee on Workers' Capital (CWC), an international labour union network for dialogue and action on the responsible investment of workers' capital. Both organizations believe that workers can leverage their retirement savings to influence how companies respect human and labour rights, remain financially sustainable, and minimize adverse impacts on the environment.[1]

In common law jurisdictions like the UK, US, or Canada, labour union pension funds have actually been among the most vocal class of shareholder activists (Fung et al. 2001; Gillan and Starks 2000; Naczyk 2016), using their ownership power to push corporate governance reforms (Schwab and Thomas 1998). Retirement savings and pension funds invested in global capital markets are valued at more than US$32 trillion (Towers Watson 2014). They have had a major impact on the pension and productive system of various countries over the past decades, notably because they enable workers to own (at least part of) the means of production (see Drucker 1976 for the US). Central to this mechanism is the role of trustees. The trustees are people, acting separately from the employer, who are responsible for the assets invested in the pension scheme for the benefit of the scheme's members. It is these individuals who are ultimately responsible for the investment decisions of the fund.

Since the shift from a 'pay-as-you-go' retirement system to a funded pension system is much more recent in continental Europe and South America than in the US or Canada, the role of trustees in these countries is quite new and the modalities of their action still under construction. 'Pay-as-you-go' means that workers' current contributions pay for pensioners' current benefits—a system managed by the state, which redistributes pensions. The alternative means of financing retirement incomes is through a funded system, where workers' contributions are invested, namely through pension funds or retirement savings plans, which funds are entrusted to trustees. Accumulated contributions and investment returns on those contributions then pay for pensions. The meeting I was participating in was designed explicitly to help trustees affiliated to trade unions from various countries meet and exchange knowledge

---

[1] Source: <http://www.workerscapital.org/>, accessed 1 May 2016.

about their initiatives. Not surprisingly, then, most participants of the conference were socially engaged trade unionists from pension schemes from all over the world.

While conversing with participants during a coffee break, I could not prevent myself from observing more closely what seemed to appear to me a strange interaction. Representatives of the most reformist French trade union were deep in conversation with a representative of the most Marxist French trade union, whose presence at this conference had already surprised me. What could a trade union against the very existence of capital markets have to do with a trade union often denounced by its peers for being too close to employers? Intrigued, I walked towards them, hoping for the kind of lively, even conflictual discussion that any French citizen would expect from such a situation.

When I arrived, the discussion was drawing to an end. 'Thanks, we'll see each other there, then.' This sentence in itself was enough to trigger my interest. Given these two trade unions almost never agreed on anything, I could not believe that these people would want to meet; usually they barely accepted appearing together in public. I thought to myself that something of prime importance was going on; I worried that a veritable French revolution was being prepared. What I did not know at this time was that I would be lucky enough to attend this meeting and all the following ones. This was not an insurrection against the French government, but a rebellion against the way financial markets were working. Trade unionist trustees from all the French public contributory professional retirement savings plans were about to decide to take power in the investment chain. Their aim: to use their role as trustees to get sponsoring companies to better integrate environmental, social, and governance (ESG) criteria. Their means: collaborating across French pension schemes to leverage forces and assets.

What these trustees had not yet realized though was that to be able to impact companies, they would have to move the whole investment chain. Trustees were at one end of the chain—the beneficiaries being the ultimate actors—while the companies they planned to target were at the other end (see Figure 1.1). In between there were many actors to convince before these trustees could reach their targets: in particular, investment managers, brokers, trade unions, and rating agencies. The use of retirement savings as weapons against the exploitation of workers required French trade unionists to rethink their entire mode of reasoning and action. Strikes were useless: beneficiaries were not all employees of the companies in which their money was invested. Lobbying against the French government was pointless: it did not control the investment chain. Pressuring companies was hopeless: the amount of money that was actually invested in each company was not significant enough to give these funds any bargaining power. Trustees believed that the only way to make a difference with the savings they had been entrusted was to create ripples that would run along the entire investment chain. The investment chain, however, turned out to be stickier than they anticipated.

Elaborating on these findings, this chapter shows that the expansion of the investment chain over the past decades has rendered the action of trade unions more difficult than might have been envisaged forty years ago when Drucker (1976) predicted that socialism would come to America through the ownership of the means of production by the workers themselves, by way of their pension funds. Through regulation, the US constrains pension funds' ability to influence investment decisions (McCarthy 2014).[2] This chapter suggests such regulation might now have become superfluous, since the way in which constituents of the chain are linked to one another thwarts any attempt at autonomous action by a single actor such as a pension fund, even in a country with a strong tradition of centralized state intervention like France. Contrary to what Drucker imagined, the 'unseen revolution' might not come from the pension funds but from the investment chain itself.

Coordinating as Trustees

I went back to my seat, thinking about what had just happened, immediately writing down a brief description of the episode on a piece of paper. Trained as an ethnographer, I used to take notes on almost every event I judged to be significant in my life. As an inductive field researcher, I had no plan. If something gripped me, I simply followed it. And this intrigued me. At lunch I succeeded in sitting at the table of the French trade unionists. I sat down close to my friend, a trade unionist I had met during my PhD and who had invited me to the conference. He introduced me to his peers in such a nice way that people were immediately well disposed towards me. Lunch was ending; everybody was going back to the lecture theatre, except the French trade unionists. They were talking about their next meeting. I started asking questions: 'But what is your plan?' 'We don't really know. We want to do something big. We need to collaborate.' 'But is it something official?' 'Not really, you know it is difficult for us to join together.' 'So, who is your target?' 'We have several plans, but we all agree that this company is a big problem.' The more we spoke, the more curious I became, and the more passionate they were. I asked, 'Do you think that I could attend? I mean, you know I am an ethnographer by training, I could just come and gather information on what

---

[2] For instance, the Employee Retirement Income Security Act (ERISA) of 1974 is a federal law that establishes minimum standards for pension plans to ensure that plan assets are not misused.

happens; this would be great for science!' They smiled at me. 'Yes, sure, come. It would be a very good thing if academics started paying attention to us.'

A few weeks later, I was at the meeting, together with a colleague who knew US pension funds very well. I thought it would be helpful for the French trustees to have his insights if needed. My colleague was as intrigued as I was. The meeting took place in the boardroom of one of the largest French public contributory professional retirement savings plans. Trustees were entering the room. The member of the Marxist trade union I saw at the conference sat down in front of me, silent. A trustee belonging to the most reformist trade union came and started teasing him: 'Does your confederation know you are here? I will take a picture of you and post it on Facebook!' As the reformist trustee took his phone out, laughing, the Marxist trustee turned pale. 'Are you kidding me?' he complained. 'Stop that. This is not funny.' For trade unions normally so opposed to one another, to collaborate was unusual and the trustees were aware of this extraordinary situation.

Everybody introduced themselves. There were around twenty trustees in the room, belonging to different trade unions, representatives of all the French public contributory professional retirement savings plans. These funds were created at the beginning of the twenty-first century as a consequence of the shift from a pay-as-you-go retirement system towards a funded pension system. They were jointly administered by employers and employees' unions. In practice, this meant that half of the trustees were appointed by the trade unions (eight trade unions in total), and half by the French government (trustees who were sometimes members of a trade union themselves). People in the room were well educated, often high up in the hierarchy of their trade unions, and had important political connections. One person was not a trade unionist but a politician, representing the regions of France,[3] a former member of the French Socialist Party, but by that time a member of the French Green Party. I swiftly understood that he was closely involved in what was happening.

This was actually the first meeting of what its members had named RAIR (*Réseau d'Administrateurs pour l'Investissement Responsable*, the Network of Trustees for Responsible Investing). Altogether, these members represented €42 billion and six million beneficiaries (all the employees of French central and local government), the latter a number which was expected to grow in the following decade since the national pay-as-you-go retirement system was in trouble because of the inability of working generations to pay the pensions of the elderly who were living longer (Roche 2015). Participants explained in general terms to their peers what was happening in their funds and trade

---

[3] That is to say he had been elected to a *Conseil régional*, a body representing one of the French regions.

unions. Almost all participants had received warning emails from their superiors: trade unions themselves tended to disapprove of the meeting. It was not normal for French trade unions to work together. The biggest problem, however, was that several trade unions were against the public use of workers' capital to influence companies. Publicly engaging as shareholders might give the impression that these trade unions were endorsing the use of capital markets to provide pensions. Several trade unions regarded this capitalist system as individualistic and dangerous; they were instead in favour of a national retirement system based on solidarity between generations.

To address this problem, trustees agreed that their network would remain informal. 'This is not an official trade union meeting. We are just individuals who want to share knowledge and ideas as trustees. We have the right to do that.' The meeting ended with this agreement. I asked several participants if I could interview them, under a confidentiality agreement with the RAIR. They laughed at me: 'Didn't you understand that we don't exist!' Our cooperation would be based on trust, as with everybody in the room, although, unlike the others, I had nothing to lose. They were activists aiming to transform the use of the retirement funds at their own risk, for the simple reason that they believed they had a social duty to do so.

Bringing Together the Investment Chain

In the following months, I interviewed five members I had identified as leaders of the movement. The funds they were managing integrated ESG criteria and the trade unions they belonged to were somehow supportive of the use of pension funds to put pressure on companies. Consequently, they had little issue with going public. They were nevertheless fully aware of the difficulties faced by their peers—issues that these trustees later confirmed to me. Their question hence was, 'How can we trigger change inside companies, without going public, while protecting workers' jobs?' The network agreed on a strategy: favouring a collaborative and discreet form of shareholder engagement throughout the investment chain. Public naming and shaming campaigns that might endanger trustees and workers' jobs had to be avoided.

Several months after the first meeting, the second meeting was about to happen, at 2 p.m. I had succeeded in booking a lunch with the politician at 1 p.m. He was there to size me up. One hour later, he knew everything about my life and I knew nothing about him. Why was he a member of the RAIR? What was his role? What was the position of the French regional authorities? I had no idea. The second meeting started and I could immediately sense that many discussions had happened in between. The network had its press release ready, difficulties with the trade unions seemed to have been managed, and everybody agreed quickly on organizing RAIR's first official workshop.

This workshop was scheduled for 23 October 2013. The room was crowded: the main leaders of French responsible investing were present—investment managers, social rating agencies, brokers, trustees of both public and private pension funds, consultants and proxy voting companies—together with trade unionist board members of French listed companies.[4] The topic of the workshop was the 'Fair Dividend'. The RAIR trustees started to explain who they were and what they wanted:

> We funded this network because we want to increase our competences to favour responsible investing.[5] We work together with the eight representative trade unions of the country so as to put together, in due course, a shareholder engagement policy that would be able to influence annual meetings. There is no media in the room. There won't be any minutes of the meeting. We are here to work together on important topics in a thorough manner.

Several academics had been invited to present their work on the cost of capital and the links between dividends and economic, social, and environmental performance. The overall topic of the workshop was better to understand what a 'fair dividend' might be. In other words, trustees wanted to estimate the amount of dividends a company should distribute so that value created by the company might be shared in an adequate and fair manner between employees, shareholders, and other stakeholders. Workshop participants had a very good knowledge of the workings of financial markets and were happy to discuss these concerns together. Most asset owners and investment managers in favour of RI indeed believed that it was better for a company to re-invest most of its profits rather than distributing everything to shareholders. The meeting was anything but a superficial chat over coffee. One conversation ran thus:

TRUSTEE 1: Our role is to show that we are responsible investors when it comes to our expectations. If we use a 6 or 7 per cent discount rate in our retirement system, by implication we're asking equity markets to do 15 per cent.[6] This is a planned catastrophe.

---

[4] In 2014, 18 per cent of conventional funds managed in France were said to systematically integrate ESG criteria into their investment processes (known as ESG integration) while funds that labelled themselves 'socially responsible' represented 7 per cent of total French assets under management (Novethic 2015).

[5] Responsible investing is understood here as investing assets in a way that favours the development of a sustainable real economy, which will ultimately benefit workers while protecting the planet.

[6] Fifteen per cent is regarded as the minimum return on investment necessary in order to provide adequate benefits on retirement, particularly in the case of defined benefit pension plans (see Chapter 3).

TRUSTEE 2: But the problem is that we are obliged to ask for 15 per cent to give our beneficiaries more than the inflation rate.

TRUSTEE 3: We are the markets. Markets are not anonymous people; how can we meet our fiduciary duty?[7] We manage assets and we have a role to play in the economy, of which we are one constituent element.[8]

INVESTMENT MANAGER 1: We are only investment managers; this is your role as asset owners to decide what you want.

TRUSTEE 4: Let's be frank. The French government also plays a role. I mean some companies have been saved only because of political reasons.

INVESTMENT MANAGER 2: Companies don't know how to communicate. That is the reason why they increase the dividends. It is a just a signal for comfort.

After three hours of discussion, informed by several academic studies, the meeting ended and everybody agreed that it was a good initiative. According to workshop participants, there was nowhere all those in the industry interested in being more socially responsible could meet. RAIR trustees were happy overall, but would have been much happier if more trustees had come, especially from private pensions and employee savings funds. Building on this success, however, the RAIR began to publish a series of position papers in the media, dealing with various topics including stock options, tax evasion, climate change, and the social economy.

On 4 January 2014, I received an email inviting me to RAIR's second workshop, scheduled for a few days later.

> You are invited to our forthcoming seminar on January 15, organized with and proposed by the United Auto Workers (UAW), on the subject of 'Trade Union Freedom'. Trade union freedom is under threat: can Corporate X's[9] case be tackled with shareholder dialogue?

I was surprised to see a company name in the workshop title. Although I wasn't expecting any journalists to be present, I wondered whether the RAIR had decided to start a public naming and shaming campaign. The room was much bigger than for the previous workshop, and crowded. People had obviously heard about the first workshop and were intrigued by the title of the second one. The public contributory professional retirement savings funds were managing dozens of billions of euros; what trustees thought about

---

[7] Fiduciary duty does not exist as such in France but trustees still use this term to refer to their responsibilities (cf. later in this chapter for more explanations).

[8] In French the trustee in question used the term *agencement*, difficult to translate into English; readers familiar with the sociology of Bruno Latour and Michel Callon, or the philosophy of Deleuze and Guattari which influenced the former, will know that it is often translated as 'assemblage'. Here we have opted for the simpler concept of 'constituent element', but the idea is implied that 'the economy' is a series of heterogeneous constituent elements arranged in relation to other elements, as opposed to a uniform 'thing'.

[9] Corporate X is a pseudonym, and refers to an automotive company.

145

this company therefore mattered to the rest of the industry. I sat down, looking at the audience, and noticed an African-American woman sitting close to the organizers, speaking in English to some other Americans. On the table were headphones for English and French translation. On the wall was a videoconference system. There was something odd about this workshop. It was 4 a.m. in New York (i.e. 10 a.m. in Paris), but someone planned to speak to us. People in the room wondered what was happening. It was no longer just the actors of the French responsible investing world talking to each other; the US had stepped in too.

The RAIR trustees welcomed everybody and explained:

> We have organized this workshop together with the International Union, United Automobile, Aerospace and Agricultural Implement Workers of America (UAW),[10] because they have an issue in Mississippi and we can help them. It happens to be that Corporate X—of which we are all shareholders or connected to—has plants in this state where trade unions are not allowed. The goal of this workshop is to understand the situation and see what we can do together. There is no journalist in the room, we're among friends, and we have the power to make a change. Let's do it.

I was astounded. It was the first time that French institutional investors had decided to engage in such a manner. None of the members of the RAIR had told me about this initiative. Indeed, it was a complete surprise for everybody in the room.

The meeting proceeded as follows. First, the person in New York—who was the Director of an influential NGO, known worldwide—explained to us what was happening in Mississippi and what could be done. Then, a famous engaged academic disclosed what he had found when studying Corporate X in this state. According to the academic, Corporate X did not seem to authorize workers to form trade unions. At this moment, the African-American woman I had noticed when I entered the room started to speak. She was a worker at one of the plants in question and the people sitting beside her were UAW representatives. She explained to us in considerable detail what her daily life at the plant was like: the difficult working conditions, the long hours, the low salaries, the fear of being fired if workers formed a union, the risk she had taken to come and speak to us. She was close to tears. Everybody in the room was moved. The situation was, however, somewhat surreal. We were in the centre of Paris, drinking espresso and eating croissants, expecting an intellectual debate, of the kind the French cherish—and we ended up jumping into what we had hitherto imagined to be African-American life in Mississippi as it might have been in the 1950s. The person sat down, everybody applauded and

---

[10] UAW because it is usually known by its abbreviated name, the United Auto Workers Union.

congratulated her on her courage. Following this, UAW representatives and a lawyer also spoke, explaining the legal situation in detail.

The RAIR politician concluded the presentation: 'This is the situation. Nobody in this room can any longer pretend to ignore it. We are responsible for it. We have shares or we work for or we evaluate this company. We can do something. Let's talk.' The debate could start. One exchange went as follows:

INVESTMENT MANAGER 1: You are the asset owners; you decide if you want us to divest. This is your choice.

TRUSTEE 1: You know that there is no fiduciary duty in France, we have little power,[11] the French government has more power. And you know perfectly well that your investment management company manages its own assets, so you are a shareholder too.

INVESTMENT MANAGER 1: OK, let's imagine that you want us to divest from this company. How can I do that if I have no dedicated mandate? I mean your assets are pooled with other investors' assets who might not share your viewpoint. So we cannot divest the entire fund just because of one investor. And even if we had a dedicated mandate, there are still the other asset owners for whom we are working and they might disagree.

TRUSTEE 2: Divest your own assets to start with! In addition, as an investment management company, you are required to vote, you have the power.

INVESTMENT MANAGER 1: No, we manage on behalf of asset owners, we cannot decide for them.

TRUSTEE 2: You're kidding. What about all the mutual funds you are managing for your parent company? At least you can raise the issue during the annual meeting.

INVESTMENT MANAGER 2: How could we do that? Once again, it would mean that the entire investment management company would have to engage with the company. We cannot, we have other funds and some of our clients would disagree.

TRUSTEE 3: I confess; it is a really sad situation. But these are only a few plants. This company is global. Should we divest just for that? I mean, in such a case, we should divest from all companies. . . . And how come this company is well assessed by social rating agencies? I had no clue that was happening.

SOCIAL RATING AGENCY ANALYST: You know, it is only a small part of the criteria we are using to assess companies; we factor many things into our evaluation.

INVESTMENT MANAGER 3: Can we talk to the company's trade unionists? We have several trade unionist board members of the company here. Let's ask them.

---

[11] Explained later in the chapter.

TRADE UNIONIST BOARD MEMBER OF CORPORATE X: It is so difficult, this is another country and we have no power on their jurisdiction. I mean this plant belongs to the Y brand, which is not legally based in France. You know there was this merger. You should contact the trade unions in the other country. And we have already so many problems to deal with here, I mean in France.

TRUSTEE 1: But come on, the CEO is the CEO of both brands! He does not wake up the morning as CEO of X and go to bed in the evening as CEO of Y. This is ridiculous.

TRADE UNIONIST BOARD MEMBER OF CORPORATE X: Yes, but, the law is the law, there is nothing we can do really.

TRUSTEE 4: So trying to propose a resolution at the French annual general meeting is pointless?

INVESTMENT MANAGER 1: First, I doubt that you would gather enough investors to join you, and you know you need to attain a threshold to be able to propose a resolution. Plus, this resolution has to be linked to the agenda of the meeting, so you need to frame it in a way that is legally acceptable. And anyway, this plant belongs to the other brand.

TRUSTEE 4: What about going to the media, making people aware of the situation, our beneficiaries for instance?

BROKER: Do you really think that the French would care about what happens in Mississippi while people are losing their jobs in the automotive industry here?

TRUSTEE 2: The French government should step in.

TRUSTEE 3: Are you serious? Commenting on what is happening in Mississippi?

TRUSTEE 2: Or the media. Or consumers.

TRUSTEE 3: Which ones? There, they don't care. Here, maybe, but us, what can we do in practice? Nothing really. This is what NGOs are for.

TRUSTEE 2: What about the national contact point at the OECD?[12]

TRUSTEE 3: Yes, good idea. But again not our duty, right? More of a trade union move?

TRUSTEE 2: As investment managers, could you talk to the company in private and tell them that some of your investors have raised the issue?

INVESTMENT MANAGER: Yes, we can do that.

SOCIAL RATING AGENCY ANALYST: As social rating agencies, we can do that as well. If that helps.

---

[12] The OECD Guidelines for multinational enterprises are supported by a mechanism of National Contact Points (NCPs), agencies established by adhering governments to promote and implement the Guidelines. NCPs assist enterprises and their stakeholders to take appropriate measures to further the observance of the Guidelines. They provide a mediation and conciliation platform for resolving practical issues that may arise with the implementation of the Guidelines. Source: <http://www.oecd.org>, accessed 2 June 2016.

INVESTMENT MANAGER 1:   But really, you are the asset owners, you are the
ones who decide.

TRUSTEE 1:   We already explained it to you. We are trying our best to
mobilize everybody but we are appointed with no real power. If we do
something that is disapproved of by our organization, we are out. There is
no fiduciary duty in this country, just duty. And beneficiaries have no
clue really that their money could be used to trigger change, they focus on
their pensions and I understand that.

The meeting ended. I was very struck by what I had seen. The entire investment chain was there: from the worker in Mississippi to the trustee, including
investment managers, social rating agencies, brokers, board members of the
company under fire, trade unions, and also lawyers and NGOs. Almost no
actor had been forgotten; participants evoked the possibility of reaching the
beneficiaries, government, OECD, the media, and even French citizens. Everybody was trying to find a way to help the underpaid African-American woman
sitting in front of them, yet nobody could find any viable solution. Each time
the responsibility of a particular actor in the investment chain was evoked,
that actor just passed the responsibility to another. It was as if the investment
chain was slipping through the hands of those who were its very components.

Why is the Investment Chain so Difficult to Move?

The fact that this meeting took place at all is in itself exceptional. Exchanges
along the investment chain tend to be either confined to particular links of the
chain (see Chapters 2 and 4) or instead disembodied in the form of 'collective
calculative devices' (Callon and Muniesa 2005) (see Chapter 5). Almost never
do actors from along the length of the chain convene. Additionally, few
industry actors are ready to play a societal role. The French context is rather
unique in this respect, since it has long been commonplace in France (even for
economists) to assume that financial markets and society are intertwined
(Paris Europlace 2015). The fact that most of the participants belonged
to trade unions and/or the world of responsible investing also facilitated
these exchanges. Although rarely dedicated to the solving of a specific social
issue, such arenas of discussion do nevertheless exist in other countries, albeit
in different forms: trustees' education networks (e.g. in common law jurisdictions), political governance structures (e.g. Scandinavian countries), or
professional conferences, among others. Such discussions might hence *theor-
etically* occur everywhere.

When exchanging views, the participants of the meeting identified several
reasons that rendered shareholder engagement with Corporate X difficult to

Table 7.1 The investment chain and the attempted transformation of Corporate X's attitude towards unionization

Actors	Potential leverage for change	Elements preventing change
Asset owners and trustees	Collaborative and discreet shareholder engagement; Public naming and shaming campaign; Divestment; Proposing a resolution at the AGM.	Minority shareholding: not enough shares to propose a resolution at the annual meeting; Do not want to threaten jobs at Corporate X; No fiduciary duty: limited responsibility and limited power.
Asset owners and beneficiaries	Pressure on the trustees to engage/divest from Corporate X.	Not aware of the situation; Remote issue compared to problems in the French automotive industry; Perceived as potentially costly in terms of financial performance.
Investment managers	Engagement with the company; Proposing a resolution at the AGM.	Manage on behalf of asset owners: cannot voice their concerns as an investment management company; Diversity of clients and therefore viewpoints.
(Social) Rating agencies and brokers	Reduce the company's (social) rating; Engagement with the company.	Mississippi's plants are a very limited part of the activities of Corporate X; Cannot trace all these types of issues worldwide.
French government	Ask for more regulation.	Not the responsibility of the French government.
French trade unions inside Corporate X	Put some pressure on their US counterparts to authorize unions.	Different jurisdiction; Corporate X belongs to the company's other brand (following the merger).
Media and NGOs	Public name and shame campaign.	Too far away for French citizens to be interested in the issue.

implement (see Table 7.1)—almost all these attempts at justification actually referred to the links of the investment chain. Key in this chain is the relationship between asset owners—embodied by the trustees—and investment managers. When asset owners have dedicated mandates—which is often the case for large retirement funds—investment managers have to implement trustees' decisions when it comes to voting and divestment. However, when funds are invested in collective investments in transferable securities (UCITS), known in the US and Canada as mutual funds, it is often investment management companies that decide.[13] Since investment managers manage assets on behalf of their clients, who are diverse, they are usually reluctant to appear too socially engaged.

In the case of shareholder engagement per se, even when there are dedicated mandates, investment managers usually refuse to engage. Contrary to voting

---

[13] At least in France, following the implementation of the LSF Law no. 2001–420, 15 May 2001 concerning new economic regulations, French investment management companies are required to define a voting policy, exercise their rights, and account for their voting practices for all the assets they manage.

policy or divestment decisions, shareholder engagement is indeed carried out at the asset management company level not at the portfolio one, raising reputational issues for the asset management company. Knowing that, trustees during the workshop tried to convince investment managers to act based on the fact that they often manage the assets of their parent company, an internal client that is often effectively the largest asset owner for which they work.[14] In other words, the trustees hoped that the parent company could act as an asset owner, not as an investment manager. Few investment managers, however, want to engage,[15] notably because the target company is itself frequently a client of the parent company (often a bank or an insurance company) (Davis 2008; Useem 1996).[16] The ramifications of the investment chain are actually so numerous that any decision has abundant potential consequences that actors usually want to avoid.

It was apparent that social rating agencies and brokers also had limited power: the company's problem with the unions was of so little importance when compared to the sheer size of the company that based on the criteria analysts used to assess companies, its ratings would not have been affected (see Chapter 6). The French trade unionist board members of Corporate X bemoaned the situation, but could not do anything either since the plant belonged to another brand based overseas. The media, NGOs, and the French government were all invoked, but none of them appeared to be a good candidate because the issue was not a national one. Trustees could neither divest nor conduct a name and shame campaign to protect workers' jobs, because many of the trade unions feared going public. Nor could trustees put forward a resolution at the annual general meeting because the percentage of shares they held was too low, and resolutions had to conform to the meeting agenda. Lastly, trustees did not believe that they could convince their beneficiaries, since the latter were rarely aware of how their money was invested, focusing instead on the pensions they received. The only solution proposed was consequently to ask investment managers, social rating agencies, and brokers to tell Corporate X that some investors were concerned by the lack of union rights in Mississippi.

---

[14] This is not the case for independent boutiques, however.

[15] However, some insurance and bank companies have started divesting from some industries. For instance, AXA divested from high-risk coal funds in 2015 and from the tobacco industry in 2016. In 2016, the fossil fuel divestment movement included 527 institutions worldwide, representing $3.4 trillion. See <http://gofossilfree.org/commitments/>, accessed 9 June 2016.

[16] Another possibility is to pool money into a fund managed by a proxy voting company whose goal is explicitly to engage with companies. The identity of the investors who participate in such a fund can remain unknown to prevent sanctions in case of conflicts of interests (i.e. if the parent company is a bank or an insurance company). Such funds are nevertheless marginal in France and not much used by savings retirement funds because of disclosure requirements, meaning that these funds can only conceal where they invest with great difficulty.

While I was in the metro coming back from the meeting, watching the stations come and go, I wondered, 'What can I do as an academic?' Like everybody else in the room, I believed I was too small to have an impact. I was thinking about what I'd heard at the first workshop: 'We are the markets.' 'Am I the market?' 'Am I responsible for this person suffering?' I perceived myself as someone who cared about others and was aware of her societal impact, but I had to admit that I was the first one to complain if something was going wrong with my pensions or the prices of products I was buying. I was the market, but so was everybody else in the room. The markets were everybody, and because they were everybody, it was difficult to change them.

The Problem of Fiduciary Duty

French trustees in particular appeared to be stuck: 'We try our best to move everybody but we are just appointed with no real power.' How could this be possible? I had to interview the person who uttered this sentence: the politician. I chased him for months, eventually meeting him by chance in a multi-stakeholder meeting organized by the French Ministry of Ecology and Sustainable Development, in which I participated as an expert. At the coffee break he explained to me that 'We need a fiduciary duty that is broader than financial obligation, because without fiduciary duty, we don't have much power.'[17]

In common law jurisdictions, that is to say in countries where legal rules are generally interpreted in light of the precedent of relevant court decisions, such as the US, UK, or Canada, fiduciary duty applies to institutional investors. Where institutions or individuals are the trustees or fiduciaries of funds, they are mandated by the law to manage or supervise the management of assets in the best interests of the individual beneficiaries or investors (Hawley et al. 2014: 1). In common law countries, institutional investors are usually governed by the modern prudent investor rule, which incorporates both a duty of care—the duty to act prudently—and a duty of loyalty—all investment decisions must be motivated by the interests of the funds' beneficiaries and/or the purposes of the fund. As a trustee put it to us:

> As a trustee, remember, you've got limited upside and you've got unlimited downside. You realize that actually your risk of going to jail has just gone up a bit because if something ever goes wrong, if the regulator says, we warned you and

[17] This problem of fiduciary duty has also been identified elsewhere as critical and is briefly explained later in the chapter (see Black 1990; Camara 2005; Davis 2008 for further explanation).

you disregarded our warning, you guys are clearly negligent. Once you have introduced the negligent word, you're in real trouble.... You are the responsible person; you're the one who will go to jail. My understanding is you cannot dispose of your fiduciary duties; you can't subcontract and say, that's me done. So you still have that go to jail outlet. You can hire someone to do work for you as a fiduciary himself or herself, I think you still remain fiduciary. In other words, you are responsible.

Even if in most countries the law does not explicitly mention what the best interests of the beneficiaries consist in, trustees have often understood their role as maximizing short-term financial performance. In the US the use by pension funds of their assets to pursue non-shareholder value maximizing objectives remains highly controversial and potentially against the law (Agrawal 2012). The position in the UK has notably been influenced by the *Cowan v. Scargill* case (1985) which became an important precedent for interpreting fiduciary duty as mere financial performance, though the judge later insisted that his ruling had been misinterpreted. Scholars have identified this narrow but widespread financial interpretation of fiduciary duty as one of the main reasons that has prevented the systematic integration of ESG factors into investment practices to date (Deringer 2005; Sandberg 2011).

Although the short-term financial understanding of fiduciary duty still dominates, other interpretations of what the best interests of the beneficiaries are have also emerged (see Principles for Responsible Investment 2015). The England and Wales Law Commission's report on the fiduciary duties of investment intermediaries has notably explained that the consideration of ESG factors by pension fund trustees is entirely consistent with their fiduciary duty to beneficiaries (Law Commission 2014). Several decades ago already, the US case known as the *Board of Trustees v. Mayor of Baltimore City*[18] destabilized the singular focus on profit maximization. More recently, in April 2015, sixty large institutional investors, representing a combined $1.9 trillion in assets, sent a letter to the Securities and Exchange Commission, expressing concern that oil and gas companies were not disclosing sufficient information in their financial statements about carbon asset risks and the possibility of reduced global demand for oil. Given these recent developments, an increasing number of financial actors claim that climate change, among other non-financial topics, should be part of the fiduciary duty of care, diligence, and prudence (Gold and Scotchmer 2015).

Civil law jurisdictions, such as France, Germany, and Japan, do not mention fiduciary duty as such. However, these countries impose a similar set of core responsibilities on institutional investors, usually including a duty to act

---

[18] *Board of Trustees v. Mayor of Baltimore City*, 317 Md. 72, 562 A.2d 720 (1989), cert. den. sub nom. *Lubman v. Baltimore City*, 493 U.S. 1093.

conscientiously, to seek profit, and to take into account the fundamentals of the modern portfolio approach to investment, that is to say diversification as a way of reducing risk. The absence of fiduciary duty has often been described as facilitating the integration of ESG concerns into investment processes (Richardson 2013). Trustees in these countries are indeed legally authorized to pursue non-financial goals in addition to providing financial return for their beneficiaries. For instance, the French retirement reserve fund (FRR—Fonds de Réserve des Retraites), responsible until 2040 for the management of assets entrusted to it by public authorities in order to supplement the basic pension fund, officially endorses the goal of encouraging the development of a 'sustainable finance'.[19] The lack of fiduciary duty also has a side-effect, however, one the politician explained to me. In comparison to their UK or US peers, the RAIR trustees felt that they lacked power. Since they were not legally responsible for the investment decisions they made, they believed that they were more accountable to the supervisory authorities employing them than their common law peers.[20] Though they would like to trigger change within the investment chain towards sustainability, they could not act without the political support of the ministry, company, or trade union they belong to. Yet this support was complicated to obtain, resulting most often in the maintenance of existing investment practices.

So Near, Yet so Far

While conversing with the politician, I started to understand what he was doing in the RAIR. He was pushing a law that would oblige French institutional investors to disclose the ESG aspects of their investment processes. Later, he sent me an invitation for a discreet lobbying action planned at 8 p.m. at the French parliament while the law was being discussed. Together with some members of parliament and other RAIR members, he had convened a small meeting bringing together investment managers, brokerage companies, journalists, and asset owners to speak with politicians about responsible investing and the need to adopt this law. It occurred to me that now politicians were joining the investment chain too.

At the end of the meeting, I went over to the RAIR members; I was about to leave the country and knew that my data collection was ending. 'I will

---

[19] The aim of the FRR is to promote sustainable wealth creation and job growth, in a way that is consistent with certain shared values that promote balanced economic, social, and environmental development. Source: <http://www.fondsdereserve.fr/en>, accessed 1 June 2016.

[20] The need for political support is also present in common law countries, but the RAIR trustees believed they had less power because of the absence of fiduciary duty. More research is needed to be able to compare both legal regimes in this regard.

certainly write a book chapter about the second workshop, you know, with this person from Mississippi. I would like to know how you organized it and what happened afterwards. Can we talk about it?' At that moment the politician appeared. 'You should ask him', a trade unionist told me. The politician agreed to meet me at a café, a few weeks later.

We started talking. 'I cannot believe that the law was adopted.[21] It is crazy!' He concurred: 'I know; I didn't think that it would be the case either.' I asked: 'So, can you explain this Mississippi story to me?' The politician told me the whole story. Some RAIR members had participated in a conference in Washington in 2013 organized by the Committee on Workers' Capital, where they exchanged ideas and experiences with their North American peers. During these exchanges they discovered what was happening in this company. Upon their return, the RAIR trustees decided to do something. For some months the French trustees went back and forth with the UAW, the NGOs, and other US trustees. The main problem they faced was that the US employees and US trade unions themselves did not see why these French trustees wanted to investigate the situation. They were suspicious. Why would an institutional investor in a far away country want to help them? According to the US employees' representatives, shareholders were the evil people demanding the 15 per cent return on investment that forced them to work like beasts. The notion of a 'fair dividend' meant nothing to them. It therefore took months for the RAIR members to convince their US counterparts that they were actually on their side and could help them because they were related to each other through the flow of capital.

Curious, I asked: 'But what was the result of the workshop? What happened afterwards?' The politician answered: 'Nothing, really, at least in this company. Some investment managers raised questions, social rating agencies made a tiny change in their evaluation, and we discussed the topic at board meetings. But you know, it is really difficult to move. At least there will be something written about it now, thanks to you.' Leaving the café, I did not know what to think: should I rejoice because of the fact that everybody got together and attempted to do something, or should I get depressed because nothing happened? The only thing I was sure of was that it was the investment chain that made us all meet and it was the same investment chain that made us all move apart.

---

[21] By adopting law no. 2015-992 on energy transition for green growth, France became the first country to introduce disclosure requirements for asset owners on their management of climate-related risks, and, more broadly, on the integration of ESG parameters into their investment policies. The law is perceived by the French investment industry to be the most advanced worldwide when it comes to non-financial concerns.

8

Conclusion

In this book, we have outlined the investment chain and explored its key components and attributes. We have shown that the chain enables as well as constrains. The actors that constitute the chain make decisions that are heavily influenced by their own position within it, and this influence does not come from their narrow financial interests alone. Closely connected to the chain's influence on decision-making is its enabling function. Figure 1.1 (Chapter 1) shows an investment chain structured around the flow of money from savers to the companies and governments that utilize those savings. Actors external to the chain strongly influence particular links (in the case of governments and regulatory authorities, arguably every link) in the chain through their advice, judgement, and regulation. Even within the chain, however, we have demonstrated that what is flowing—both up and down the chain—is not only money. The chain enables money to move, but it also enables the flow of information, advice, performance, and relationships. These all have an influence on how decisions are made at individual links within the chain, and ultimately on how the final decision is taken as to the investments that are made.

Our analysis of an investment chain comes at a time when the superficially competing view of financial markets as networks (e.g. Uzzi 1999; Allen and Babus 2009) is influential. We do not see this as a rival theory. As noted in Chapter 1, we see the investment chain as a subset of financial market networks. A number of the issues we address in this book to do with the nature of the interaction between actors constituting various links in the chain are consistent with those sociological approaches to financial markets that approach them by way of the concept of embeddedness, approaches which often focus on networks (e.g. Granovetter 1985). The chain is, however, a way of thinking about financial markets that serves to make clearer the character of the various interactions. This results from a focus on the different roles actors play within the investment chain, and therefore within financial markets. Network-based approaches can encompass these different roles—Kellard et al.

(2016), for example, cover material somewhat similar to our Chapter 4—but the methodological challenges of using networks to consider all the links we highlight in the investment chain are very considerable. The complexity of such an approach may well obscure much of the real tenor of the interactions this book discusses.

The concept of the investment chain also allows a complementary approach to the question of where influence resides *within* finance. For network-based approaches, simply put, the strongest power flows are those that emanate from the most connected node in the network. This risks down-playing the different roles played by financial market actors and the influence that results. It also means that important roles in finance remain under-researched: investment consultants are one such area, as discussed in Chapter 3. The focus of research has tended to be on those who make the final invest-ment or lending decision, fund managers or banks, with other market actors being seen as hierarchically arranged below these 'decision-makers', where they are acknowledged at all. To us, this misunderstands the nature of the investment process and the multiple influences on decisions. This does not imply, however, that equality of influence is the rule across the investment chain. Some actors are clearly more influential than others, and understand-ing this variation and the reasons behind it remain an important area for further research.

The investment chain matters to outcomes in financial markets. As this book has demonstrated, more academic study of the chain is needed if we are to understand current markets and change within them. Throughout the book, we have emphasized a range of outcomes in which the workings of the investment chain are important. These include a range of issues with broad societal consequences. We have focused on investors' investment time-horizons (see also Kay 2012), responsible investment broadly (see Chapter 6), and, in Chapter 7, attempts by trade unionists to use the pension fund invest-ments of their members to influence a company's treatment of its workers. In each case, the investment chain had a major influence. In particular, the fund manager 'link' increases the likelihood of short-term investment and thwarts trade union efforts. The discussion of responsible investment shows in add-ition how the investment chain within an investment management company can act as a hindrance, in this case to responsible investment (see also Chapters 2 and 4). A wide-ranging literature has seen a link between longer-term perspectives and company policies that favour other stakeholders than simply the providers of capital (e.g. Hall and Soskice 2001; Jackson and Petraki 2011). Numerous official reports, going back in the UK at least until the 1930s, have worried about the economic impact of a lack of long-term capital (Macmillan Committee 1931). We could have as easily focused on issues around climate change and attempts to ensure that investors both encourage climate change mitigation efforts and incorporate the investment risks inherent in some of that mitigation (for example, for producers of the fossil fuels that will be not usable; e.g. Carbon Tracker 2011; Ansar et al. 2013), or alternatively inherent in climate change itself (including increased damage to infrastructure and higher insurance claims). Just as the Kay Commission on short-termism in UK equity investment focused heavily on investment chain issues (see also Garratt and Hamilton 2017), so those considering environmental issues, and responsible investment more broadly, are forced to address the investment chain (see, for example, Principles for Responsible Investment 2016: 7). Taken together, it is difficult to see a more important set of issues for all societies currently than economic growth, workers' rights, and climate change. The investment chain has implications for all three, and, in case more was needed, Chapter 1 raises the question of the implications for inequality. Despite the investment chain's importance, and its ubiquity in official reports across a variety of concerns with financial market operations, the chain, as Chapter 1 notes, is rarely the subject of explicit academic enquiry. It is even less often the subject of public debate. If a poorly functioning investment chain contributes to lower growth, inequality, poor workers' rights, and a hotter planet, its functioning should be a matter of urgent political enquiry.

At its heart, there are two main issues with the operation of the investment chain. First, and a main focus of official reports, is how the views of asset owners—often, perhaps naïvely, assumed to be inherently long-term, responsible investors—can ensure that their preferences flow down the investment chain, to be reflected in the choices of investment and the nature of engagement with investee companies and countries. The second set of issues refers to the unintended consequences of attempts to solve what are broadly seen as principal–agent problems (see Chapter 3 for concerns with this approach). These issues, as outlined in Chapter 1, include herding, 'closet benchmarking', and the worsening of short-termism. In this concluding chapter, we consider the implications of the book for the main types of solutions offered to these two issues. At the risk of accusations of excessive negativity, we start with our overall conclusion: there are no simple solutions to the problems of the investment chain.

Attempts to Address Problems in the Investment Chain

It is clear throughout this book that there can be no guarantee that final investors' preferences will flow down the investment chain to be reflected in the ultimate investment decisions. In wider discussions of why this is not the case, the most common frame has been the principal–agent problem and its sibling, information asymmetries. This framing has in turn shaped the nature of a range of suggested solutions. As we discuss in the following, there are issues with the effectiveness, when they are considered in isolation, of them all.

Increased Information Disclosure

The problem of information asymmetries—of some actors having greater information than others and being able to exploit that advantage—would seem to have an obvious solution in greater disclosure. And unsurprisingly, increased disclosure as a solution to problems in finance has become something akin to Lily the Pink's Medicinal Compound: 'most efficacious in every case'.[1] The Asian Financial Crisis of 1997–8 begat the International Monetary Fund's Data Dissemination Initiative (Alexander et al. 2008), just as it is hoped that improved disclosure of climate change risks will bring greater financial market influence on mitigation efforts (Task Force on Climate Related-Financial Disclosures 2016); however, 'the demand for more disclosure is a process with no end' (Kay 2012: 46). For the *Kay Review*, increasingly frequent data provision can increase the incentive to short-termism. Available information is certainly already beyond available processing capacity, requiring strategies to deal with this overload (Simon 1955; Abolafia 1996). One of our number, perhaps betraying his own background in investment management, but also almost certainly right, doubts in Chapter 2 that investors into funds can ever fully understand. They 'deserve an explanation, and yet by virtue of not having themselves participated in the discussions leading to investment decisions, can never fully understand. Further explanation is always possible, and never comprehensive'. In other words, the principal–agent problem cannot ever be fully resolved by providing more information. It is not clear how guidelines or even regulation requiring certain standards of disclosure aimed at improving its utility can address information overload and inherent limits to the comprehensibility of specialized work. The presentation of information about performance is always itself a performance involving (possibly some dark) narrative arts, as emphasised in Chapter 2. The *Kay Review*'s (2012: 13) recommendations both to remove the requirement for quarterly reporting while encouraging 'succinct narrative reporting' risks increasing rather than decreasing the opportunities for such performance, and many readers will have plentiful experience of the subjectivity of explanations of underperformance, from their children and, for UK readers, their rail companies, if not their financial adviser.

---

[1] 'Lily the Pink' by The Scaffold. See <https://www.youtube.com/watch?v=2x8D4T–0v4>.

Equally fundamentally, increased information about investment perform-ance, however well organized, seems likely to increase the incentive to dele-gate. More information also highlights to its recipients their inability to analyse it. Analysis of the investment chain makes this clear. In Chapter 3, we discuss how both individuals and pension fund trustees react to their own limitations by employing the services of various other links in, or influences on, the investment chain, most obviously fund managers, independent finan-cial advisers, and investment consultants. However, a lack of information may also lead to 'unconscious loyalty' (Hirschman 1970: 91) from investors who fail to recognize poor performance. The continued existence of large numbers of mediocre-performing or 'closet benchmarking' retail funds would appear to suggest such unconscious loyalty, and other examples of apparent inaction by individual investors include their high propensity for accepting (by not indi-cating a preference) the default investment options in defined contribution pension schemes.

Seen in the context of the investment chain, this inactivity is a delegation, and a delegation that increases the length of the chain. Time- or expertise-constrained individual investors can of course still invest directly in shares or bonds, thereby delegating decision-making to company management. This was the situation in the 1950s and 1960s in the US and UK, the high point of management autonomy, or 'managerialism', and not a positive experience for those seeking 'shareholder value'. The increasing complexity of the invest-ment process, and the additional information flow attached to it, are as influential as the desire to diversify risk and increase liquidity that is often seen as a good reason for investors to employ fund managers. A similar logic applies to an investor who delegates part of the process of assessing fund managers to a company such as Morningstar. The *Kay Review* (2012: 30) sees the lengthening of the investment chain as a result of regulation and profes-sionalization, '[b]ut a principal driver of the growth of intermediation has been the decline of trust and confidence in the investment chain'. These three influences are all important, but an emphasis on problems of regulation, and especially on the decline of trust, risks obscuring the powerful underlying logic of the processes of delegation.

Two areas of increased disclosure do, however, appear more than justified. As highlighted in Chapter 1, fees and individual rewards are high in the invest-ment chain, and financial intermediation generally has not improved its efficiency since the nineteenth century in the US (Philippon 2015) and at least the 1950s in Europe (Bazot 2014). This is a staggering combination of facts, leaving it tempting to conclude that a central enabling feature of the investment chain is the way in which it enables the extraction of rents. Chapter 1 sets out one calculation of the consequences for a central societal issue: pension provision. The full disclosure of investment costs, if done in a sufficiently straightforward fashion—remarkably, a significant 'if'—is a reform that empowers investors rather than highlighting complexity in a process they may well not wish to take the time to understand. This is a necessary reform (Kay 2012), but in itself unlikely to be sufficient to reduce the high cost of the investment chain and the remuneration of those involved in it.

As discussed in Chapters 6 and 7, more information about the social and environmental impacts of the investment processes would also be beneficial. The extension of fiduciary duty towards the integration of non-financial concerns may explain why asset owners are increasingly asking for more accountability and transparency on these dimensions (see Chapter 7). The multiplication of NGOs and multi-stakeholders' initiatives specifically aiming to 'put finance at the service of society' (e.g. Finance Watch)[2] is additional evidence that the investment chain is not an isolated network composed of financial professionals alone but instead a socially embedded web of connections that have effects felt throughout society (see Chapter 6). It is therefore not surprising that societal expectations vis-à-vis the financial markets are growing—especially in Europe. An outcome of this may be that actors in the investment chain become increasingly accountable for how they participate in the solving of global challenges such as climate change, poverty, health, water scarcity, and inequality.

Shortening the Investment Chain

A further suggested solution to the problems inherent in the investment chain, including its cost, is to shorten it (e.g. Kay 2012: 46). Among the *Kay Review*'s less noted recommendations is to make individual investment directly into company shares easier, thereby removing all links in the chain (but not, it should be noted, lessening the influence of some external actors on the investment chain). To shorten the chain to any material extent in this way clearly represents a significant turning back of the clock, and seems unlikely to lead to a major resolution of the issues the *Kay Review* addresses (nor indeed does the review claim it will). The institutionalization of investment, the initial influence on the development of investment chains, is now most likely irreversible. Any shortening needs to still involve institutional investors in some form.

As already noted, the analysis here suggests that the investment chain represents, in many instances, a sensible response to issues faced by asset holders. Issues of expertise have been mentioned earlier; the insertion of investment consultants' 'fiduciary management' (see Chapter 3) is a solution

[2] <http://www.finance-watch.org/home>.

to another problem: the difficulties for trustees of making decisions in a timely fashion. As the *Kay Review* (2012: 35) suggests, and our analysis supports, there is a 'bias towards action' at most links in the investment chain, and this is likely, in aggregate, to increase short-termism. However, there are also equally prevalent and unavoidable biases towards inaction that harm investment performance at certain points in the chain, which can only be solved by adding further links. These links may be there in part to demonstrate rigour (see Chapter 2), but they also solve clear problems. In addition, we show throughout this book that links in the chain exist within institutions as well as between institutions. A final investment decision—the buying or selling of a particular share or bond—represents the culmination of a number of individual decisions involving different skill sets, and likely to be best made by different individuals or teams. The quantitative skills highlighted in Chapter 4 are one example, and part of a common divide in financial markets (see also Chapter 2). The broad asset allocation function—deciding between bonds and equities, choosing geographic regions, etc.—and the more specific decisions of targeted funds to buy or sell particular securities are obviously different functions, and can be performed within or across institutions. We would of course expect greater strength of relationships and trust within institutions than between them, but we cannot simply assume that an institution can reconcile different priorities as an individual would. Indeed, Chapters 2, 3, 4, 6, and 7 all suggest that differing interests within financial institutions may be closer to the norm than commonly recognized. In a number of cases, what is described fits closely with MacKenzie's (2011) 'clusters of evaluation practices', whereby different financial market actors bring contrasting evaluation approaches to the same investment decision. The quantitative strategists of Chapter 4 fall into that category.[3] However, elsewhere we are talking about different parts of the investment decision-making process, a vertical chain in Figure 1.1 rather than the horizontal representation implied by MacKenzie's clusters. In other words, some form of investment chain is better seen as almost inevitable in financial markets than as a product of regulation—problematic though much of the latter is—or as a general societal process towards greater specialization and professionalization; a process that in itself is almost certainly largely irreversible. It is questionable whether its reversal is in any case necessarily desirable: would a concentration of all the various investment decisions in a single team, or, worse, a single person (or even a single algorithm, though this is a far broader debate), result in better investment? Disclosure of cost should at least reveal the price paid for additional expertise and specialization, but there is clearly a price at which such expertise is worth paying for.

---

[3] In contrast to the different quantitative/qualitative distinction outlined by Larminat (2013; see Chapter 2).

Passive Investment

This is not to say that the investment performance of active fund managers is in aggregate good. There is little to suggest that the ever-expanding investment chain has improved performance, even as it has increased the percentage of many countries' GDP taken up with financial intermediation (Chapter 1; Philippon and Reshef 2013). It is well known that most active managers do not, after fees, outperform the particular market index against which they are measured, and, by definition, all fund managers cannot perform well relative to each other (Kay 2012).

Investors, whether institutional or retail, have drawn an obvious conclusion from this, as evidenced by the rise of passive investment funds. As discussed in Chapter 2, these funds—charging low fees to track the performance of a chosen index—could be an existential threat to certain parts of the active fund management industry. Since 2007, such funds have grown by 230 per cent to approximately US$6 trillion globally, compared to growth of only 54 per cent (albeit to US$24 trillion) for their active counterparts.[4] The result has been fee pressure on conventional active fund managers (see Chapter 1; French 2008). Passive funds essentially solve the principal–agent problem inherent to the investment chain by removing agential discretion at this particular link in the chain. Investors are almost guaranteed a better return than the aggregate performance of active fund managers in that particular asset class, and have few, if any, of the problems of selecting fund managers. The influence of other financial market actors, such as investment consultants, is also markedly reduced. There is a very lively debate about passive funds, and whether they represent an attractive alternative to active investment. Our purpose is not to reprise that debate here, but rather to focus on passive funds as a potential solution to problems caused by the investment chain.

Increasingly popular as they are, we cannot see passive funds as the silver bullet to solve these problems. Indeed, analysis focused on the investment chain highlights how the debate about passive funds is confined to only a part of the investment process: 'stock picking', or the choosing of individual securities in which to invest, and market timing.[5] The relative importance of asset allocation, individual security selection, and market timing is much debated (e.g. Brinson et al. 1986; Ibbotson and Kaplan 2000; Chen et al. 2010), but the debate highlights the different decisions lying behind any final investment. It is perhaps telling that the world's largest fund management company, BlackRock, combines funds that make asset allocation decisions with funds that are passive in terms of stock picking.

---

[4] Source: Morningstar, quoted in Mooney (2016).
[5] Although, as noted in Chapter 3, one constraint the chain imposes is limited fund manager latitude for market timing; their investors want them to be 'in the market'.

Even after acknowledging that passive investment involves only part of the investment decision-making process, we must still consider whether it contributes to, or mitigates, some of the problems with the investment chain. Deeg and Hardie (forthcoming) argue that passive investment should be seen as relatively patient. Passive fund managers will increase or decrease their holdings of a particular security as its relative price changes, to maintain the correct weighting of that security in the relevant index. The activity can be seen as impatient or short-term. However, these are changes at the margin, and the core holdings are likely to be maintained over extended periods, providing a security's relative performance is not so poor that it drops out of the index (for example, as a result of a constituent of the FTSE 100, an index of the largest 100 UK companies by market capitalization, ceasing to be one of the 100 largest). However, this long-term investment is unlikely to demonstrate the 'stewardship' of investee companies that is sought by, for example, the *Kay Review*. Because they compete on the low level of their fees and are judged only on their ability to match the index rather than absolute or relative performance, they are likely to see engagement with companies as an unacceptable cost. Passive investment funds will also never have the sort of concentrated portfolios whose substantial holdings of few investments make engagement more worthwhile and likely more effective. Further, their engagement is also not supported by a plausible threat of exit, an important underpinning for the efficacy of voice (Hirschman 1970). The costs of exit, in terms of increased 'tracking error', or deviation from the performance of the index, are too high. Substantial passive investment is therefore likely to result not in companies being pressured into longer-term decision-making, but in high autonomy for company management, with uncertain outcomes in terms of the type of company decisions (Davis 2008: 13; Shleifer and Vishny 1997: 742) that the *Kay Review* seeks, including regarding increased research and development spending.

The result is that active managers perform a necessary role in pressuring company management, whether directly through their engagement or indirectly through their stock picking. Passive managers need that pressure, and its positive impact on share prices generally, as much as the broader economy does, but there is a collective action problem (see Chapter 7). Few active managers of a diversified portfolio of equities can benefit from stewardship, because each share is a small proportion of their investments. The Kay Commission's response is for active managers to have more concentrated portfolios, and some pension fund interviewees similarly wanted to see the fund managers they employ concentrating on a small number of their 'best ideas'. This may be appropriate for those managing only a limited portion of the assets of a pension fund that itself remains highly diversified, and their investment perspective can be long term. For those for whom the fund in question represents a higher proportion of their overall investments, the loss of diversification may have serious implications.

Much of the debate surrounding passive investment and stewardship remains firmly within a shareholder value paradigm: investors' voices should be heard in order to ensure that company management prioritize share price performance. This book has also highlighted, however, a different conception of stewardship in the form of responsible investment. Chapters 6 and 7 discuss two different forms such responsible investment can take: either seeking to change corporate behaviour directly (the attempted voice of the trade union pension funds) or exiting investments that do not meet standards of behaviour or sustainability. Passive investment can involve responsible investment when the index chosen excludes certain investments—excluding tobacco or fossil fuel companies, for example. Changing behaviour by voice would appear more likely to be successful, however, despite the problems outlined in Chapter 7. The lack of voting rights for fixed income investors (except in situations of severe financial difficulties for the borrower) is therefore an additional reason, besides those discussed in Chapter 6, why responsible investment is not influential in bond markets. These issues, and the most effective ways for responsible investment to achieve its aims, remain in need of further research.

Unintended Consequences

A significant part of the investment chain's negative consequences stems from the problems caused by seeing the central issue as a principal–agent problem, and attempting to deal with that through increased monitoring and comparison. Fund manager interviewees, as discussed in particular in Chapter 3, feel their relative performance is constantly monitored and that this monitoring has an impact on their investment behaviour. The short-term nature of the monitoring increases short-termism among fund managers, and concerns about how they are viewed encourages (in some cases) such behaviour as 'window dressing' or 'leaning for the tape' (see Chapter 1). Here fund managers attempt to appear to have performed better than is actually the case. They involve, however, two distinct concerns fund managers have. Leaning for the tape—increasing the price of shares already held to improve the price—is aimed at improving short-term numerical performance. The *Kay Review* (2012) recommends reducing the frequency of the reporting of such numbers, so limiting the incentive to 'lean' (and, more importantly, increasing the overall focus on longer-term performance). Window dressing, in contrast, is aimed at the narrative that surrounds the presentation of performance. By removing poorly performing stocks or higher yielding, less creditworthy bonds from the portfolio at the reporting date, fund managers do not improve the actual performance figures. They do, however, make the 'succinct narrative reporting' of that performance, which the *Kay Review* seeks to encourage, easier. These are, as Chapter 1 makes clear, techniques that go beyond self-presentation as Goffman (1959) sees it, but the motivation remains self-presentation nevertheless.

Performance measurement is also at the heart of issues of herding and 'closet benchmarking' (active fund managers making investments that closely match the index against which they are judged). Just as companies can be influenced into adopting business models that match the classification of research analysts (see Chapter 1), so the comparability that performance measurement requires necessitates funds acting in ways that are similar to their peers in the sector against which they are judged, as discussed in Chapter 3. Herding is therefore likely. Concern about the highly volatile returns that will result, leading to marked underperformance at some stage (and therefore the likelihood of losing investors), discourage the highly concentrated investments needed to reduce closet benchmarking. This is likely to prove a significant disincentive to the kinds of concentrated portfolios the *Kay Review* hopes will increase engagement (see Garratt and Hamilton forthcoming).

Combination Therapy

Thus far, this conclusion has been pessimistic. There are clear problems within the investment chain, we argue, and, taken individually, the solutions already presented by official reports are unlikely to solve them. However, some form of 'combination therapy'—multiple treatments of the same disease, as with HIV—may result in improvement. The *Kay Review*'s many recommendations represent just such an approach, albeit focused on a narrower outcome than the broader concerns raised in this book. Increased disclosure, as discussed earlier, can confuse as much as enlighten, and can, importantly, result in additional links in, or influences on, the investment chain, serving the purpose of simplifying that information, often down to a rating, number of stars, or metallic colour. However, transparency on fees must be seen as likely to have positive outcomes, especially in reducing the cost of (especially mediocre or poor) active management. Finance's contribution to inequality is at its heart in large part the result of financial services being so profitable. The causes of that profitability across finance are well beyond the scope of this book, but one thing is clear: we pay, directly or indirectly, too much for investment services, and those payments underpin profitability along the investment chain. Transparency as to what we pay to an industry with multiple actors and often high de facto barriers to entry should reduce fees. Chapter 1 gives the stark mathematics of what that might do to improve returns on pension savings, with the broader societal positives that would have.

Pressure on fees in active management is already starting, with, as discussed, low-cost passive investment the likely proximate cause. Particularly in highly developed financial markets, passive investment is simply a better deal for most investors. We have argued that financial markets dominated by passive investment would not be a welcome development, but its pressure on overall fee levels is welcome. They will remain an important part of financial markets; many active managers will each year underperform their index, so justifying passivity. However, if genuinely active management, as Kay advocates, is combined with lower fees, the two investment approaches can successfully coexist.

We have been wary of policy prescriptions aimed at shortening the chain, and see the different roles necessary to the investment process as making this difficult. Regulation that seeks to solve conflicts of interest often results in a link in the chain moving from within a single institution to outside, and this has potentially negative consequences, as we believe this book highlights in a number of its chapters. The impact of lower overall returns from managing investments might also lead to too much outsourcing, because the latter, whether in manufacturing, direct marketing, or finance, is often motivated by the desire to cut costs. The economies of scale of, for example, a fund assessment company such as Morningstar may become more compelling with low profitability. Increased concentration at many links of the chain may also be an outcome of cost pressures. More optimistically, increased vertical integration—doing more 'in-house'—is another possible response (see Clark and Monk 2017: chapter 11, for the scale of the cost savings that could come from this). It would not shorten the chain, but would move it to within particular organizations. As we have shown in this book, this does not remove the issues within the chain, but it does in most cases reduce them.

Relationships and Trust

The *Kay Review* recognizes 'the dependence of successful financial intermediation on trust and confidence'. This in turn depends, as the report recognizes, on 'long-term and personal relationships: trust and confidence are not generally created by trading between anonymous agents attempting to make short-term gains at each other's expense' (Kay 2012: 5). This is more likely (though far from guaranteed) within a single organization, but this book has shown that it can also exist between actors in different organizations. It has long been axiomatic across a range of academic fields (most obviously economics and comparative political economy) to see financial markets as composed of just such anonymous agents engaged in arm's-length transactions. Without some form of investment chain, that is precisely how financial markets must operate: savers, the vast majority of them small and with (tightly) bounded rationality, have very limited opportunities for effective voice and can only choose exit. They may demonstrate unconscious loyalty, but such ignorance of change can hardly be seen as a positive.

In contrast, this book has given multiple examples of financial market interactions that are far from anonymous and arm's-length. At worst, these can be seen as iterated games which bring the shadow of the future into rational self-interested actors' decisions on cooperation or defection. At best, they hold the potential for relationships of confidence and trust. The relationship between a large institutional investor and a fund manager, for example, can involve not just the constraints of clear investment guidelines which the fund manager must not contravene, but also a dialogue. As outlined in Chapter 3, this dialogue can involve the fund manager discussing an investment with the investor, when that investment is within the guidelines but may nevertheless be something with which the investor might be uncomfortable. Even the fund manager being aware of this discomfort is evidence of a link in the chain which is far from arm's-length and far more than constraining. Similarly, Chapter 4 outlines the nature of a relationship between brokerage salespeople and investors that includes reciprocity and friendship (see Montgomery 1998). In Chapter 5, we see how the move from first- to second-generation dark pools was influenced by the desire to maintain relationships between 'buy' and 'sell sides'. This is small comfort when set against the many problems, and we may fairly be accused of grasping at straws. Furthermore, the recent development highlighted by interviewees, of brokers establishing a more formal hierarchy of customers, with only the highest-ranked receiving the most complete service, raises additional issues. The connections we highlight may also provide explanations for the emergence of market failures such as herding (Kellard et al. 2016). However, the answers to many of the problems of the investment chain lie within the investment chain itself. To understand how this might be found, it is necessary, we argue, to accept the investment chain as the reality of financial markets, and as a framework for academic study of those markets and public discussion of them.

A Brief Roster of Intermediaries

What follows is a brief introduction to some of the most salient categories of inter-mediaries in the investment chain. Clearly, we could expand this list almost indefin-itely, for example to include the full range of support staff, specialist functions such as custodians and regulators, and also specialist occupations such as those of accountants, lawyers, information technology staff, compliance officers, etc. However, this list conveys something of the multiplicity of roles to be found in the investment chain.

Between the Saver and the Investment Management Firm

Financial advisers and wealth managers. Under this category we include a wide range of institutions and individuals whose roles and responsibilities vary considerably accord-ing to jurisdiction, as well as depending on the level of service their clients want or can afford. Many of these advisers are independent of institutions that manage investment funds, while others may be housed under the same overarching institutional roof (e.g. within a bank or life assurer, or a specialist retail stockbroker). Clients range from people investing relatively modest savings to high net worth individuals, but the basic service provided is the same: analysis of clients' financial positions and advice on savings, pensions, and investments, with some proportion of their assets being invested in stock markets. These investments (except for high net worth individuals receiving 'wealth management' services) tend to be directed to collective investment vehicles run by investment managers—OEICs (open-ended investment companies), unit trusts, mutual funds, investment trusts, ETFs (exchange-traded funds)—rather than individual securities. Advisers may charge fees to clients based on the assets entrusted to them (where the adviser has control of these assets, which is not the case if the role is a purely advisory one), or based on the advice given, or as a commission or flat rate charge on each purchase or sale of a fund or security following their advice.

Execution-only services. Offered by a variety of institutions, including banks and retail stockbrokers, here no advice is given to clients (who are essentially the same people as in the previous category). Clients purchase funds or securities on payment of commis-sion, a flat fee, and/or an initial or annual account charge. The institution administers the portfolio and often provides access to basic market information (prices, valuation ratios, overviews of company accounts), and executes purchases and sales through the institutional brokers with which it has relationships. As far as collective investment vehicles are concerned, execution-only firms often provide access through 'fund platforms', which are increasingly important distribution vehicles for investment managers selling retail funds. These platforms rarely offer access to all the funds in the market; rather the manager of the platform selects what it considers to be the best-performing funds in different asset classes (e.g. North American Growth, UK Income, Global Socially-Responsible Investment). In some cases execution-only firms also provide separate advisory services (see *Financial advisers and wealth managers*).

Institutional pension funds. The most important class of investors in financial markets as measured by asset value, pension funds receive money from the governments, companies, or other employers that sponsor them, as well as from employee contributions (depending on the nature of the fund) and pay out pensions to retired employees. The largest funds control billions of dollars of assets. While some have 'in-house' investment management capacities, even these typically very large funds contract management out to third parties: i.e. investment managers. Depending on size, their liability profile, and the advice of investment consultants, they will select one or more investment manager, with diversification often a question of reducing risk, but also of selecting managers who specialize in or who have better track records in particular asset classes.

Insurance and life assurance companies. Insurance companies invest a proportion of their premium income in stock markets (a proportion that is determined both by their own risk evaluations and by regulatory requirements); given their risk profiles they tend to invest mainly in fixed income securities, especially government bonds with high credit ratings. Life assurers, because of the longer-term nature of their core business, are more likely to invest in equities. Life assurance companies (in continental Europe often part of a bank under the 'bancassurance' model) also frequently have extensive investment management operations where they attract external funds from retail and institutional clients and compete with stand-alone investment managers.

Charities. A wide variety of tax-exempt organizations fall under this heading, their exact structures, functions, and names varying according to jurisdiction, from universities to medical research grant-making organizations, from religious bodies to private philanthropical foundations. Some of these have assets comparable to large pension funds, but as a whole this is a much smaller section of the institutional market. These organizations are strictly regulated, and will often seek both to grow their endowment value over the long term, and to generate annual income to satisfy legal requirements to distribute money to beneficiaries. It is not uncommon for them to have ethical restrictions related to their charitable purposes (e.g. churches will not invest in the arms trade; medical research charities will not invest in tobacco).

Investment consultants. Investment consultants are firms that advise institutional clients, mainly pension funds, on their investment programmes. Consultants often have actuarial backgrounds, and advise clients both on what types of asset to invest in and which benchmarks to adopt in order to meet their liabilities (e.g. to pensioners), and on which investment managers to select. As such they have an important role in evaluating investment managers, to which end they adopt both 'qualitative' forms of analysis (looking at managers' investment processes or the experience of key personnel) and 'quantitative' forms (investigation of risk-adjusted performance) (Larminat 2013).

Fund raters. A small number of firms (e.g. Morningstar, Standard & Poor's) analyse the performance of retail funds (various forms of collective investment vehicle), on the basis of which they compile league tables published in financial and some non-specialist press outlets ranking funds and fund managers. These are then used by financial advisers and other intermediaries when advising clients. Where results are good, they are also used by the marketing departments of investment managers to sell a particular product or products managed by highly rated managers. For this reason, at the retail end of the industry it is important for individual fund managers to build up a performance 'track record' of at least three years in order to be able to attract significant funds.

Within the Investment Management Firm

Fund managers. There are basically two models. In large firms, fund managers are portfolio managers. They have responsibility for at least one fund each, but work as a team (if they have more than one fund then there is usually some relation between them, e.g. one is more concentrated, but they are both European equity funds). They decide what to buy and sell; meet with company managements and sell-side analysts and sales staff; meet—perhaps less frequently than in the case of smaller firms—with (big institutional) clients, investment consultants, and financial advisers (where they are responsible for 'retail' products: i.e. their funds are sold to the public, usually via advisers/fund platforms/retail brokers/banks etc.) and monitor relevant stocks and markets; and have frequent meetings and discussions with colleagues, especially buy-side analysts (see *Buy-side analysts*). Fund managers will also have assistants: junior fund managers not yet responsible for the overall performance or taking decisions independent of their supervisors.

In smaller firms, fund managers also have analytical responsibilities, that is to say they divide up different industry sectors between them and have frequent contact with the sell-side and company managements. Their work is a combination of the fund managers' and the buy-side analysts' under the large-firm model, but with the proviso that they have limited time to go into depth, e.g. to build detailed models of the companies they cover.

Buy-side analysts. In terms of training, recruitment, etc. they come from similar backgrounds to fund managers, and in some firms being a buy-side analyst is a stepping-stone or a prerequisite to becoming a portfolio manager. They focus on an industry sector or sectors and develop an expertise both on industry trends and on the financial statements and strategy of specific companies. They often build detailed accounting models and projections, on the basis of which they come up with price 'targets' (predictions with a specific time-horizon) and make recommendations to fund managers. Their work is therefore similar to that of the sell-side analysts whose work is outlined later, except that buy-side analysts usually cover larger universes of stocks and their work is for internal consumption only.

Client service managers. Except in very small firms, fund managers are not involved in day-to-day contact with clients. Client service teams are well-remunerated 'front office' staff (rather than less-well-paid 'back office' administrative staff), who, as well as visiting clients (generally accompanied by senior fund managers, usually on a quarterly basis for major clients) field enquiries from them on an ad hoc basis, e.g. concerning performance, portfolio composition, the firm's investment strategy, fees, the client's investment objectives. Client service personnel are therefore supposed to be on top of both investment matters (i.e. understanding the rationale behind investment decisions, under/outperformance, risk) and administrative issues. The clients in question here are 'segregated clients', that is to say pension funds, charities, and in some firms 'private clients', high net worth individuals whose investments are large enough to be treated as a distinct portfolio rather than aggregated in a collective investment vehicle of some kind. Here there is an overlap with the 'wealth management' and 'private banking' functions of banks.

Marketing staff. Marketing is usually the first port of call for enquiries from prospective clients, and as such they work closely with client service and fund managers in order to understand the firm's products. They prepare presentations on the firm's investment process, funds, etc., although these are often given by fund/client service managers. Depending on the size and scope of the firm's activities, there will be more or less specialization. For example, the firm for which Grant worked had a member of staff who was a former investment consultant and actuary and who dealt with relationships with consultants. Where a firm has a large retail offering there will be marketing personnel dealing with financial advisers and fund platforms and arranging roadshows to show off an outperforming fund manager to new clients in this area, and also providing information to the fund raters (Morningstar, etc.) and discussing this with fund managers and the Chief Investment Officer.

Risk management. This is a function that has grown considerably through time (for example, only fifteen years ago the reasonably large investment management firm for which Grant worked had a single, junior, but mathematically advanced employee whose function it was to monitor portfolio risk). Today, any large firm will have a number of people in this role. These will be part of a more general risk monitoring apparatus, e.g. a 'risk management committee' including the chief investment officer, a couple of senior fund managers (team heads), and so on. What risk managers do in investment management firms has become increasingly elaborate through time (often prompted by pressure from regulators). For example, it is very common for fund managers to have a set 'value-at-risk' or VAR limit, a maximum level of anticipated losses with a given probability. If they approach or breach their VAR limit, they have to take immediate corrective action.

Valuations. This is a 'back office' function whose task is to use valuations software to produce quarterly and annual valuations of client portfolios: i.e. for each account there will be a list of holdings, purchase and sales prices, gains and losses, and historic performance information. These are sent out to clients ahead of quarterly deadlines, but also on an ad hoc basis, usually at the request of clients made via client service managers. They might also be produced for internal consumption (again by client service managers).

Chief investment officer. This is generally someone with long experience as a fund manager, who then becomes responsible for all the investment, risk, and client servicing functions of the firm, including being the 'public' face of what the firm does. The CIO has a central role in determining and reviewing investment philosophy and process and asset allocation (which is usually also carried out by a committee involving the CIO and heads of fund management teams, and the firm's economist(s)/strategists where these exist). The CIO reports to the chief executive/board.

Buy-side traders. Medium-sized and large investment management firms will have a small number of traders (or 'dealers') whose job it is to execute deals placed by portfolio managers (small firms tend to have an exclusive relationship with a single broker and do all their trading through them). They are in contact with traders at institutional brokers (most of which are owned by investment banks). Fund managers place orders through their electronic order management system. Traders can then simply canvas brokers for prices, and execute through the broker giving the best price. However, when the order is large, or the shares or bonds are illiquid, or the fund manager wants to reward a particular broker with whom she has a relationship, the fund manager will normally talk to the trader in order to get a feel for how the trade can be executed. Fund managers also discuss general market conditions and unusual price moves with their buy-side traders.

Economists/strategists. Smaller firms don't usually have these, and even some larger firms don't employ them on the basis that macroeconomic predictions are a fool's game, but many firms do employ an economist or two to develop a house macroeconomic view which then feeds into the investment process by way of asset allocation (usually reviewed on a quarterly basis) and possibly directly into the investment process if analysts or fund managers are supposed to incorporate the house macroeconomic view into their analysis of sectors and stocks. Economists will also communicate the house view to client service personnel, since it can often form an important part of the justificatory narrative.

Between the Investment Management Firm and the Market

Brokers (institutional stockbrokers, frequently parts of or owned by major investment banks). From the fund manager's point of view, these firms are composed of sales staff and analysts (two of the three roles of brokers being sales and research, the other being trading and market-making), as these are the groups of employees fund managers (both portfolio managers and buy-side analysts) deal with on a daily basis (trading being taken care of by buy-side traders: see *Buy-side traders*).

General sales. General sales staff cover the whole of a particular market (for example, UK shares) and their job is to sell their firm's recommendations on stocks within that market to the fund managers with whom they have a relationship. Because general salespeople are generalists their clients tend to be portfolio managers rather than buy-side analysts who are interested in more specialist knowledge. General sales staff are also involved in placements and new and secondary offerings of shares or bonds as the link between the company's advisers (investment banks) and its investors (fund managers). For example, if a major shareholder is conducting a placement the sales staff of the bank executing the placement will call their fund manager clients to ask them if they want any stock; or if there is an initial public offering (IPO) of shares, she will call to see if the fund manager wants to meet company management on their 'roadshow' or meet with the sell-side analyst who will be taking up coverage of the stock once it is listed.

Sell-side analysts. Organized by industry sector as well as geographic region (for example, European Chemicals, Latin American Banks), analysts are often trained as accountants or have industry experience (especially in the finance/treasury/accounting departments of major corporations) before becoming brokers. They build large models of the companies under coverage, based on published accounts and company guidance. Company managements or their investor relations departments will often look at these models and tell the analysts if they are on the right track. They write research notes, ranging from short pieces to major reviews of particular stocks or whole sectors, which they then both 'sell' (distribute along with efforts at persuasion) to their colleagues in general sales and to the fund managers or buy-side analysts who are their clients. Where fund managers are simply portfolio managers (in the large-firm model outlined at the start of this roster), their contact with sell-side analysts is more ad hoc: for example, when the fund manager has a particular interest in a stock and wants to get a second opinion. For fund managers who also have analytical responsibilities and for buy-side analysts contact will be more regular, with sell-side analysts calling up fund managers not only to hawk their latest piece of research but more generally to chat, get their latest thoughts, offer them meetings with company managements, etc., while fund managers/buy-side analysts will call up to request meetings, ask the analysts to come in and do a sector review (for example, at the same time the fund managers are conducting an internal review of that sector), or send over the detailed workings of their valuations or even their models.

Many analyst teams also have specialist sales staff attached to them, people whose role is less to do the basic research and more to understand the sector in depth and take a more proactive role in contacting clients, and also feed back client priorities into the research process.

Economists/strategists. They are also part of the research process, and all major brokers have a small team at least some of whom have advanced training in economics and who develop a 'house view' on macroeconomic trends, on the links between those trends and the prospects for returns in different industry sectors, and on the relative performance of different asset classes. This house view affects the research analysts carry out and is 'sold' to fund managers as part of the overall relationship they have with general sales. Strategists will also visit fund managers to tout a piece of major research.

Under dominant current relationships (see Chapter 5), the 'selling' of research is still often metaphorical rather than a literal transaction with an explicit price. The trading commissions paid to sell-side brokers by buy-side investment management firms cover all these research and sales activities, as well as actual trading. At the fund manager's end, relationships with brokers will be to a large extent on a personal basis, for example, between a particular fund manager or analyst and individual sales or research staff on the sell side. That said, senior managers do take an interest in their fund managers' relationships with brokers, particularly at smaller firms where there is less commission to go around and therefore broking relationships may be restricted to a small number of firms in order to have greater clout with them (because brokers tend to call their bigger clients first).

References

Abbott, Andrew. 2005. 'Linked Ecologies: States and Universities as Environments for Professions'. *Sociological Theory* 23(3): 245–74.

Abolafia, Mitchel Y. 1996. *Making Markets: Opportunism and Restraint on Wall Street.* Cambridge, MA: Harvard University Press.

Adams, Charles W., Herbert R. Behrens, Jerome M. Pustilnik, and John T. Gilmore Jr. 1971. 'Instinet Communication System for Effectuating the Sale or Exchange of Fungible Properties between Subscribers'. U.S. patent 3,573,747, awarded 6 April.

Agrawal, Ashwini K. 2012. 'Corporate Governance Objectives of Labor Union Shareholders: Evidence from Proxy Voting'. *Review of Financial Studies* 25(1): 187–226.

Alexander, Jeff, Linda Giordano, and David Brooks. 2015. 'Dark Pool Execution Quality: A Quantitative View'. <http://tabbforum.com>, accessed 31 August 2015.

Alexander, William E., John Cady, and Jesus Gonzalez-Garcia, eds. 2008. *The IMF's Data Dissemination Initiative After 10 Years.* Washington, DC: International Monetary Fund. <https://www.imf.org/external/pubs/ft/books/2008/datadiss/dissemination.pdf>, accessed 24 August 2016.

Allen, Franklin and Ana Babus. 2009. 'Networks in Finance'. <http://finance.wharton.upenn.edu/~allenf/download/Vita/Allen%20and%20Babus%20-%20aug%2020-08-Long-SSRN.pdf>, accessed 27 September 2016.

Alvesson, Mats. 2013. *The Triumph of Emptiness: Consumption, Higher Education, and Work Organization.* Oxford: Oxford University Press.

Angel, James J., Lawrence E. Harris, and Chester S. Spatt. 2013. 'Equity Trading in the 21st Century: An Update, June 21'. New York: Knight Capital Group.

Ansar, Atif, Ben Caldecott, and James Tilbury. 2013. 'Stranded Assets and the Fossil Fuel Divestment Campaign: What Does Divestment Mean for the Valuation of Fossil Fuel Assets?' Oxford: University of Oxford Smith School. <http://www.smithschool.ox.ac.uk/research-programmes/stranded-assets/SAP-divestment-report-final.pdf>, accessed 25 August 2016.

Arjaliès, Diane-Laure. 2010. 'A Social Movement Perspective on Finance: How Socially Responsible Investment Mattered'. *Journal of Business Ethics* 92(1): 57–78.

Authers, John. 2014. 'How Active is Your Fund Manager, and What Chance Do They Really Have of Beating the Market?' *Financial Times*, 12 March.

Authers, John. 2015. 'Chasing Hot New Funds is a Five-Star Recipe for Poor Capital Allocation'. *Financial Times*, 19 November, p. 34.

Barber, Brad M. and Terrance Odean. 2001. 'Boys Will be Boys: Gender, Overconfidence, and Common Stock Investment'. *Quarterly Journal of Economics* 116(1): 261–92.

References

Barclays. 2014. 'Supreme Court of the State of New York Index No. 451391/2014: Barclays' Memorandum of Law in Support of its Motion to Dismiss the Complaint'. <http://www.barclays.com>, accessed 26 August 2014.

Bazot, Guillaume. 2014. 'Financial Consumption and the Cost of Finance: Measuring Financial Efficiency in Europe (1950–2007)'. <https://halshs.archives-ouvertes.fr/halshs-00986912>, accessed 19 April 2016.

Bell, Brian and John Van Reenen. 2010. 'Bankers' Pay and Extreme Wage Inequality in the UK'. <http://lse.ac.uk>, accessed 5 February 2016.

Berkowitz, Stephen A., Dennis E. Logue, and Eugene A. Noser. 1988. 'The Total Cost of Transactions on the NYSE'. *Journal of Finance* 43(1): 97–112.

Bernstein, Aaron and James Hawley. 2014. 'Is the Search for Excessive Alpha a Breach of Fiduciary Duty?' In *The Cambridge Handbook of Institutional Investment and Fiduciary Duty*, edited by J. Hawley, A. Hoepner, K. Johnson, J. Sandberg, and E. Waitzer, pp. 171–80. Cambridge: Cambridge University Press.

Beunza, Daniel and Raghu Garud. 2007. 'Calculators, Lemmings or Frame-Makers? The Intermediary Role of Securities Analysts'. In *Market Devices*, edited by Michel Callon, Yuval Millo, and Fabian Muniesa, pp. 13–39. Oxford: Blackwell.

Beunza, Daniel and David Stark. 2004. 'Tools of the Trade: The Socio-Technology of Arbitrage in Wall Street'. *Industrial and Corporate Change* 13(2): 369–400.

Beunza, Daniel and David Stark. 2012. 'From Dissonance to Resonance: Cognitive Interdependence in Quantitative Finance'. *Economy and Society* 41(3): 383–417.

Bikhchandani, Sushil and Sunil Sharma. 2001. 'Herd Behavior in Financial Markets'. *IMF Staff Papers* 47(3): 279–310.

Black, Bernard S. 1990. 'Shareholder Passivity Reexamined'. *Michigan Law Review* 89(3): 520–608.

Blume, Marshall E. 1993. 'Soft Dollars and the Brokerage Industry'. *Financial Analysts Journal* 49(2): 36–44.

Boffey, Daniel. 2011. 'Revealed: How City Fees Are Eating Into our Pensions'. *The Observer*, 18 December, pp. 1 and 7.

Borch, Christian and Ann-Christina Lange. 2016. 'High-Frequency Trader Subjectivity: Emotional Attachment and Discipline in an Era of Algorithms'. *Socio-Economic Review*, <https://doi.org/10.1093/ser/mww013>.

Brinson, Gary B., L. Randolph Hood, and Gilbert L. Beebower. 1986. 'Determinants of Portfolio Performance'. *Financial Analysts Journal* 42(4): 39–44.

Brooks, David. 2010. *Bobos in Paradise: The New Upper Class and How They Got There.* New York: Simon & Schuster.

Brundtland, Gro H. 1987. *Our Common Future: The World Commission on Environment and Development.* Oxford: Oxford University Press.

Brunnermeier, Markus K., Luis Garicano, Philip R. Lane, Marcus Pagano, Ricardo Reis, et al. 2011. 'ESBies: A Realistic Reform of Europe's Financial Architecture'. In *The Future of Banking*, edited by Thorsten Beck, pp. 15–20. London: Centre for Economic Policy Research.

Callon, Michel, Yuval Millo, and Fabian Muniesa, eds. 2007. *Market Devices*. Oxford: Blackwell.

Callon, Michel and Fabian Muniesa. 2005. 'Peripheral Vision: Economic Markets as Calculative Collective Devices'. *Organization Studies* 26(8): 1229–50.

Camara, K. A. D. 2005. 'Classifying Institutional Investors'. *Journal of Corporate Law* 30: 219–53.

Carbon Tracker. 2011. 'Unburnable Carbon: Are the World's Financial Markets Carrying a Carbon Bubble?' London: Carbon Tracker Initiative. <https://www.carbontracker. org/wp-content/uploads/2014/09/Unburnable-Carbon-Full-rev2-1.pdf>, accessed 25 August 2016.

Carhart, Mark M., Ron Kaniel, David K. Musto, and Adam V. Reed. 2002. 'Leaning for the Tape: Evidence of Gaming Behavior in Equity Mutual Funds'. *Journal of Finance* 57(2): 661–93.

Carrie, Carl. 2008. 'Illuminating the New Dark Influence on Trading and U.S. Market Structure'. *Journal of Trading* 3(1): 40–55.

Carruthers, Bruce and Wendy Nelson Espeland. 1991. 'Accounting for Rationality: Double-Entry Bookkeeping and the Rhetoric of Economic Rationality'. *American Journal of Sociology* 97(1): 31–69.

Chapman, Peter. 2012. 'Barclays Polices Dark Pool'. *Traders Magazine Online News*, 25 April. <http://www.tradersmagazine.com>, accessed 25 April 2012.

Chen, Yong, Wayne Ferson, and Helen Peters. 2010. 'Measuring the Timing Ability and Performance of Bond Mutual Funds'. *Journal of Financial Economics* 98: 72–89.

Chevalier, Judith and Glenn Ellison. 1997. 'Risk Taking by Mutual Funds as a Response to Incentives'. *Journal of Political Economy* 105(6): 1167–200.

Chevalier, Judith and Glenn Ellison. 1999. 'Career Concerns of Mutual-Fund Managers'. *Quarterly Journal of Economics* 114(2): 389–432.

Choi, James J., David Laibson, and Brigitte C. Madrian. 2010. 'Why Does the Law of One Price Fail? An Experiment on Index Mutual Funds'. *Review of Financial Studies* 23(4): 1405–32.

Christie, William G. and Paul H. Schultz. 1994. 'Why do NASDAQ Market Makers Avoid Odd-Eighth Quotes?' *Journal of Finance* 49(5): 1813–40.

Clark, Gordon L. 2000. *Pension Fund Capitalism*. Oxford: Oxford University Press.

Clark, Gordon L. 2003. *European Pensions and Global Finance*. Oxford: Oxford University Press.

Clark, Gordon L. and Ashby H. B. Monk. 2017. *Institutional Investors in Global Markets*. Oxford: Oxford University Press.

D'Antona, John Jr. 2014. 'Top 2014 Trends: FINRA Requires ATS to Report Trade Data'. *Traders Magazine Online News*, 24 December. <http://www.tradersmagazine.com>, accessed 24 December 2014.

Davis, Gerald F. 2008. 'A New Finance Capitalism? Mutual Funds and Ownership Re-concentration in the United States'. *European Management Review* 5(1): 11–21.

Deeg, Richard and Iain Hardie. Forthcoming. 'What is Patient Capital and Who Supplies It?' *Socio-Economic Review*.

Deringer, F. B. 2005. *A Legal Framework for the Integration of Environmental, Social, and Governance Issues into Institutional Investment: Report Produced by the Asset Management Working Group, UNEP Finance Initiative*. Geneva: United Nations Environment

Programme. <http://www.unepfi.org/fileadmin/documents/freshfields_legal_resp_20051123.pdf>.

Desmartin, J.-P., N. Jacob, B. Cavalier, and F. Bossy. 2014. *Public Debt and the Eurozone: After Greece and Cyprus, What Might the New ESG Signals Be?* Paris: Oddo Securities.

Desrosières, Alain. 2008. *L'argument statistique: Pour une sociologie historique de la quantification.* Paris: Presse des mines.

Dincer, Oguzhan, Russel B. Gregory-Allen, and Hany A. Shawky. 2010. 'Are you Smarter than a CFA'er?' <http://ssrn.com/abstract=1458219>, accessed 22 November 2010.

Dixon, Adam D. (2008). 'The Rise of Pension Fund Capitalism in Europe: An Unseen Revolution?' *New Political Economy* 13(3): 249–70.

Domowitz, Ian and Benn Steil. 1999. 'Automation, Trading Costs, and the Structure of the Securities Trading Industry'. *Brookings-Wharton Papers on Financial Services Annual* (June): 33–92.

Drucker, Peter F. 1976. *The Unseen Revolution: How Pension Fund Socialism Came to America.* New York: Harper & Row.

Economides, Nicholas and Robert A. Schwartz. 1994. 'Making the Trade: Equity Trading Practices and Market Structure—1994'. <http://www.stern.nyu.edu/networks/making.html>, accessed April 29 2015.

Edwards, Mark and Wayne H. Wagner. 1993. 'Best Execution'. *Financial Analysts Journal* 49(1): 65–71.

Eyal, G. 2013. 'For a Sociology of Expertise: The Social Origins of the Autism Epidemic'. *American Journal of Sociology* 118(4): 863–907.

Fabozzi, F. J., S. M. Focardi, and C. Jonas. 2007. 'Trends in Quantitative Equity Management: Survey Results'. *Quantitative Finance* 7(2): 115–22.

Fabozzi, F. J., S. M. Focardi, and C. Jonas. 2008. *Challenges in Quantitative Equity Management.* New York: CFA Institute.

Ferraro, F., J. Pfeffer, and R. I. Sutton. 2005. 'Economics Language and Assumptions: How Theories Can Become Self-Fulfilling'. *Academy of Management Review* 30: 8–24.

Financial Services Authority. 2013. *Retail Distribution Review Newsletter.* Issue 9, February. <http://www.fsa.gov.uk/static/pubs/newsletters/rdr9.pdf>, accessed 7 August 2014.

Fligstein, Neil. 1990. *The Transformation of Corporate Control.* Cambridge, MA: Harvard University Press.

French, Kenneth R. 2008. 'Presidential Address: The Cost of Active Investing'. *Journal of Finance* 53(4): 1537–73.

Fridson, M. 2013. 'Book Review of "Inside the Yield Book: The Classic That Created the Science of Bond Analysis" by Leibowitz, M. L., Homer, Sidney and Kogelman, S., John Wiley & Sons, 2103'. CFA Institute. <https://blogs.cfainstitute.org/investor/2013/11/29/book-review-inside-the-yield-book-the-classic-that-created-the-science-of-bond-analysis/>.

Fulton, Mark and Reid Capalino. 2014. 'Investing in the Clean Trillion: Closing the Clean Energy Investment Gap'. <https://www.ceres.org>, accessed 12 October 2015.

Fung, Archon, Tessa Hebb, and Joel Rogers. 2001. *Working Capital: The Power of Labor's Pensions.* Ithaca, NY: Cornell University Press.

Ganatra, Amrish. 2016. 'Research Payments: Funding Options Explained'. <http://tabbforum.com/opinions>, accessed 3 June 2016.

Garratt, Tim and Kathrin Hamilton. 2017. 'Patience in Practice: The Loneliness of the Long-Term Investor'. *Socio-Economic Review*.

Geertz, Clifford. 1973. *The Interpretation of Cultures: Selected Essays*. New York: Basic Books.

Gennaioli, Nicola, Andrei Shleifer, and Robert Vishny. 2015. 'Money Doctors'. *Journal of Finance* 70(1): 91–114.

Gillan, Stuart L. and Laura T. Starks. 2000. 'Corporate Governance Proposals and Shareholder Activism: The Role of Institutional Investors'. *Journal of Financial Economics* 57(2): 275–305.

Gitlin, Todd. 2012. *Occupy Nation: The Roots, the Spirit, and the Promise of Occupy Wall Street*. New York: HarperCollins.

Godechot, Olivier. 2007. *Working Rich: Salaires, bonus et appropriation du profit dans l'industrie financière*. Paris: La Découverte.

Godechot, Olivier. 2013. 'Financiarisation et fractures socio-spatiales'. *L'Année sociologique* 63(1): 17–50.

Goede, Marieke de. 2005. *Virtue, Faith, and Fortune: A Genealogy of Finance*. Minneapolis: University of Minnesota Press.

Goffman, Erving. 1959. *The Presentation of Self in Everyday Life*. New York: Doubleday.

Gold, Murray and Adrian Scotchmer. 2015. *Climate Change and the Fiduciary Duties of Pension Fund Trustees in Canada*. Toronto: Koskie Minsky LLP.

Gond, J.-P. and E. Boxenbaum. 2013. 'The Glocalization of Responsible Investment: Contextualization Work in France and Quebec'. *Journal of Business Ethics* 115(4): 707–21.

Gorham, Michael and Nidhi Singh. 2009. *Electronic Exchanges: The Global Transformation from Pits to Bits*. Amsterdam: Elsevier.

Goyal, Amit and Sunil Wahal. 2008. 'The Selection and Termination of Investment Management Firms by Plan Sponsors'. *Journal of Finance* 63: 1805–47.

Goyer, Michel. 2011. *Contingent Capital: Short-Term Investors and the Evolution of Corporate Governance in France and Germany*. Oxford: Oxford University Press.

Granovetter, Mark. 1985. 'Economic Action and Social Structure: The Problem of Embeddedness'. *American Journal of Sociology* 91(3): 481–510.

Greenwood, Robin and David Scharfstein. 2013. 'The Growth of Finance'. *Journal of Economic Perspectives* 27(2): 3–28.

Guyer, Jane. 2009. 'Composites, Fictions and Risks: Toward an Ethnography of Price'. In *Market and Society: The Great Transformation Today*, edited by Keith Hart and Chris Hann, pp. 203–20. Cambridge: Cambridge University Press.

Hager, Sandy Brian. 2014. 'What Happened to the Bondholding Class? Public Debt, Power and the Top One Per Cent'. *New Political Economy* 19(2): 155–82.

Hägglund, P. 2000. 'The Value of Facts: How Analysts' Recommendations Focus on Facts Instead of Value'. In *Ökonomie und Gesellschaft: Facts and Figures, Economic Representations and Practices*, edited by H. Kalthoff, R. Rottenburg, and H.-J. Wagener, pp. 313–37. Marburg: Metropolis.

Hagstrom, Warren O. 1965. *The Scientific Community*. New York: Basic Books.

Haldane, Andrew. 2014. 'The Age of Asset Management?' Speech given at the London Business School, London, 4 April. <http://www.bankofengland.co.uk/publications/Pages/speeches/default.aspx>.

References

Hall, Peter A. and David Soskice, eds. 2001. *Varieties of Capitalism: The Institutional Foundations of Comparative Advantage*. Oxford and New York: Oxford University Press.

Hanlon, Michelle, Edward L. Maydew, and Jacob R. Thornock. 2015. 'Taking the Long Way Home: US Tax Evasion and Offshore Investments in US Equity and Debt Markets'. *Journal of Finance* 70(1): 257–87.

Hardie, Iain and Donald MacKenzie 2007. 'Constructing the Market Frame: Distributed Cognition and Distributed Framing in Financial Markets'. *New Political Economy* 12: 389–403.

Harrison, Debbie. 2007. 'Parties Foster Closer Links to Build Expertise'. *Financial Times*, 30 July.

Hawley, James P., Andreas G. F. Hoepner, Keith L. Johnson, Joakim Sandberg, and Edward J. Waitzer, eds. 2014. *The Cambridge Handbook of Institutional Investment and Fiduciary Duty*. Cambridge: Cambridge University Press.

Hirschman, Albert O. 1970. *Exit, Voice, and Loyalty*. Cambridge, MA and London: Harvard University Press.

Holmes, Douglas and George E. Marcus. 2005. 'Cultures of Expertise and the Management of Globalization: Toward the Re-Functioning of Ethnography'. In *Global Assemblages: Technology, Politics, and Ethics as Anthropological Problems*, edited by Aihwa Ong and Stephen Collier, pp. 235–52. Malden, MA: Blackwell.

Hong, Harrison, Jeffrey D. Kubik, and Amit Solomon. 2000. 'Security Analysts' Career Concerns and Herding of Earnings Forecasts'. *RAND Journal of Economics* 31(5): 121–44.

Ibbotson, Roger G. and Paul D. Kaplan. 2000. 'Does Asset Allocation Policy Explain 40, 90, or 100 Percent of Performance?' *Financial Analysts Journal* 56(1): 26–33.

Instinet. 1989. 'The Crossing Network User Manual'. Copy in interviewee's private papers.

Investment Association. 2015. *Asset Management in the UK 2014–15*. <http://www.theinvestmentassociation.org>, accessed 4 August 2016.

Investment Management Association. 2009. *Asset Management in the UK 2008*. <http://www.theinvestmentassociation.org>, accessed 4 August 2016.

Investment Management Association. 2011. *Asset Management in the UK 2010–11*. <http://www.theinvestmentassociation.org>, accessed 4 August 2016.

Investment Management Association 2013. *Asset Management in the UK 2012–13*. <http://www.theinvestmentassociation.org>, accessed 18 August 2015.

Investment Management Association. 2014. *Asset Management in the UK 2013–14*. <http://www.theinvestmentassociation.org>, accessed 18 August 2015.

Jackson, Gregory and Anastasia Petraki. 2011. *Understanding Short-Termism: The Role of Corporate Governance*. Stockholm: Glasshouse Forum.

Jenkinson, Tim, Howard Jones, and Jose Vicente Martinez. 2016. 'Picking Winners? Investment Consultants' Recommendations of Fund Managers'. *Journal of Finance* 71(5): 2333–70.

Jopson, Barney, Stephen Foley, and Caroline Binham. 2015. 'Fund Managers Relieved as Threat of Tougher "Sifi" Regulation is Dropped'. *Financial Times*, 15 July, p. 1.

Jung, Jiwook and Frank Dobbin. 2012. 'Finance and Institutional Investors'. In *The Oxford Handbook of the Sociology of Finance*, edited by Karin Knorr Cetina and Alex Preda, pp. 52–74. Oxford: Oxford University Press.

Kay, John. 2012. *The Kay Review of UK Equity Markets and Long-Term Decision Making*. London: HM Government of the United Kingdom. <https://www.gov.uk/government/news/kay-review-publishes-report-on-uk-financial-sector>, accessed 15 October 2014.

Kay, John. 2015a. *Other People's Money: Masters of the Universe or Servants of the People?* London: Profile.

Kay, John. 2015b. 'Shareholders Think They Own The Company: They Are Wrong'. *Financial Times*, 11 November, p. 11.

Keim, Donald B. and Ananth Madhavan. 1996. 'The Upstairs Market for Large-Block Transactions: Analysis and Measurement of Price Effects'. *Review of Financial Studies* 9(1): 1–36.

Keim, Donald B. and Ananth Madhavan. 1998. 'The Cost of Institutional Equity Trades'. *Financial Analysts Journal* 54(4): 50–69.

Kellard, N., Y. Millo, J. Simon, and O. Engel. 2016. 'Close Communications: Hedge Funds, Brokers and the Emergence of Herding'. *British Journal of Management*, forthcoming.

Knorr Cetina, Karin. 1999. *Epistemic Cultures: How the Sciences Make Knowledge*. Cambridge, MA: Harvard University Press.

Knorr Cetina, Karin and Urs Bruegger. 2002. 'Global Microstructures: The Virtual Societies of Financial Markets'. *American Journal of Sociology* 107: 905–50.

Knorr Cetina, Karin and Alex Preda, eds. 2012. *The Oxford Handbook of the Sociology of Finance*. Oxford: Oxford University Press.

Koenig, Peter and Con Keating. 2015. 'German Discount Rates: Biases in Pension Accounting'. *Investment and Pensions Europe*, November. <http://www.ipe.com/pensions/pensions/briefing/german-discount-rates-biases-in-pension-discounting/10010440.fullarticle>.

Kolhatkar, Sheelah and Sree Vidya Bhaktavatsalam. 2010. 'The Colossus of Wall Street'. *Bloomberg Businessweek* (December): 60–7.

Kricheli-Katz, Tamar and Tali Regev. 2016. 'How Many Cents on the Dollar? Women and Men in Product Markets'. *Science Advances* 2(2): 1–8.

Lakonishok, Josef, Andrei Shleifer, Richard Thaler, and Robert Vishny. 1991. 'Window Dressing by Pension Fund Managers'. *American Economic Review* 81(2): 227–31.

Langley, Paul. 2008. *The Everyday Life of Global Finance*. Oxford: Oxford University Press.

Larminat, Pierre de. 2013. 'Entre "quantitatif" et "qualitatif". Comment les investisseurs professionnels évaluent les gérants d'actifs financiers'. *L'Année sociologique* 63(1): 77–105.

Latour, Bruno. 1987. *Science in Action: How to Follow Scientists and Engineers Through Society*. Cambridge, MA: Harvard University Press.

Latour, Bruno. 2004. *The Politics of Nature: How to Bring the Sciences into Democracy*. Cambridge, MA: Harvard University Press.

Latour, Bruno. 2005. *Reassembling the Social: An Introduction to Actor-Network Theory*. Oxford: Oxford University Press.

Law Commission. 2014. *Fiduciary Duties of Investment Intermediaries*. LAW COM No. 350. London: Law Commission.

Lépinay, Vincent A. 2011. *Codes of Finance: Engineering Derivatives in a Global Bank*. Princeton, NJ: Princeton University Press.

Levine, Amy. 2005. 'Transparency and Conspiracy'. *PoLAR: Political and Legal Anthropology Review* 28(1): 160–5.

Lewis, Michael. 2010. *The Big Short: Inside the Doomsday Machine*. New York and London: Norton.

Lounsbury, Michael and Paul M. Hirsch. 2010. 'Markets on Trial: Toward a Policy-Oriented Economic Sociology'. In *Research in the Sociology of Organizations 30: Part A*, edited by Michael Lounsbury and Paul M. Hirsch, pp. 5–26. Bingley, West Yorkshire: Emerald.

McCarthy, Michael A. 2014. 'Turning Labor into Capital: Pension Funds and the Corporate Control of Finance'. *Politics & Society* 42(4): 455–87.

McFall, Liz. 2011a. 'The Practical Heart of Markets'. *Journal of Australian Political Economy* 68: 149–68.

McFall, Liz. 2011b. 'A "Good, Average Man": Calculation and the Limits of Statistics in Enrolling Insurance Customers'. *Sociological Review* 59(4): 662–84.

McFall, Liz. 2015. 'What's Changing Cultural Economy?' *Journal of Cultural Economy* 8(1): 1–15.

MacKenzie, Donald. 2006. *An Engine, Not a Camera: How Financial Models Shape Markets*. Cambridge, MA: MIT Press.

MacKenzie, Donald. 2007. 'The Material Production of Virtuality: Innovation, Cultural Geography and Facticity in Derivatives Markets'. *Economy and Society* 36(3): 355–76.

MacKenzie, Donald. 2008. 'What's in a Number?' *London Review of Books* 30(18): 11–12.

MacKenzie, Donald. 2011. 'The Credit Crisis as a Problem in the Sociology of Knowledge'. *American Journal of Sociology* 116(6): 1778–841.

MacKenzie, Donald. Forthcoming. 'Shaping Algorithms: A Historical Sociology of High-Frequency Trading'. Working paper.

Mackenzie, Michael and Helen Thomas. 2009. 'SEC Looks to Get to the Bottom of "Dark Pools"'. *Financial Times*, 28 October, p. 35.

McKinsey Global Institute. 2013. 'Financial Globalization: Retreat or Reset'. <http://www.mckinsey.com/insights/mgi/research/financial_markets>.

Macmillan Committee. 1931. *Committee on Finance and Industry Report*. London: HMSO.

Matsaganis, M. 2013. *The Greek Crisis: Social Impact and Policy Responses*. Berlin: Friedrich Ebert Stiftung.

Mennicken, Andrea and Peter Miller. 2014. 'Michel Foucault and the Administering of Lives'. In *The Oxford Handbook of Sociology, Social Theory, and Organization Studies: Contemporary Currents*, edited by Paul S. Adler, Paul Du Gay, Glen Morgan, and Michael Reed, pp. 11–38. Oxford: Oxford University Press.

Messner, Martin. 2009. 'The Limits of Accountability'. *Accounting, Organizations and Society* 34(8): 318–38.

Montazemi, Ali Reza, John J. Siam, and Akbar Esfahanipour. 2008. 'Effect of Network Relations in the Adoption of Electronic Trading Systems'. *Journal of Management Information Systems* 25(1): 233–66.

Montgomery, James D. 1998. 'Towards a Role-Theoretic Conception of Embeddedness'. *American Journal of Sociology* 104: 92–125.

Mooney, Attracta. 2016. 'Passive Funds Grow 230% to $6 tn'. *Financial Times*, 29 May. <http://www.ft.com/cms/s/2/2552ce62-2400-11e6-aa98-db1e01fabc0c.html#axzz4J Me26GXH>.

Morey, Matthew R. and Edward S. O'Neal. 2006. 'Window Dressing in Bond Mutual Funds'. *Journal of Financial Research* 29(3): 325–47.

Mosley, L. 2003. *Global Capital and National Governments*. Cambridge: Cambridge University Press.

Muniesa, Fabian. 2011. 'Is a Stock Exchange a Computer Solution? Explicitness, Algorithms and the Arizona Stock Exchange'. *International Journal of Actor-Network Theory and Technological Innovation* 3(1): 1–15.

Muniesa, Fabian, Yuval Millo, and Michel Callon. 2007. 'An Introduction to Market Devices'. In *Market Devices*, edited by Michel Callon, Yuval Millo, and Fabian Muniesa, pp. 1–12. Oxford: Blackwell.

Naczyk, M. 2016. 'State Regulators' Institutional Entrepreneurship, Pension Funds' Shareholder Activism and the Push for Patient Capital in the US and UK Economies'. Unpublished working paper.

Nadler, R. 1999. *The Rise of Worker Capitalism*. Policy Analysis No. 359. Washington, DC, Cato Institute.

Næs, Randi and Bernt Arne Ødegaard. 2006. 'Equity Trading by Institutional Investors: To Cross or Not to Cross?' *Journal of Financial Markets* 9(2): 79–99.

Newlands, Chris. 2015. 'The Endangered Female Fund Manager'. *Financial Times*, 8 June, p. 6.

Niessen-Ruenzi, Alexandra and Stefan Ruenzi. 2015. 'Sex Matters: Gender Bias in the Mutual Fund Industry'. <http://ssrn.com/abstract=1957317>.

Novethic. 2015. *2014 Figures on Responsible Investment in France*. Novethic Studies. <http://www.novethic.fr/fileadmin/user_upload/tx_ausynovethicetudes/pdf_com plets/2014-figures-on-responsible-investment-in-France.pdf>.

Ortiz, Horacio. 2014. *Valeur financière et vérité: Enquête d'anthropologie politique sur l'évalation des entreprises cotées en bourse*. Paris: Presses de Sciences Po.

Ortiz, Horacio. 2015. 'Imaginaires politiques et moraux des pratiques financières'. In *La fabrique de la finance. Pour une approche interdisciplinaire*, edited by I. Chambost, Y. Tadjeddine, and M. Lenglet, pp. 59–66. Lille: Presses Universitaires du Septentrion.

Paris Europlace. 2015. *Attentes et pratiques des acteurs de la Place de Paris en matière d'ISR et de RSE*. Paris: Europlace.

Pelkmans, Mathijs. 2009. 'The "Transparency" of Christian Proselytizing in Kyrgyzstan'. *Anthropological Quarterly* 82(2): 423–45.

Pénet, P. 2015. 'Rating Reports as Figuring Documents: How Credit Rating Agencies Build Scenarios of the Future'. In *Making Things Valuable*, edited by M. Kornberger, L. Justesen, A. Koed Madsen, and J. Mouritsen, pp. 62–88. Oxford: Oxford University Press.

Pezzuto, I. 2012. 'Miraculous Financial Engineering or Toxic Finance? The Genesis of the U.S. Subprime Mortgage Loans Crisis and its Consequences on the Global Financial Markets and Real Economy'. *Journal of Governance and Regulation* 1: 114–25.

Philippon, Thomas. 2015. 'Has the US Finance Industry Become Less Efficient? On the Theory and Measurement of Financial Intermediation'. *American Economic Review* 105(4): 1408–38.

Philippon, Thomas and Ariell Reshef. 2012. 'Wages and Human Capital in the U.S. Finance Industry: 1909–2006'. *Quarterly Journal of Economics* 127(4): 1551–609.

Philippon, Thomas and Ariell Reshef. 2013. 'An International Look at the Growth of Modern Finance'. *Journal of Economic Perspectives* 27(2): 73–96.

Poovey, Mary. 1993. 'Figures of Arithmetic, Figures of Speech: The Discourse of Statistics in the 1830s'. *Critical Inquiry* 19(2): 256–76.

Porter, Theodore. 1995. *Trust in Numbers: The Pursuit of Objectivity in Science and Public Life*. Princeton, NJ: Princeton University Press.

Power, Michael. 2003. 'Auditing and the Production of Legitimacy'. *Accounting, Organizations and Society* 28(4): 379–94.

Pozner, J.-E., M. K. Stimmler, and P. M. Hirsch. 2010. 'Terminal Isomorphism and the Self-Destructive Potential of Success: Lessons from Subprime Mortgage Origination and Securitization'. In *Research in the Sociology of Organizations 30: Part A*, edited by Michael Lounsbury and Paul M. Hirsch, pp. 183–216. Bingley, West Yorkshire: Emerald.

Preda, Alex. 2009. *Framing Finance: The Boundaries of Markets and Modern Capitalism*. Chicago, IL: University of Chicago Press.

Principles for Responsible Investment. 2015. *Fiduciary Duty in the 21st Century*. <https://www.unpri.org/download_report/6131>.

Principles for Responsible Investment. 2016. *How Asset Owners Can Drive Responsible Investment*. <https://www.unpri.org/download_report/6385>.

Rabinow, Paul. 2003. *Anthropos Today: Reflections on Modern Equipment*. Princeton, NJ: Princeton University Press.

Rabinow, Paul and George E. Marcus, with James Faubion and Tobias Rees. 2008. *Designs for an Anthropology of the Contemporary*. Durham, NC: Duke University Press.

Randall, Tom. 2014. 'Renewable Energy at $254 Billion? Let's Make It a Clean Trillion'. <http://www.bloomberg.com/news/articles/2014-01-16/renewable-energy-at-254-billion-let-s-make-it-a-clean-trillion>, accessed 9 October 2015.

Rees, Tobias, instigator. 2007. 'Concept Work and Collaboration in the Anthropology of the Contemporary'. *ARC Exchange* 1(July).

Responsible Investor Insight. 2014. *Fixed Income: ESG in the World's Largest Asset Class*. <https://www.responsible-investor.com/reports/P20/>.

Richardson, Benjamin J. 2013. *Fiduciary Law and Responsible Investing: In Nature's Trust*. New York: Routledge.

Ritholtz, Barry. 2014. 'Guess How Much Money Bill Gross Made Last Year'. *Bloomberg View*, 14 November. <http://www.bloombergview.com>, accessed 8 October 2015.

Roche, G. 2015. *Ramener durablement notre système de retraite à l'équilibre*. <https://www.senat.fr/notice-rapport/2014/r14-624-notice.html>.

Roscoe, Philip J. 2013. 'Constructing the Retail Investor: Performativity and Power in the Markets for Investment Services'. <https://research-repository.st-andrews.ac.uk/bitstream/10023/3516/1/P_Roscoe_perf_and_power_April_2013.pdf>.

Rovnick, Naomi. 2015. 'Fund Managers Face Pressure on Hidden Fees'. *Financial Times*, 17 November, p. 7.

Sandberg, Joakim. 2011. 'Socially Responsible Investment And Fiduciary Duty: Putting the Freshfields Report into Perspective'. *Journal of Business Ethics* 101(1): 143–62.

Schneiderman, Eric T. 2014. 'The People of the State of New York against Barclays Capital, Inc, and Barclays PLC: Summons'. <http://www.americanlawyer.com>, accessed 27 August 2014.

Schumann, William. 2007. 'Transparency, Governmentality, and Negation: Democratic Practice and Open Government Policy in the National Assembly for Wales'. *Anthropological Quarterly* 80(3): 837–62.

Schwab, Stewart J. and Randall S. Thomas. 1998. 'Realigning Corporate Governance: Shareholder Activism by Labor Unions'. *Michigan Law Review* 96: 1018–94.

Schwartz, Robert A. and Benn Steil. 2002. 'Controlling Institutional Trading Costs'. *Journal of Portfolio Management* 28(3): 39–49.

Shah, Ajay and Kshama Fernandes. 2000. 'The Relevance of Index Funds for Pension Investment in Equities'. Policy Research Working Paper 2494. Washington, DC: World Bank.

Shleifer, Andrei and Robert W. Vishny. 1997. 'A Survey of Corporate Governance'. *Journal of Finance* 52(2): 737–83.

Simon, Herbert. 1955. 'A Behavioral Model of Rational Choice'. *Journal of Quarterly Economics* 69(1): 99–118.

Smith, Adam. 1976 [1759]. *The Theory of Moral Sentiments*. Oxford: Clarendon Press.

Smith, Randall. 1984. 'Fee War: Pension Funds Feud with Money Managers over Brokers' Rebates'. *Wall Street Journal*, 4 October, p. 1.

Stan, Sabina. 2007. 'Transparency: Seeing, Counting and Experiencing the System'. *Anthropologica* 49(2): 257–73.

Stasavange, David. 2003. *Public Debt and the Birth of the Democratic State: France and Great Britain 1688–1789*. Cambridge: Cambridge University Press.

Stiglitz, Joseph E. 2009. 'The Anatomy of a Murder: Who Killed America's Economy?' *Critical Review: A Journal of Politics and Society* 21: 329–39.

Strathern, Marilyn. 2000. 'The Tyranny of Transparency'. *British Educational Research Journal* 26(3): 309–21.

Svetlova, Ekaterina. 2013. 'Evaluation in Financial Markets'. Presentation at the University of Edinburgh, 9 January.

Taleb, Nassim. 2007. *The Black Swan: The Impact of the Highly Improbable*. New York: Random House.

Task Force on Climate-Related Financial Disclosures. 2016. *Phase 1 Report of the Task Force on Climate-Related Financial Disclosures*. <https://www.fsb-tcfd.org/wp-content/uploads/2016/03/Phase_I_Report_v15.pdf>, accessed 24 August 2016.

Taussig, Michael. 1999. *Defacement: The Public Secret and the Labor of the Negative*. Palo Alto, CA: Stanford University Press.

TheCityUK. 2013. 'Fund Management 2013'. <http://thecityuk.com>, accessed 13 October 2015.

TheCityUK. 2014. 'UK Fund Management 2014'. <http://www.thecityuk.com>, accessed 13 October 2015.

Tomaskovic-Devey, Donald and Ken-Hou Lin. 2011. 'Income Dynamics, Economic Rents, and the Financialization of the U.S. Economy'. *American Sociological Review* 76(4): 538–59.

Towers Watson 2014. *Global Pensions Asset Study 2014*. <http://www.%20Towerswatson. Com/En/Insights/IC-Types/Survey-Research-Results/2014/02/Global-Pensions-Asset-Study-2014>.

Tuckett, D. and R. Taffler. 2012. *Fund Management: An Emotional Finance Perspective*. New York: CFA Institute Research Foundation.

US Financial Crisis Inquiry Commission. 2011. *The Financial Crisis: Inquiry Report*. <https://www.gpo.gov/fdsys/pkg/GPO-FCIC/pdf/GPO-FCIC.pdf>.

Useem, Michael. 1996. *Investor Capitalism: How Money Managers are Changing the Face of Corporate America*. New York: Basic Books.

Uzzi, Brian. 1997. 'Social Structure and Competition in Interfirm Networks: The Paradox of Embeddedness'. *Administrative Science Quarterly* 42(1): 35–67.

Uzzi, Brian. 1999. 'Embeddedness in the Making of Financial Capital: How Social Relations and Networks Benefit Firms Seeking Financing'. *American Sociological Review* 64(4): 481–505.

Vargha, Z. 2011. 'From Long-Term Savings to Instant Mortgages: Financial Demonstration and the Role of Interaction in Markets'. *Organization* 18(2): 215–35.

Wade, Robert. 2008. 'The First-World Debt Crisis of 2007–2010 in Global Perspective'. *Challenge* 51: 23–54.

Wansleben, Leon. 2012. 'Financial Analysts'. In *The Oxford Handbook of the Sociology of Finance*, edited by Karin Knorr Cetina and Alex Preda, pp. 250–71. Oxford: Oxford University Press.

Weisberger, David. 2015. 'Is There a Dark Pool Witch Hunt Going On?' *Traders Magazine Online News*, 29 May. <http://www.tradersmagazine.com>, accessed 1 June 2015.

Whyte, W. F. 1943. *Street Corner Society: The Social Structure of an Italian Slum*. Chicago, IL: University of Chicago Press.

Wolf, Martin. 2011. 'Why Cutting Fiscal Deficits is an Assault on Profits'. *Financial Times*, 23 November, p. 13.

Wong, Simon. 2010. 'Why Stewardship is Proving Elusive for Institutional Investors'. *Butterworths Journal of International and Financial Law* (July/August): 406–11.

Woolley, Paul and Dimitri Vayanos. 2012. 'Taming the Finance Monster'. *Central Banking Journal* (December): 57–62.

Wright, William. 2015. 'Feeling the Squeeze? What's Happening with Pay at Investment Banks and Asset Managers'. <http://www.newfinancial.eu>, accessed 20 February 2015.

Wunsch, Steve. 2014. 'The Tradeoff between Fairness and Liquidity is an Old Story'. <http://www.tabbforum.com>, accessed 10 April 2015.

Zajac, E. J. and J. D. Westphal. 2004. 'The Social Construction of Market Value: Institutionalization and Learning Perspectives on Stock Market Reactions'. *American Journal of Sociology* 69: 433–57.

Zaloom, Caitlin. 2006. *Out of the Pits: Trading and Technology from Chicago to London*. Chicago, IL: University of Chicago Press.

Zaloom, Caitlin. 2009. 'How to Read the Future: The Yield Curve, Affect, and Financial Prediction'. *Public Culture* 21(2): 245–68.

Zhu, Haoxiang. 2014. 'Do Dark Pools Harm Price Discovery?' *Review of Financial Studies* 27(3): 747–89.

Zilbering, Yan. 2014. 'Why is the Fund's Return Better Than Mine?' <http://www.vanguardcanada.ca>, accessed 21 January 2016.

Zindler, Ethan and Ken Locklin. 2016. 'Mapping the Gap: The Road from Paris. Finance Paths for a 2-Degree Future'. PowerPoint slides. <http://www.ceres.org/resources/reports/mapping-the-gap-the-road-from-paris/>.

Zuckerman, Ezra W. 1999. 'The Categorical Imperative: Securities Analysts and the Illegitimacy Discount'. *American Journal of Sociology* 104(5): 1398–438.

Zuckerman, Ezra W. 2000. 'Focusing the Corporate Product: Securities Analysts and De-Diversification'. *Administrative Science Quarterly* 45(3): 591–619.

Zysman, John. 1983. *Governments, Markets, and Growth*. Ithaca, NY and London: Cornell University Press.

Index

Tables, figures and notes are indicated by an italic *t*, *f*, and *n* following the page number.

active management 13, 40, 66
algorithmic trading 112
alpha 116
Alvesson, Mats 79
Amazon 17
Aon Hewitt 71
Apple 17
Arizona Stock Exchange 105 *n*. 12
Arjaliès, Diane-Laure 15, 20, 23, 122 *n*. 4, 139
Asian Financial Crisis 1997–8 159
asset allocation funds 60, 77*f*
asset management 1, 2
ATC (Alternative Trading Systems) 111
audit trails 29, 36–7, 38
automotive plants 23, 138, 146
AXA 151 *n*. 15

back-testing 83, 87
banks, investment 5*f*, 8–9, 100–1, 110
Barclays Bank 101, 115–16
Bazot, Guillaume 11
benchmarks 133, *see also* closet benchmarking
Beunza, Daniel and Garud, Raghu 17
BlackRock 1, 2, 3, 163
Board of Trustees v. Mayor of Baltimore City 153
bonds 65–6, 131–2
    green 137
    trading 118–19
Brewer Dolphin 58–9
brokers 5*f*, 89, 91–3, 103–4, 108, 109–10, 173
Buttonwood Agreement 1792 103
buy side 8, 101
    analysts 171
    traders 10, 77*f*, 173

Cable & Wireless 34
CAC 40 index 122
calculative techniques 45
Callon, Michel 11
car plants 23, 138, 146
Carrie, Carl 107
CFA 36

chains *see* investment chains
charities 170
Charles Schwab 50 *n*. 1
Chevalier, Judith and Ellison, Glenn 10, 17
chief investment officers 77*f*, 172
child orders 112
Clark, Gordon 18–19
clients 32–3, 44*t*
client service staff 31–2, 44*t*
    managers 33–4, 35, 77*f*, 171–2
Climate Bonds Initiative (CBI) 137
climate change 2, 138, 153, 155 *n*. 21, 157–8
closet benchmarking 40, 47, 55, 67, 158, 160, 166
clusters of evaluation practices 121, 162
collective calculative devices 149, *see also* market devices
companies 5*f*, 10, 16, 17
composite prices 42–3
confidence 167–8
Corruption Perceptions index 123–4
Cowan v. Scargill 1985 153
credit rating agencies 5*f*, 132–3, 135, 151
Credit Suisse 101, 111, 113
    Advanced Execution Service department 112
Credit Suisse First Boston 89
Crossfinder 99 *n*. 1, 101, 111, 113
Crossing Network 105, 106

dark pools 5*f*, 22, 98–119, 168
    first-generation 99, 102–10, 113
    second-generation 99–100, 110–17
databases 87, 90, 91
Data Dissemination Initiative 159
Deeg, Richard and Hardie, Iain 164
Desrosières Alain 43
Dincer, Oguzhan 17
disclosure, information 159–61, 166
discount rate 65, 66
distributed framing 25, 38
diversification 70

Drucker, Peter 141
duration 95

economic growth 158
Economides, Nicholas and Schwartz,
    Robert A. 102, 104, 106–7
economists/strategists 5*f*, 173, 174
efficient market hypothesis 10, 41
emotional finance 82, 87, 97
Employee Retirement Income Security Act
    (ERISA) 1974 [USA] 63 *n*. 20, 65,
    141 *n*. 2
energy, renewable 2
environmental, social and governance (ESG)
    aspects 121, 123, 124, 126, 129, 153
epistemic cultures 122, 135
equity markets, defined 28
ETFs (exchange traded funds) 92
ethnography 33, 122, 131 *n*. 17
European Central Bank 135
Eurozone 120, 135
evaluation practices 136
Evaluation Practices in Financial Markets v
Everyday Life of Global Finance, The 19
execution-only services 169–70

Fabozzi, F. J. 84
fair dividends 144, 155
fees 166–7
Fidelity 50
fiduciary duty 145, 152–4
fiduciary management 73–4, 161–2
filter systems 81
financial advisers and wealth managers 169,
    see also IFAs; wealth managers
financial analysis 16–17
Financial Conduct Authority 74
financial crisis 2008 120
financial intermediation 11–13
Financial Reporting Council 63
Financial Services Authority Retail Distribution
    Review (RDR) 59–60
Financial Stability Board 3
Financial Times 13–14
firms 5*f*, 10, 16, 17
fixed income investment 125, 130, 131–6
    defined 133
    short-term nature 132
Flash Boys 115
Fligstein, Neil 16
Foucault, Michel 19, 45
framing, distributed 25, 38
France 149
    regulations 128, 150 *n*. 13, 155
    responsible investment 123, 155
French, Kenneth 13
FRR (Fonds de Réserve des Retraites) 154

fund managers 8, 26, 47–75, 77*f*, 82, 84,
    86, 171
    career considerations 17
    clients' impact 21
    self-presentation 14, 34, 35, 36, 165–6
    spreadsheets use of 38–9
fund of funds sector 59
fund platforms 5*f*, 50, 59, 169–70
fund raters 5*f*, 44*t*, 170–1

Geertz, Clifford 33
gender 18, 93–4 *n*. 17
general sales staff 173
Germany 130 *n*. 16
global microstructures 138
Global Peace index 123
Global Union Committee on Workers' Capital
    (CWC) 139
Godechot, Olivier 100
Goffman, Erving 14, 34
Goldman Sachs 109, 113, 119
Goyal, Amit and Wahal, Sunil 71
Goyer, Michel 16
grandiosity 79
Grant, Philip 20, 26–30, 31
Greece 56, 120, 121, 128, 129–30,
    132–3, 135
    government bonds 23, 134
green bonds 137
Greenwood, Robin and Scharfstein David 13
guidance 82
Guyer, Jane 42–3

Haldane, Andrew 1, 2, 3
Hardie, Iain and MacKenzie, Donald 25
Hargreaves Lansdown 50
hedge funds 2, 13, 40, 57, 70, 73
Heidegger, Martin 45
herding 15–16, 61, 158, 166, 168
high frequency trading (HFT) 20, 101, 102,
    113, 114, 115
Hirschman, Albert 49
Hong, Harrison 17

Iceland 135
IFAs 5*f*, 49–50, 53, 59–60
income funds 57
inequality 158, 166
information asymmetries 159
information disclosure 159–61, 166
Information Ratio (IR) 88
Instinet 104–5, 106
insurance companies 5*f*, 6, 62, 66–7, 170
intermediaries *see* investment intermediaries
intermediation, financial 11–13
internalization 111
International Accounting Standards Board 63

International Monetary Fund Data
     Dissemination Initiative 159
interviews conducted 20, 27, 49, 76–7, 102
Investment Association 54, 55, 56, 57–8
investment banks 5*f*, 8–9, 100–1, 110
investment chains 5*f*, 9, 18–19, 44*t*
  collective struggles through 23–4, 138–55
  conclusions on 24, 156–68
  Corporate X 150*t*
  internal 77*f*
  nature of 156
  shortening 161–2
  use explained 4, 15, 25
investment consultants 5*f*, 7, 44*t*, 48, 50, 70–5,
     157, 163, 170
investment intermediaries 4, 9–11, 49–51,
     see also fund platforms; IFAs; wealth
     managers
Investment Management Agreement (IMA) 68
investment management firms 5*f*, 7–8, 10, 44*t*
  assets, amounts of 1
  hierarchies 32, 123, 124–5
  pay 2
investment time-horizons 157
Investmentzertifikat 81 *n.* 5
Investor Capitalism 16
investors 5*f*
  individual 5–7, 48, 51–8
  institutional 48, 61–75
Ireland 135
Italy 121, 128, 129–30, 132–3, 135
  government bonds 55, 134

Jenkinson, Tim 72

Kay Commission on short-termism 158
Kay, John 10
Kay Review 10, 159, 160, 161, 162, 164, 165,
     166, 167
Keim, Donald and Madhavan, Ananth 104
Kellard, N. 89, 156–7
Kerviel, Jérome 127–8
Knight and Getco 110 *n.* 15
Knorr Cetina, Karin 122
Knorr Cetina, Karin and Preda, Alex 11

labour unions *see* trade unions
Langley Paul 19
Larminat, Pierre de 30–1
Latour, Bruno 4 *n.* 3, 42
leaning for the tape 17–18, 21, 165
Lewis, Michael 115
liability-driven investment 62–7
Libor 100 *n.* 2
life assurance companies 170
Light Pool 101
Liquidity Profiling 116

Liquidnet 105–6, 107, 111, 113
lit markets 117–18
Loiselet, Éric v
long-only investment 40, 92 *n.* 12
loyalty 49, 58–9, 61, 160
LX 99 *n.* 1, 115–16

McFall, Liz 99
MacKenzie, Donald 11, 100, 162
managerialism 160
market devices 99, 100
marketing 83–4, 89–90
marketing staff 32, 44*t*, 77*f*, 172
Marx, Karl 42
mediators 4 *n.* 3
Mennicken, Andrea and Miller Peter 100
Mercer 71
Merrin, Seth 105–6
Messner, Martin 42 *n.* 6
metrological realism 43
micro-mechanisms 136
midpoint peg orders 114 *n.* 16
MIFID (Market in Financial Instruments
     Directive) II 109 *n.* 14
Mississippi 23, 138, 146
mobilizations 23–4, 138
money 14, 100
monitoring 165
Montazemi, Ali Reza 118
Morgan Stanley 89
Morningstar 7, 52, 60, 167, 170–1
MSCI World index 92
multiples 81
Muniesa, Fabian 99
mutual funds 6, 150

Nasdaq (National Association of Securities
     Dealers' Automated Quotation system) 103
naturals 99
neoliberalism 45
networks 156–7
New Financial 2
New York Attorney General's office 101
New York Stock Exchange (NYSE) 103, 118
Niessen-Ruenzi and Ruenzi 18
NJ2 99
Northern Rock 127
numbers 14, 26, 38–40, 41–2, 43, 44–6, 165–6

OECD Guidelines for multinational
     enterprises 148
order management systems 105
Ortiz, Horacio 19, 25, 26, 45, 73

participant observation 20, 27, 77
passive investment 13, 66, 163–5, 167
Pension Fund Capitalism 18–19

pension funds 6–7, 13–14, 61, 62–4, 139, 160–1, 170
  trade union 139–41
  trustees 5*f*, 7, 71–2, 74–5, 139, 152–3, 154
pensions, pay as you go 139
Pensions Regulator 63
performance 3, 14
performance figures *see* numbers
Philippon, Thomas 11–12
PIMCO (Pacific Investment Management Company) 2, 3
ping destinations 110 *n.* 15
platforms, fund 5*f*, 50, 59, 169–70
Polanyi, Karl 42
Poovey, Mary 36
portable alpha products 92
Porter, Theodore 42
portfolio managers *see* fund managers
Portugal 135
Posit (Portfolio System for Institutional Trading) 105, 106, 115
Pozner, J.-E. 136
prices 45
  composite 42–3
principal–agent issues 49, 67, 158–9, 163
principal–agent relationships 51
principal–agent theory 47–8
public secrets 41

qualitative analysts 30
quantitative analysts (quants) 30
quantitative asset management 21–2, 76–97, 162

RAIR (Réseau d'Administrateurs pour l'Investissement Responsable) 142–9, 154, 155
Rathbones 58
rating agencies 5*f*, 132–3, 135, 151
Regulation National Market System (Reg NMS) 111
relationship value 9, 119
renewable energy 2
research, authors' 19–20
responsible investment 23, 43, 120–37, 157–8, 165
  defined 123 *n.* 7
  France 123, 142, 144, 155
retail investors *see* investors, individual
returns, maximizing of 67–70
risk 55
risk management 69–70, 77*f*, 94–6, 172
Ritholtz, Barry 2
rules 81

sales staff, general 173
savers *see* investors

Schneiderman, Eric T. 101
Schwartz, Robert and Steil, Benn 104, 108
screening models 81
secrets, public 41
Securities and Exchange Commission (SEC) 101, 111
sell side 8, 101
  analysts 5*f*, 173–4
Shah, Ajay and Fernandes, Kshama 48
shares 98
short gamma 90
short-termism 48, 67–8, 74, 158, see also *Kay Review*
  fixed income investment 132
Sifis (systematically important financial institutions) 3
Sigma X 113
smart order routers 112–13
Smith, Adam 33
social economy sector 123
social studies of finance 11, 15–16, 19, 83–4
Société Générale bank 127–8
society 121, 135–6
soft-dollar arrangements 19, 22–3, 93, 94 *n.* 17, 107–9, 110
Spain 135
Stan, Sabina 42
Standard & Poor's 7, 170–1
star managers 61
St James Place 59
stock picking 163
Strathern, Marilyn 38
Street Corner Society 122
subprime crisis 120, 127, 136
sustainability 123
Svetlova, Ekaterina 15, 20, 77
swaps 92

TABB Metrics 114 *n.* 16
Task Force on Climate-Related Financial Disclosures 159
Taussig, Michael 41
tax evasion 138
TheCityUK 1
third market 105
time value of money 65 *n.* 22
Traders Magazine 113–14, 115
Trade Union Advisory Committee (TUAC), OECD 139
Trade Union Pension Trustees, Seventh International Meeting 139
trade unions 138, 157
Transformation of Corporate Capital, The 16
transparency 38, 166
trust 73, 75, 167–8
trustees *see* pension funds, trustees
truth 26, 43, 44, 45

UCITS 150
United Automobile, Aerospace and Agricultural
    Implement Workers of America (UAW) 146
Useem, Michael 16
US Financial Crisis Inquiry Commission
    2011 120–1

Valeur financière et vérité 19
valuations 32, 172
value 19, 26, 44–5
value-at-risk limit 172
Vanguard 3 *n.* 2
Viridian 29–30

wealth managers 5*f*, 49–50, 53,
    58–9, 60
Wealth Managers Association 60
Whyte, William Foot 122
window dressing 17, 21,
    165–6
women 18, 93–4 *n.* 17
Woodford, Neil 61
Woolley, Paul and Vayanos, Dmitri 67
workers' rights 158
Wunsch, Steve 104

Zaloom, Caitlin 11, 133